INVENTING SUPERSTITION

INVENTING
SUPERSTITION

FROM THE HIPPOCRATICS
TO THE CHRISTIANS

DALE B. MARTIN

HARVARD UNIVERSITY PRESS

Cambridge, Massachusetts
London, England
2004

Library of Congress Cataloging-in-Publication Data

Martin, Dale B., 1954–
    Inventing superstition : from the Hippocratics to the Christians / Dale B. Martin.
      p.   cm.
    Includes bibliographical references and index.
    ISBN 0-674-01534-7 (alk. paper)
    1. Philosophy, Ancient.   2. Philosophy and religion—Greece.   3. Philosophy and
religion—Rome.   4. Superstition—Religious aspects—History—To 1500.   I. Title.

B187.R46M37   2004
398'.41'0901—dc22

2004047407

To Wayne A. Meeks

Contents

Preface

In a previous book, *The Corinthian Body,* I found myself making a statement that seemed to me self-evident. In speaking of certain early Christian beliefs, such as the resurrection of the body, I commented that educated Greeks would generally have rejected these beliefs and even found them to smack of "superstition," but I added that their reasons for doing so had nothing to do with any rejection of "supernaturalism." I argued in that book that the category of "the supernatural" didn't really exist in the classical world, so dependence on "supernatural causation" would not have been the issue in rendering a belief or action "superstitious" in the eyes of an ancient intellectual. After finishing that book, it haunted me that I had not provided any alternative description of what actually counted in the ancient world as "superstition" and why, nor did I know of any study that had done so. I set out to find answers to those questions, and this book is the result.

I have attempted to write for a generally educated audience, hoping that more than scholars of antiquity will find my topic interesting. The scholarship on the subjects addressed by this book —ancient and comparative religion, medicine, science, and philosophy—is vast. (And I have limited my treatment to ancient Greek and Roman cultures, leaving out, for instance, the Ancient Near East.) Yet in keeping with my goal of producing a generally accessible book, I have kept the dialogue with other scholarship to a minimum and simply laid out my own case unless there seemed to be a real need to place my ideas within the context of contemporary scholarly debate, and even then, I have tried to relegate most of that comment to the notes. Moreover, the notes and references are kept to a minimum, though I do occasionally point readers in the direction of other scholarship should they wish to pursue a topic further, and of course I cite sources on which I directly depend. Likewise, Greek is quoted only when I felt it was necessary to make a point or signal a nuance, and the Greek has been transliterated. All translations from Greek or Latin are my own unless otherwise noted.

Though I give reasons throughout the book for certain translations, I should here explain my decision about the translation of one particular Greek word because it occurs so often. In almost every instance I have rendered the Greek *daimōn* as "daimon" rather than "demon." The ancient Greek category of *daimones* (the plural form) could include anything from a god, to a junior sort of divine being, to a being intermediary between divinities and humans. They could be good or bad, helpful or harmful, consistently ethical (as most of the philosophers thought) or capricious and ambivalent (as I take them to have been in most popular thought).

Often modern scholars hesitate to use the English term *demon* for such figures since that word refers almost exclusively to the sorts of beings depicted as evil in Jewish and Christian mythology. But it can also be misleading to use *daimones* when referring to the more classical Greek beings while reserving *demons* for the Christian referent. The early Christians did not think they were referring to different beings from those called *daimones* by the Greeks—that Zeus or Athena, say, were benign deities who existed simply alongside evil demons. On the contrary, the Christians took precisely those beings considered either benevolent or morally ambivalent by traditional Greek culture and insisted that those very "gods" were in fact evil, without exception. We should not imagine that the ancient debate was about two different kinds of beings; rather the debate was precisely about the ethical status of the very same beings. Since I felt it would be misleading to go back and forth from "daimon" to "demon" and since most of this book covers non-Christian texts, I use the term "daimon" throughout as less "loaded" with the later connotations of the unmitigated evil of "demons" and in recognition that the ancient debate was much more than a disagreement about terminology.

I have been working on this topic for many years and have incurred many debts—so many, in fact, that I fear I will not be able to acknowledge everyone who has offered help, suggestions, or encouragement. Those who have provided financial support, of course, deserve explicit thanks. The project was begun during a year-long fellowship in Tübingen sponsored by the Alexander von Humboldt Foundation of Germany. I most gratefully thank the Foundation and my host, Hubert Cancik. Professor Cancik and Hildegard Cancik-Lindemaier went out of their way to offer help on the project as well as gracious hospitality. Support was also given by the Duke University Research Council, and leave was made possible by the generosity of my colleagues in the Department of Religion at Duke.

Many of the questions I discuss in Chapters 3 and 6 were earlier explored in my essay, "Hellenistic Superstition: The Problems of Defining a Vice," published in *Conventional Values of the Hellenistic Greeks,* Studies in Hellenistic Civilization VIII, ed. Per Bilde et al. (Aarhus, Denmark: Aarhus University Press, 1997).

I have vetted ideas at many schools and conferences, too many to name, but I would especially like to thank friends at Ohio State University, Drew University, the University of Oslo, and the University of Copenhagen for invitations to present my work. Graduate students in seminars at Duke University, the University of North Carolina at Chapel Hill, and Yale University have patiently listened as I tried to clarify my ideas; they offered many excellent observations. I am indebted to them all, as well as to my current students and colleagues at Yale.

Friends have kindly read the manuscript and helped make it better. I especially wish to thank Elizabeth A. Clark, John Barclay, Judith Farquhar, Margaretta Fulton, and Diana Swancutt. Even more deserving are two brave souls who read the entire manuscript in three different (sometimes *very* different) drafts and provided invaluable advice: Bart Ehrman and Wayne Meeks. Without their steadfast encouragement this project probably would not have been completed. The book is dedicated to Wayne Meeks, who was my teacher and advisor during my graduate education at Yale. Returning to Yale has been made much more pleasant by the opportunity to enjoy again his company. I continue to benefit from his mentoring and friendship.

1

Superstitious Christians

In the year 112 CE, Pliny the Younger, at the time Roman governor of Bithynia (the northern part of modern Turkey), wrote to the emperor Trajan requesting instruction on how to deal with some Bithynians who had apparently been accused by their neighbors of being Christians. Pliny admits that he has never been present at an inquisition concerning Christians, and he is unsure how to proceed. Should they be punished merely for bearing the name "Christian"? Or must some specific crime accompany the name? Should differences in age be taken into account? What about people who had once been Christians but had recanted? Should they be punished as well?

Much has been written about this correspondence between Pliny and Trajan, so I will not rehearse all the issues.[1] The important point for my study is Pliny's assumption that Christianity itself is perceived as a threat to society and the Roman order. Pliny admits that he has found nothing very criminal about the groups. After torturing a couple of female deacons, Pliny passes on what he has learned. The Christians meet on certain days before light, but only to sing a few hymns to Christ "as to a god." Together they take an oath, but not a criminal one such as those taken by bandits or rebels; rather they promise not to defraud people, steal, commit adultery, lie, or refuse to return a deposit. They sometimes come back together later to eat food, but quite innocent food. And they had ceased even that practice after Pliny announced that all such private societies *(hetaeriae),* which were usually considered suspicious by Roman rulers, were forbidden. In the end Pliny admits that he found nothing very important here, just a "depraved, immoderate superstition" *(superstitio)* (Ep. 10.96). From Pliny's point of view, the Christians' stubbornness alone, in their refusal to sacrifice to the gods and the emperor when requested, was enough to merit death.

In spite of the fact that Pliny admits to finding nothing terribly incriminating, he seems to feel the need to nip the movement in the bud. It is, he says, a "contagious superstition" *(superstitio).* Like a disease, it has spread not only throughout the cities of the province but also into the countryside and villages. Pliny blames Christianity for the fact that some temples had become almost deserted, that religious festivals had been neglected, and that people selling the meat of sacrificed animals were finding it difficult to find buyers, perhaps reflecting the fact that Christians (and perhaps others under their influence) refused to buy or eat meat that had been sacrificed to a deity. Pliny, as is typical for Roman upper-class authors writing about "foreign" religions, thinks of Christianity as a contagious disease. The body politic may be protected if the "contagious superstition" is destroyed in time.

One of Pliny's contemporaries, the Roman historian Tacitus, writing about the same time as Pliny but about events that took place in Rome in the 60s, calls Christianity a "recurrent superstition" *(rursum superstitio)* and a spreading disease that invaded Rome from Judea *(Annals* 15.44). Tacitus, in this famous passage from his *Annals,* is relating the events surrounding a devastating fire in Rome. To divert suspicions that he himself was responsible for the fire, Nero blamed the Christians, a group already unpopular with the city's other residents. Tacitus then gives some background on the sect. He explains that Christians were named after Christus, who had been sentenced to death by Pontius Pilate during the reign of the Emperor Tiberius. Though repressed for a while, the "recurrent superstition" had spread from Judea, its place of origin, and had broken out in Rome, "where every horrible and shameful thing from everywhere in the world collects and is even celebrated" (*Annals* 15.44). Tacitus here brings together typical Roman depictions of foreign religions that were perceived as a threat by the Romans, or at least by the conservative upper class: Christianity is of foreign origin; it is disgusting and shameful; it resembles a contagious and pestilential disease that must be repeatedly suppressed to discourage it from breaking out over and over again in different locations.

Another Roman contemporary of Pliny and Tacitus, the historian Suetonius, is the third early Roman writer to label Christianity a *superstitio.* The citation occurs in a context in which Suetonius lists various accomplishments of the Emperor Nero for the improvement of Roman civic life, especially his attacks on excesses of all sorts. Nero limited expenditures for public celebrations and banquets; he forbade the sale of luxurious delicacies in roadside taverns; he put an end to public misconduct by chariot drivers; and he banished pantomime actors and other disreputable characters from the city. Right in the middle of this list, Suetonius, without further comment, mentions that Nero had also punished the Christians, "a kind of human in the grip of a new and maleficent *superstitio*" (*Nero* 16.2).[2] The context makes it clear that Suetonius considered Christianity not only a public nuisance but a threat to the health of the state. Its suppression was necessary for the well-being of the body politic.

What was it about Christianity that provoked such responses? What bothered these Roman authors about this relatively insignificant social movement? In spite of the common notion that Christians suffered severe persecution from the Romans from the inception of the new religion—an idea that owes more to Hollywood and famous films like *The Robe* or *Ben-Hur* than to historical evidence—modern scholars are united in the opinion that the Romans actually took quite a while to notice Christianity at all.[3] At first, they would have had difficulties distinguishing Christians from Jews. Scholars have debated whether we may have an early reference to Christianity in Suetonius's account of the expulsion of the Jews from Rome in 49 CE. According to Suetonius, Claudius ordered the Jews to leave Rome "because of constant disturbances precipitated by Chrestus" (*Life of Claudius* 25.4; see also Acts 18:2). It is tempting to read this, taking the name "Chrestus" as a mistake for "Christ," as a confused reference to a dispute between Jews and Christians (or Jews who were followers of Jesus—that is, before the term "Christian" had gained currency). This is all speculation, but if it is true, we have here one piece of evidence that there were Christians in Rome before 49 CE, that there were disputes between them and members of the Jewish community in Rome, and that the Romans didn't distinguish the followers of Jesus from other Jews.

The next time we see Romans taking notice of Christians is in the incident previously cited from Tacitus, when Nero blamed Christians for the fire he was suspected of setting himself. As we have seen, Tacitus is no fan of Christians, but he nonetheless seems disgusted at their brutal treatment at the hands of Nero, who had them clothed in the skins of wild animals and torn apart by dogs, or nailed up and burned on crosses to serve as torches lighting an evening festival (*Annals* 15.44). And as we have noted, Suetonius also related Nero's "punishment" of Christians. These incidents are described, though, as the rather spontaneous actions of a perhaps mad, or only conniving, emperor, not as anything like "official" or concerted attempts to suppress Christianity. Moreover, they appear to have been totally local events and can in no way be interpreted as reflecting an empirewide persecution. That sort of official, widespread, concerted persecution of Christianity did not occur until the third century.

By the time Pliny wrote to Trajan in 112, however, Christianity had come to the attention of Roman rulers to the extent that they could now certainly distinguish Christians from Jews. Furthermore, the letter provides evidence that it had not been uncommon to arrest and try Christians in Rome. After all, Pliny explains to Trajan that he is asking for advice on how to deal with the Christians in Bithynia because he has never been present at such a trial, implying that he knew such "inquiries" had taken place. Thus, although the Romans did not attempt to "hunt down" and exterminate Christians altogether—Trajan himself tells Pliny not to seek out Christians but to deal with them only when they have been turned in by others—Roman leaders were sufficiently bothered by Christianity to imprison, torture, and kill Christians who stood publicly accused.

To this point I have not mentioned what may be the earliest account we have of someone labeling Christianity a "superstition." I say "may" because the interpretation of the passage is uncertain. In the Acts of the Apostles, taken by most scholars to have been written in the 80s or thereabouts, Paul, having been arrested and held by the Romans in the city of Caesarea in Palestine, is made to plead his case before Festus, Roman procurator of Judea, and the Jewish king Agrippa. In bringing the king up to date on the case, Festus explains that he can find no charge on which to convict Paul. Festus suggests, rather, that the entire conflict between Paul and the Jerusalem leadership was attributable to "some kind of dispute about their own *deisidaimonia*" (Acts 25:19). *Deisidaimonia* is the Greek word most commonly translated as "superstition," but it is not certain whether that is its meaning here. As we shall see in the next chapter, the word could also mean simply "piety" or "religion." Thus a reader of Acts could take Festus merely to be referring to Judaism (including the followers of Jesus within Judaism, as we have seen was the case in the early period of the movement) as a "religion." After all, Festus is speaking with the Jewish king. Would the author of Acts want to present the Roman ruler as intentionally insulting the king by referring to Judaism as a "superstition"? Not likely, according to most modern interpreters. Armin Moellering, for example, says that *deisidaimonia* in Acts 25:19 "is used in a neutral, objective sense for 'religion.'"[4] Most English translations reflect the same opinion.[5]

On the other hand, a careful—or clever—ancient reader may have noticed that the person speaking here is a *Roman* ruler. Perhaps Festus's use of the Greek *deisidaimonia* would have evoked for this reader the Latin *superstitio,* which *did* almost always carry the negative connotations of "superstition" and which often referred particularly to the religion of some "barbarian" people (discussed in Chapter 9 below). Such a meaning would, after all, make perfect sense in the context: Festus, as the "sophisticated" Roman official stuck in the "boondocks" of Judea, dismisses the Jewish religion as a "superstition." But by using the potentially ambiguous word *deisidaimonia,* Festus veils his insult (again, in the mind of our clever reader) for the benefit of his royal Jewish guest. The reader might also take this to be a veiled insult, on the lips of a Roman ruler, of Christianity, which is being lumped together with the "superstition" of Judaism. We have here, therefore, a designation of Judaism (and Christianity) as either a "religion" or a "superstition"—depending on how the reader takes the admittedly ambiguous word.

Some scholars have suggested that the author of Acts intentionally manipulates that ambiguity when he has Paul use the term (here in the form of a comparative adjective) in a speech delivered to Athenians on the Areopagus (Acts 17:22–31). According to the account, Paul is troubled by the number and variety of different deities honored in Athens. He begins his speech, therefore, by saying, "Men of Athens, I see that you are in every way the most . . ." (17:22). But should we translate the next Greek word as "the most religious" or "pious" or "the most superstitious"? In this case scholars are more divided than in their interpretations of Acts 25:19.

On the one hand, a reader in the first century may well have thought that Paul was here beginning his Athenian sermon with an accusation against "superstition." Since a main purpose of Paul's Areopagus sermon is to oppose the cult images and various shrines of Athens (17:24, 29), one could easily take Paul's use of the term to signify his disapproval of Athenian religion—perhaps in its "excesses" or simply because the Athenians were worshipping "daimons" in the guise of "gods." For some readers, it may have seemed significant that Paul uses the term when speaking with *philosophers.*[6] Should the situation be taken to indicate that the word was *intended* in its negative sense?

On the other hand, would Paul (as portrayed in Acts, we must remember) be such a bad orator as to begin a speech by insulting his audience? Should we rather understand Paul to begin with a *captatio benevolentiae,* a compliment to his audience intended to win their sympathy? "Men of Athens, I see that you are the most pious of people, for not only have I seen many and varied shrines. I have even seen one dedicated to 'the Unknown God.'" Paul's language could be taken either way.

Or both ways. In fact, according to some interpreters, the word is used by the author of Acts precisely because its meaning would be ambiguous.[7] Mark Given, for example, has offered a complicated but compelling interpretation of the passage along these lines.[8] According to Given, the text of Acts repeatedly de-

picts Paul as rather cunning in his rhetoric—*and* the author of
Acts as rather cunning in his intentional use of ambiguity. The
entire narrative of Acts has portrayed Paul as a staunch critic of
idolatry and an accomplished speaker. Since we've already been
told that Paul's "spirit was much provoked within himself" by all
the idolatry in Athens (Acts 17:16), we, as readers "in the know,"
are included in the "inside secret" that Paul is only *apparently*
complimenting his audience as "pious" while actually convicting
them of "superstition." Along with this double entendre, Paul's
speech offers several other ambiguities. To cite only one, when
Paul says that he proclaims a god whom the Athenians worship
"unknowingly," he could be excusing them for their ignorance or
accusing them of willfully engaging in improper worship (Acts
17:23).[9] According to Given, the author of Acts intentionally presents Paul as an orator like Socrates who purposefully engages in
irony, double meaning, and even deception—for the good of his
audience and because he is privy to special knowledge, to be sure.
The ambiguity of the term *deisidaimôn*—"pious" or "superstitious"?—offers a perfect opportunity for Paul and the author to
criticize the "pagan" culture of idolatry while presenting Christianity as not superstition but the only true philosophy.[10]

It is impossible, of course, to know what the author of Acts intended to communicate by his uses of the term *deisidaimonia*.
Was he using the term to refer to what we would call simple "religion" or "piety"? Or was he already engaged in the charges and
countercharges of "superstition" that would later become more
common between Christians, on the one side, and Greeks and
Romans, on the other? Do his texts hint at an early sensitivity on
the part of Christians to the charge of superstition? Though his
own intentions are impossible to discern, we may certainly imagine how his language may have been heard in the first century.
And one of the ways it may have been interpreted was as the beginning of a debate over whether Christianity was superstition.

This brief survey of early charges against Christianity demonstrates that outsiders did sometimes see it as a "superstition." But it is not yet clear what precisely about Christianity bothered its Greek and Roman critics. And what was the precise meaning of "superstition" for these ancient writers? To begin to answer those questions, I turn now to a discussion of the difficulties of defining *superstition* for the ancient world.

2

Problems of Definition

What is "superstition"? To those of us who don't think of ourselves as superstitious, superstitions are beliefs or practices that presuppose a faulty understanding about cause and effect, usually by assuming notions of causality that have been rejected by modern science but may represent long-standing popular beliefs or practices. So people for centuries have believed that certain numbers are unlucky and others lucky. Modern science has uniformly rejected beliefs underpinning "lucky" and "unlucky" numbers, but we still have buildings and elevators with no thirteenth floor. In the modern world, therefore, "superstitions" are often seen as vestiges of older popular beliefs and practices that survive somewhat out of place in modern culture, influenced as it is by modern science and its notions of what is rational and irrational.[1] Even for modern persons who may describe themselves as superstitious, the term usually indicates their recognition that they are accepting certain beliefs—or at least that they act in ways that might be taken as accepting certain beliefs—that are admittedly rejected or marginalized by scientific culture. They may say, "Oh, I'm a bit superstitious," but by putting it that way, they show that they know such things are ridiculed by one dominant, powerful discourse of the modern world: science.

Of course, this doesn't really answer the question of what specific practices are superstitious. Most people might agree that lucky and unlucky numbers are a sign of superstition, or that it is superstitious to fear stepping on a crack or crossing paths with a black cat. But other things may be more debatable. Is it superstitious to believe that wearing a copper bracelet will alleviate arthritis pain? If so, why? Disagreements about such questions sometimes reveal certain confusions in attempts to define "superstition." This kind of problem is revealed when some scholars try to define it and provide definitive examples. Iona Opie and Moira Tatem, for example, in their *Dictionary of Superstition* claim that they include superstitions but *not* mere "fallacies that are straightforward misunderstandings of nature, or herbal remedies that have no magical element."[2] Yet the authors end up including all sorts of beliefs that have no "magical element," unless one takes "magical" to refer simply to a "misunderstanding of nature." They include what are in some cultures quite common beliefs—for instance, that the presence of a menstruating woman will turn beer or milk sour or will spoil meat. The use of the term "magical" for such assumed activities simply misleads. What the authors are actually looking for are in fact "misunderstandings of nature" that appear superstitious to us modern, educated Westerners. The authors fail to *define* "superstition" in a way that holds true to their actual practices of inclusion and exclusion for the purposes of their dictionary.[3]

Disagreements about what counts as "superstition" will usually be exacerbated when we move from one culture to another. During a sabbatical in Germany, I was regularly frustrated when traveling on trains in hot summer weather. On the sometimes stifling, non-air-conditioned trains, I would attempt to sit by an open window to catch the breeze once the train began moving. Regularly, though, as soon as the train picked up speed, a German (often but not always an older person) would get up and close the window, leaving the entire car sweltering in humid, stale air. When I, the foreigner, looked at the culprit in disbelief and exasperation, he or she would usually explain to me, as if to a dense child, that wind blowing on an unprotected neck would render the person ill with something like, as best I could tell, "stiff neck." Not only had I never heard of the illness, but it was unfathomable to me (once a boy from Texas, after all) how a bit of cool breeze on a hot day could make me sick. To me, these Germans just seemed to be senselessly suffering, sitting there all summer in torrid train cars, all because of some superstitious folk belief. To the Germans, I needed some instruction on elementary principles of disease etiology. Where is superstition here?

Importantly, the way people argue about the issue tells us much about what superstition is in the modern world. If the arthritic man with a copper bracelet on his wrist wants to convince me that he is not thereby superstitious, he will probably offer some kind of account, using as much scientific-sounding language as he can muster, that explains how the known properties of copper interact with the known mechanisms of arthritis, and if possible he will interpret all those properties and mechanisms as ones recognized, at least in appearance, by modern physics, chemistry, or biology. He will not likely invoke a category of demonic possession or sympathetic magic. He may end up sounding like a chemist, but he will not likely sound like an exorcist—*if*, that is, he really wants to defend his practice against the charge of superstition. In other words, the definition of "superstition" in the modern world is parasitic on whatever is taken to be "scientific." "Superstition" is the "other" to "science."

What happens, though, when we turn our attention to the ancient world? Obviously, modern science did not exist in the ancient world. We could simply label as superstitious anything we see in ancient culture that looks superstitious by modern standards. This is, in fact, the way most scholars have used the term in speaking about ancient beliefs.[4] Any ancient acceptance of dream interpretation or astrology, for instance, is sometimes called superstition. Usually in modern discussions the common denominator for what is taken to be "superstition" ends up centering around notions of "the supernatural." The assumption is that "we" all know what may be accepted as "natural" cause and effect, and any cause understood as intervening from outside that nexus of nature may be taken to be "supernatural," and any assumption of supernatural causation betrays superstition. There are definite problems, however, in assuming that appeals to "supernatural intervention" will aid us in identifying what the *ancients* considered "superstitious."

Problems with "Supernatural"

One of the basic arguments of this book is that, contrary to many modern assumptions, the category of "the supernatural" did not exist in ancient culture *as a category*. Neither popular notions, held by the vast majority of inhabitants of the ancient world, nor philosophical notions (we could say "scientific" with due consideration for the possible anachronistic connotations of the term) assumed that reality was split up into two realms, one "natural," containing things like "matter" and "natural forces" such as gravity or electricity, and another "supernatural," to which gods and similar beings (demigods, angels, demons, ghosts) could be assigned. Elsewhere I have argued that the invention of the modern category of the supernatural may be attributed to René Descartes in the sixteenth century.[5] Other scholars may disagree with that particular dating, preferring to point to Thomas Aquinas or perhaps even to certain thinkers of late antiquity. I have no interest in debating the precise time and place of the invention of the supernatural as an intellectual category. What is important for my purposes is that the category was not available, either explicitly or by assumption, for persons in the classical Greek and Roman worlds.[6]

The Greeks and Romans certainly had no *word* that was equivalent to the modern English "supernatural." Their word for *nature* was *physis,* from which we derive *physical, physics,* and such terms. But there was no such word as *hyperphysis,* which would be a literal translation into Greek of the English *supernatural.* Even the term *metaphysics,* which certainly looks Greek and is derived from combining two Greek words, was not a classical Greek term. We may imagine that someone *could* have coined "metaphysical" in the ancient world to refer to what we in the modern world call "the supernatural," but no one did. To be sure, English readers of translations of ancient Greek texts will sometimes come across the term *supernatural* in their translations, but those translations, I argue, are misleading. They are translating Greek terms that more precisely mean something like "the divine" *(theios)* or that refer to *daimones* ("demons"), beings or forces that were taken to be divine or quasi-divine. None of these terms encompasses all those entities moderns mean when they use the term *supernatural.*

I do not, however, want just to quibble about words. Classical Greek and Latin had no term for what passes in the modern world as "the supernatural" precisely because the ancients did not separate out divine forces and beings from "nature" and relegate them to a separate ontological realm that could be designated by its own label. Generally, for ancient people whatever does exist exists in "nature." Almost without exception the Greek term *physis* (nature) refers to "all that is." People might argue that the gods did not exist or that some particular daimon or god or superhuman being did not exist (I know of no ancient author who argued for actual atheism in the modern sense). But in that case, they said that the disputed entity simply did not exist, not that it might exist in some other realm of reality, such as the "supernatural." Ancient philosophers might argue that lightning was not caused by a god, but they did not do so by pointing out that lightning occurs in the "natural" realm and that the gods exist in the "supernatural" realm and that the two realms are not supposed to interact with one another.[7] Ancient people took the gods, and all other beings we would think of as "supernatural," to be *part* of nature if they existed at all.

Another terminological confusion is related to this one. Modern writers will regularly claim that one or another ancient philosopher is rejecting divine or supernatural *intervention* into nature. Obviously, if the ancients took divinities to be *part* of nature (which they all did if they believed in them at all), then talk of "intervention" is misleading. In order for something to "intervene" in some process, it must come from outside that process. Ancient writers may well have believed, for example, that deities did not personally interject themselves into the normal course of a disease, but it is anachronistic to portray that as the rejection of divine *intervention* into nature. Those writers who insisted that a god did not cause the disease did so for reasons other than that they believed, in principle, that deities did not intervene in nature. But we will be unable to recognize those reasons or understand *their* concerns if we rush to characterize the debate as one about divine intervention into nature.

Finally, assuming that ancient intellectuals criticized superstition because they were rejecting supernatural causation basically begs the question. It simply assumes that superstition is belief in the supernatural and doesn't tell us *why* they rejected supernatural causation. I will demonstrate in this book not only that the ancient critics of superstition did *not* reject "supernatural intervention" in nature but also that they had no reason to do so. That entire way of thinking about the problem is a modern one and absent in ancient discussions. But we will never be able to recognize the precise reasons for the *ancient* criticism of superstition if we assume that it was motivated by what have actually been only modern concerns. If we want to discern precisely *what* counted as superstition in the ancient world and *why*, we must avoid invoking the category of "the supernatural" and must instead look for the *ancient* logic of nature that made certain beliefs and actions seem superstitious to intellectuals of that time.

Superstition and Popular Culture

Ancient writers, indeed, often mention beliefs that look something like modern superstitions, such as a belief that when entering a room, people should step with the right foot first, or that medicine set on a table before use might lose its potency, or that after eating eggs or snails, one should break the shells to avoid bad luck.[8] Ancient writers instruct their readers to sprinkle black hellebore, a poison, around their homes to ward off evil spirits, and we have many references to people spitting down their chests to ward off madness or the "evil eye."[9] Other advice looks to us more like "folk" beliefs or simply the remedies of popular culture. Pliny the Elder, whose *Natural History* is a mine of such trivia, mentions that wearing a garment to a funeral will keep moths away from it, and that rinsing the mouth an uneven number of times in the morning with cold water will guard against toothache (see 28.6.32, 28.14.55). He relates that some men are afraid of exposing their penis to the sun or moon when urinating; others believe that people should not let their urine fall on someone else's shadow; but still others believe that letting a drop of "morning urine" fall on one's foot will protect against sorcery (28.19).[10]

But once we begin attempting to compile a list of such beliefs, it is difficult to know where to draw the line separating "superstition" from science, religion, or simply popular culture in the ancient world. Pliny himself, for example, certainly did not consider most of these beliefs to be superstitious. To mention another example, when Cicero ridicules the popular belief that it is a bad omen when statues sweat or when two yoked animals defecate at the same time, we may fairly assume that he took these beliefs to be superstitious.[11] But what about the common belief that the blood of bulls was poisonous, a belief that was apparently part of popular culture but nonetheless given a "scientific" explanation by ancient intellectuals, who were themselves on the watch for "superstition"?[12]

Other practices we might initially categorize as superstitions resemble, on closer scrutiny, normal, "legitimate," religion of the ancient world. In his agricultural manual, for example, Columella writes that farmers should perform certain sacrifices in order to ensure the purity of a wine cellar; that certain kinds of farm work may be done on a holiday only after sacrificing a puppy; that initiating a task on January 1 bodes well for it but that farmers generally should not work the soil until January 13; and that the training of oxen should begin on a storm-free day and not on a holiday.[13] To anyone familiar with Roman religion, with its concerns about proper sacrificial propriety, holy days, and omens, these admonitions are not surprising or strange in the least. And Columella himself, an educated Roman gentleman, certainly did not take them to be superstitious.

Readers who want to survey ancient practices that would be considered superstition by modern standards have many resources at their disposal. Besides Pliny's *Natural History* and Columella's *On Agriculture,* one could browse ancient books on astrology, pharmacology, and medicine, not to mention Greek and Roman fiction.[14] But such a survey, interesting though it may be in itself, will not inform us about what *the ancients themselves* took to be "superstitious," and why.

Looking for the Right Words

One possible solution is to find out what the ancient Greeks themselves *call* superstition. This involves a word study that is not without its own problems, mainly because there is no ancient Greek word that fully encompasses what we moderns mean by "superstition" (or Latin word, for that matter, which I address in Chapter 9). That is, there is no one Greek word that is used in ancient texts to refer to everything rejected by ancient philosophy or science because of a misunderstanding about the basic mechanisms of cause and effect. So no word study, no matter how exhaustive or nuanced, will deliver an accurate portrait of ancient superstition, taking the term in the modern sense.

On the other hand, analyzing the Greek word most often rendered into English as "superstition" is not a bad place to start. By seeing what ancient writers meant—and did not mean—by *deisidaimonia,* we will make some headway toward discovering the boundaries of ancient superstition.

The basic definition of *deisidaimonia,* according to ancient writers, is "fear *(deisi)* of daimons *(daimones).*" But this is accurate only if both halves of the term are allowed a wide range of meanings. *Deisi* could refer to awe or respect rather than actual fear. And *daimones* could be taken to refer to gods or goddesses, semidivinities, or any kind of superhuman being (like "lower grade" gods, "heroes," daimons/demons, or what moderns might think of as ghosts or angels).[15] Thus *deisidaimonia* could be a positive or neutral term, as we have seen in the previous chapter, referring to piety or the respect of sacred things that most people would have considered quite appropriate. But it could also be taken to be a term of reproach, referring to irrational or exaggerated fear of benign or nonexistent beings and forces. Hence the term, even in its basic definitional sense, spanned the range of meanings from "respect for the gods" or "awe appropriate to sacred things" to "craven and irrational fear of divinities or demons."

In its earliest occurrences *deisidaimonia* seems not to have carried any stigma, referring simply to appropriate piety; it was relatively interchangeable with Greek words related to religion that were never pejorative, such as *eusebeia, eulabeia,* or *theosebeia* (each of which could be translated as "piety" or even "religious service"). Xenophon praises rulers who avoid arrogance, pay proper respect to the gods, and honor even foreign cults and temples, in one instance approvingly calling a ruler a *deisidaimōn,* perhaps best translated here as "a god-fearing man" (*Agesilaus* 11.1–2, 8). Elsewhere Xenophon says that Cyrus's soldiers sang hymns to boost their courage, because those who fear the gods *(hoi deisidaimones)* need not fear men (*Cyropaedia* 3.3.58). Aristotle uses the term similarly, noting that it is good politics for tyrants to attend to the gods zealously so as to appear to be "god-fearers" *(deisidaimōn);* such tyrants may even claim the gods as their allies (*Politics* 5.9.15 [1314b.39–1315a4]). Some forms of excessive religiosity are condemned by these writers, but the term *deisidaimonia* refers to appropriate piety, the proper deference towards the gods, sacred places, and holy people.

An earlier generation of scholars believed that this positive or neutral meaning of *deisidaimonia* was later completely displaced by the negative meaning, that under the influence of philosophy the term came to be exclusively one of reproach in the sense of "an irrational cravenness before divine and superhuman forces."[16] The situation is not quite so simple. We find many references in Diodorus Siculus's first-century BCE work *Library of History* in which *deisidaimonia* is used in a nonproblematic, positive sense. Even much later the term *deisidaimonia* occurs in a popular setting (as opposed, that is, to a philosophical text) with no pejorative connotation: a Greek inscription from Rome, probably from the third century CE, was erected by a woman named Kasia for her dead husband whom she calls a *deisidaimōn* as well as "honorable" *(teimios)* and "worthy" *(axios)*. Obviously the word, which at the time would have been unanimously taken by philosophers to mean "superstitious," is here a positive term. In fact, in the inscription itself it is equated with *eusebēs,* "pious."[17]

The problem with depending on a word study for ascertaining what counted in the ancient world as "superstition," moreover, is not only that throughout the ancient world *deisidaimonia* could refer simply to "piety," but also that ancient writers often rail against popular beliefs and practices without using the actual term *deisidaimonia.* As several of the following chapters will make clear, ancient authors reject many popular beliefs because they were thought to offend the basic assumptions about "how nature worked" as promulgated by the intellectuals themselves. Since my goal is to ascertain what counted as the ancient equivalent of the modern category of superstition and why, I will not limit my analysis to a word study of *deisidaimonia.* We must search for the line separating "legitimate" from "illegitimate"—or "rational" from "irrational"—belief and then seek to construct the logic and assumptions that made that line so obvious, and important, for the ancient intellectuals drawing the line. Having pointed out the limitations of a word study, nonetheless in the next chapter I will begin with a word study, by focusing on how one philosopher, Theophrastus, shaped his criticism of superstition by appropriating precisely the Greek term *deisidaimonia.*

}

Inventing *Deisidaimonia*

Theophrastus, Religious Etiquette, and Theological Optimism

A man in Athens in the fourth century BCE is seen walking around town with a sprig of laurel in his mouth all day. Although he has been washing his hands repeatedly, he also sprinkles himself with water from a roadside shrine. When he arrives at the outskirts of town, he comes across a pile of stones at the side of the road, presumably marking some kind of sacred spot. He stops and pours oil over them and then bows down before the pile several times. Further out of town, a weasel happens to cross the road in front of him; he freezes in his tracks and won't proceed until he throws three stones across the road. He hears an owl hoot in the woods, and immediately calls out the name of Athena. When he returns home, he has his house "purified," though he's done so many times recently, because he is convinced that otherwise Hecate, the goddess of the underworld, may possess his home.

Another man, watching all this activity, shakes his head, turns to the students gathered around him, and exclaims the word "superstitious!" The first man could have been anyone in ancient Athens who was particularly scrupulous about religion and folk customs. The second could have been Theophrastus.

Theophrastus and the "Character Sketches"

The portrait of the scrupulous fellow painted above is a composite sketch from "The Superstitious Man" written by the Greek philosopher Theophrastus (ca. 370–285 BCE). Though he was born on the island of Lesbos, in the town of Eresus, Theophrastus spent much of his life in Athens.[1] He studied with Aristotle and took over the leadership, after Aristotle's death, of his school. Theophrastus was an important philosopher in his day, writing many significant books on all sorts of topics of speculative philosophy and natural history, including studies of plants and minerals as well as religion and ethics.[2] He is said to have had 2,000 students at his school. In the premodern history of philosophy he was sometimes mentioned along with Plato and Aristotle as a significant ancient thinker and researcher. Oddly enough, however, he has been most famous in the modern world for a little work that can hardly be called "philosophy" at all: a book of "Character Sketches." One small section of that work renders Theophrastus important for my study, for his depiction of "The Superstitious Man" (deisidaimōn) furnishes us with the earliest surviving use of deisidaimonia as a term of reproach from the pen of a philosopher.

Theophrastus's *Character Sketches* is an entertaining spoof on different kinds of men one may have met in Athens in 320 BCE, the date around which scholars guess the piece was written. Yet we may use the work to ascertain what would have counted as "vices" and corresponding "virtues" for a gentleman of Theophrastus's station—that is, for an upper-class intellectual. Though the work is a rather lightweight piece, unlike some of the weighty philosophical treatises he wrote on everything from religion to pharmacology, it provides a valuable entrée into Theophrastus's thoughts and assumptions about nature, the gods, and religion. Precisely because Theophrastus, in this entertaining little piece, is *not* writing heavy theology and philosophy, the work yields, with careful reading, unguarded comments on ancient beliefs and practices.[3]

The text presents a series of portraits of typical "personality types" or, to be more accurate, caricatures: the Flatterer, the Talker, the Boor, the Gossip, the Absent-minded, the Grouch, the Slob, the Cheat, and the Coward, to name a few. Often one character is balanced by one or more that represent the opposite extreme of vice. So the Obsequious Man is mocked on the one hand, and the Arrogant on the other; the Filthy on one side, the Fastitidious on the other (see *Characters* 5.6–10). The *Deisidaimōn* (Superstitious Man) is someone who, among other things, is excessive in his observation of religious piety. We are probably expected to see his opposite in types such as the man who scratches himself during a sacrifice or the one who drops his cup and laughs while others are praying and pouring libations— that is, someone who is not pious *enough* (see *Characters* 19.4 and 9).

Athenian "Superstitions"

Merely listing the variety of superstitions condemned in the piece provides a fascinating glimpse into ancient Greek popular culture. Besides the behaviors noted above, Theophrastus also mocks: avoiding gravestones, corpses, women in childbirth, or polluted persons out of fear of polluting oneself; purifying one's house with boiled wine and spices on specified days; consulting dream interpreters, *manteis* (seers), or bird-omen readers; initiating oneself often in mysteries; sprinkling oneself with sea water for purification; avoiding madmen (or epileptics), and spitting down one's chest for protection against the madness. The Superstitious Man, according to Theophrastus, pays far too much attention to signs and omens. If he finds a snake in his house, he calls on the god Sabazios; if it is a holy snake, he builds a hero shrine on the spot. If a mouse eats a hole in a sack of grain, the man runs off to an "exegete," a person given the task of interpreting omens, and when the "exegete" tells him to forget about it and just sew the sack back up, the Superstitious Man performs elaborate religious expiations instead.

One of the values of Theophrastus's satirical portrait of the Superstitious Man is that it does list various activities that no doubt were practiced by many people of his society.[4] Though he is critical, we should imagine that many people would have seen nothing wrong with calling on Athena for good luck when hearing an owl hoot or taking certain events to be either good or bad luck. So for the historian of religion, Theophrastus's text is valuable as a repository of ancient Greek "folk" beliefs or popular religious practices. But the text also presents a problem for the historian of religion in ascertaining the *logic* of the list. What holds together these different behaviors and makes them all "superstitious"? What is the rationality that these beliefs and practices transgress? Before answering those questions, we should note what we know of Theophrastus's own religious beliefs.

Theophrastus's Religion

In the first place, we must note that Theophrastus has nothing against the traditional public cults. Theophrastus never rejected common and public religious activities of the Greek city. He certainly was not opposed, for example, to Greek sacrificial cult, as we can see throughout his *Character Sketches*. He also wrote a work *On Piety,* which survives only in fragments, mainly in a citation furnished by Porphyry (see Chapter 12). The work included a substantial critique of *blood* sacrifice. Though it is difficult to ascertain what wording came from Theophratus's pen and what is due to the possible reworking by Porphyry, there is little doubt that Theophrastus provided a fanciful and rather mythological history of sacrifice for the purpose of discouraging the killing of animals. But he did not criticize sacrifice in general.

Theophrastus apparently taught that human beings had originally sacrificed leaves, roots, and shoots of plants for "the visible gods of the heavens" (that is, the celestial bodies).[5] The sacrifice of animals was a late and degenerate form of worship. Gradually, human beings sank even to human sacrifice and great bloodshed. Such injustices led some people, according to Theophrastus, to despise and neglect the gods entirely—a consequence of impiety that Theophrastus himself clearly wants to avoid. He blames extravagant blood sacrifices for the production, in a roundabout way, of atheism (7.3–8.3)![6]

Theophrastus therefore urges (according to Porphyry's citations) that humans offer fruits as sacrifices and avoid any sort of harm to persons or animals (12). The gods themselves, moreover, have shown that they are pleased with simple, inexpensive, easily procured materials as sacrifices (15.1). Most important, the worshipper must approach the gods with a "purified character" (*kathēramenous to ēthos*, 19.4), thinking holy things (*phronein hosia*, 19.5), and with simple offerings and libations. What Theophrastus urges is moderation, the avoidance of luxury and extravagance, which for him includes the avoidance of any blood sacrifice, and the notion that a "pure heart and mind" are the best sacrifice. All this is common philosophical theology, with the addition of a complete rejection of blood sacrifice, which most philosophers did not advocate.[7] There is no hint of a wholesale criticism of religion or a rejection of "the supernatural."

In fact, if we may trust Porphyry's citations further, Theo-

phrastus even admitted that the behavior of the gods could be altered by sacrifices to them—a notion that could have been interpreted as "bribing" the gods and thus rejected by other ancient
intellectuals. According to Porphyry, Theophrastus taught that
there are three reasons people sacrifice to the gods: to render
them honor, to thank them for what they have already done, and
to procure from them the things we desire (24.1). The impli-
cation is that Theophrastus accepted a notion of sacrifice that
included reciprocal "giving," including the belief that sacrifice
could indeed influence the gods and dispose them more favorably
toward those who worship them. It was only extravagance in sacrifice that led to superstition: *deisidaimonia*.[8]

In line with such attitudes are several other indications of
Theophrastus's religiosity elsewhere in his *Character Sketches*. He
does *not* condemn, for example, having oneself initiated into
the mysteries or being especially devoted to some particular god
or goddess; nor is there anything wrong with dedicating votive
oferings at sanctuaries or paying one's respects at a shrine of
Heracles (27.5, 8). Thus on the one hand Theophrastus condemns people who do not show *enough* respect toward sacred
things: a true gentleman will not tastelessly curse the gods (19.8).
On the other hand, "superstition" is the "too much" extreme of
which impiety is the "too little." Theophrastus labels as "superstitious," therefore, all sorts of religious practices and attitudes that
he considers excessive.

The Mean, Balance, and Moderation

At work here is the ancient ideological notion of "balance" or
"the mean," famous from the works of Aristotle. And the principle informs not just Theophrastus's attitudes toward religion but,
as we will see throughout this book, all sorts of notions held by

philosophers about appropriate behavior and belief. So in his *Character Sketches* he berates men who are too religious or not religious enough (2.10, 19.8). He despises men who have no shame and dance in public even when they are not drunk and even though they've been asked only once (6.3, 12.14); but he also criticizes men who are too proud and refuse to dance even when they are drunk (15.10). Theophrastus even condemns those who are overly concerned to attain "honor," in spite of the fact that *philotimia,* the "love of honor," was usually considered one of the highest virtues among upper-class Greeks (21). *Deisidaimonia* for Theophrastus is any sort of excess in one's attitudes or behaviors with respect to divinities and the beings, persons, places, and things connected with them.

Ethics or Etiquette?

But how is the ancient person supposed to know how much is too little, how much is too much? Theophrastus does not give any prescriptions or abstract rules whereby one could predict ahead of time what behavior would be taken as appropriate and what as excessive. For example, why is it proper to invoke Athena for the protection of the city or household and yet superstitious to invoke her for personal protection when an owl hoots? Why is it proper to devote a bronze ring at a shrine but excessive to polish it every once in a while (see 21.10)? We are dealing here not so much with theology as with propriety—and even then, not so much *ethics* as *etiquette.* Theophrastus does not provide a theological argument intended to demonstrate why such behavior is wrong. He never provides "rules" people could use to gauge their behavior. Rather, he merely describes behavior taken to be self-evidently embarrassing or socially inappropriate, and he expects his reader to understand why.

In his other character sketches, for example, Theophrastus lists things that a "proper person" simply does not do: debasing himself by flattery (2); answering his own front door (4); being too familiar with the servants or playing with children (5.5); enduring insults or abuse (6); shopping for himself (11.7); or walking behind his slave (18). As we might expect from someone in a culture that highly prized gift-giving, benefaction, hospitality, and generosity, Theophrastus is so disgusted with stinginess that he provides portraits of four different kinds of "cheapskates" (see 30). Of course, Theophrastus never explains *why* such behaviors are considered shameful. But that is the way etiquette usually works. People who must have such things spelled out for them thereby advertise their lack of refinement.

Which raises the issue of class and status. We should be clear that what is appropriate behavior for a person in Theophrastus's world depends completely on the social status of the person in question. There is an assumed *hierarchy of personal station* that is supposed to be matched by a *hierarchy of appropriate behavior,* as becomes obvious when we review the list in the immediately preceding paragraph with different social roles in mind. Slaves, for example, *had to* open front doors, play with the children, shop for the household, and walk behind the master. They—and poor people in general—could hardly get by without the skillful use of flattery; they often had to endure insults and abuse. Theophrastus's approbation of benefaction and his repeated castigation of stinginess, moreover, would have had little meaning for the vast majority of Athenian residents, who had too little money to create much of a reputation for themselves as great benefactors. The etiquette that Theophrastus assumes, therefore, is really an upper-class etiquette. It assumes that his audience comprises mainly men of his own station—or at least that the people who could live up to his "virtues" are mostly men of that station.

The virtues and vices reflected in Theophrastus's sketches are implicated in a firm social and axiological hierarchy. The coordination between these two hierarchies means that people of higher station are simply expected to behave differently—better—than people of lower station. And higher is better in all ways. Once we see the importance of hierarchy for Theophrastus's views, we can discern other "logics" underwriting his condemnation of some beliefs and practices as "superstitious."

Fear and Shame

One of the central assumptions of Theophrastus's account of *deisidaimonia* is that fear of divinities is irrational and shameful. This is made explicit in the opening sentence of the section, where *deisidaimonia* is defined as "fear with regard to divine forces" (*deilia pros to daimonion,* 16.1).[9] The Superstitious Man is repeatedly pictured as fearful and cringing. He is afraid of weasels, Hecate, owls hooting, people in crossroads, madmen, and epileptics. He shamelessly prostrates himself before oiled stones along the road and worries about which divinities he should be propitiating. *Deisidaimonia* is despicable partly because it is unnecessary fear and because it incites shameful behavior.

It is easy to see why this should be the case in the honor-shame culture of ancient Greece with its hierarchical social structure and assumption that honorable people will behave honorably. According to such notions, fear of the gods is wrong because it humiliates human beings. To the Greeks, the Eastern barbarians looked ridiculous when they prostrated themselves before the Great King of Persia. Greek gentlemen, at least according to their self-congratulatory ideology, do not do such things. Even if a tyrant is fearsome, the philosopher—or the aristocratic Greek general or ambassador for that matter—will show no fear. Besides, fearing the gods implies that they are themselves vicious and mean. If it is shameful for a ruler to mistreat his subjects, how much more so for a god? If it is shameful for a philosopher to be controlled by anger, jealousy, or desire, how much more for a god? Thus those aspects of popular belief or religious practice that incite or display fear are labeled superstition and rejected because they contradict upper-class, philosophical notions of honorable behavior. Firm notions of honor and shame, therefore, play roles in the definition of superstition. The social hierarchy of honor and shame and an assumed etiquette of "moderation" and "excess" provide the assumed framework for Theophrastus's criticism of superstition.

Appropriate Place

The rigid hierarchy of ancient society and its honor-shame system reflects, of course, a cultural anxiety, at least of those of the upper class, about wanting everything "in its place." Just as hierarchy emphasizes "place," so Theophrastus's concerns about "superstition" reflect his concerns about appropriate place with regard to religious activities. Though Theophrastus never rejects the public cult, for example, he does disapprove of its being privatized. Hero shrines belong in public, not in one's living room. Hero worship belongs to the *polis,* the political body, not the *oikos,* the private citizen's household. There are household gods and rituals that are perfectly appropriate for the household, and it would be just as tasteless to take those into the marketplace as it would be to build a hero's shrine in the bedroom. The public cults must not be inappropriately appropriated for oneself. When Theophrastus mocks the Superstitious Man for building a hero shrine in his home, therefore, the offensive aspect of the action is apparently the fact that it is "out of place": it is the offensive privatizing of what should be a public cult.

Honor and the Rejection of Contagion

The rejection of shameful behavior on the part of beings who should be honorable may also explain why Theophrastus, reflecting a concern common to most ancient Greek philosophers and intellectuals, includes fears of pollution in his portrait of the Superstitious Man. The *deisidamōn* avoids stepping on gravestones, remaining in the presence of a corpse, or visiting a woman in childbirth, and he gives as his reason his desire to avoid being "polluted" (*miainesthai*, 16.9). He "purifies" *(katharai)* his house frequently (16.7). He joins people who sprinkle themselves with seawater, probably another reference to purity concerns (16.12). If he encounters someone who may be "polluted," such as a person wearing garlic at a crossroads, he purifies himself scrupulously (16.13). Crossroads were often taken in ancient Greece as a site of pollution, and garlic, then as in modern times, was sometimes taken to ward off evils. If the Superstitious Man even comes near a madman or epileptic, he spits down his chest—another common means among ancient Greeks for warding off pollution or, in this case, the "contagion" associated with insanity and fits (16.14). One of the innovations of ancient philosophers was to reject popular notions of pollution, whether in religion or medicine. Theophrastus does not explain *why* he rejects beliefs in contagion and pollution. But apparently at least one reason was because beliefs in pollution tended to assume that gods, beings considered honorable by philosophers, would be the cause of pollution. It offended the philosophers' sensibility to believe that something "holy" would or could render someone "dirty."

The logic of Theophrastus's condemnation of popular beliefs and practices as "superstitious" is constructed with a combination of these different cultural assumptions: the value of balance, the mean, and moderation; the assumption of rigid hierarchies; the rejection of fear in an honor-shame system; the concern about "appropriate place"; and the dismissal of contagion and pollution. These different assumptions provide the "rules" by which a person of philosophical training could differentiate "superstition" from appropriate religious piety.

Pharmacology and Propriety

But these ideas are not limited to Theophrastus's works explicitly devoted to religion. Theophrastus's assumptions about nature and the divine—especially the *lack* of any rejection of "the supernatural"—can be seen also in his other "scientific" writings, such as his *Inquiry into Plants,* which contains much advice about what plants are good for what ailments and how best to gather them. Theophrastus passes on different common beliefs about the precautions one should take when gathering or cutting dangerous plants, and he does so mostly without condemnation. For example, he notes that some urge people when cutting *thapsia* (among other plants) to anoint their bodies with oil beforehand and to stand upwind from the plant while cutting. Otherwise, he says, the body will swell up. He mentions that some plants are more safely gathered by night, others by day, and some just before the sun strikes them. He points out that hellebore must be dug only in intervals, to keep it from making one's head heavy, and that hellebore gatherers often eat garlic and drink unmixed wine to offset the effects of the poison (*Inquiry into Plants* 9.8.5–6). All these precautions Theophrastus accepts as possibly good ideas.

Theophrastus, though, rejects some other ideas. In particular, he thinks it is far-fetched to believe that peony should be dug only at night to avoid being seen by a woodpecker. According to popular belief, if a woodpecker witnesses someone digging peony, the person will lose his eyesight (though we aren't told how) and his "anus will fall out."[10] It is not completely clear why Theophrastus rejects this opinion. But we can be sure that "supernaturalism" is not the issue. Just after this section, Theophrastus admits that it is not unreasonable ("out of place," *atopos*) to believe that people should watch out for buzzard-hawks while cutting feverwort, and even that praying while doing so might be a good idea. He goes on then to say that some other precautions are absurd, such as the idea that one should place sacrificial offerings of fruits and cakes in the ground in compensation for any "all-heal" one has dug up, apparently as appeasement to Asclepius (who is assumed to "own" the "all-heal"?). He also rejects recommendations that people cut certain drugs only with a two-edged sword, or that one should first draw a circle around a plant three times, or that the first piece should be held up in the air while the rest is being cut (9.8.7).

Theophrastus is apparently uncomfortable with mixing religious and sacrificial rituals with plant-cutting. For example, he disputes the opinion

> that one should draw three circles round mandrake with a sword, and cut it with one's face toward the west; and at the cutting of the second piece one should dance round the plant and say as many things as possible about the mysteries of love. . . . One should also, it is said, draw a circle round the black hellebore and cut it standing toward the east and saying prayers, and one should look out for an eagle both on the right and on the left; for there is danger to those that cut, if your eagle should come near, that they may die within the year. (9.8.8)[11]

Theophrastus does not call these beliefs "superstition" *(deisidaimonia)* but "superfluous" *(epithetos)*. Yet we can see how they may be rejected precisely because they offend the same sensibilities we have discerned in his writings more explicitly on religion.

The beliefs seem to take ritual activities that may be more at home in the normal sacrificial cults and to move them out into the forests and fields, from the hands of religious devotees and into the hands of drug merchants and pharmacists. The beliefs also sometimes imply that gods or other superhuman beings might be motivated by jealousy to guard plants under their care and keep them from being used by humans, or that gods or the ground would require "payment" in the form of fruits and cakes in exchange for human use of healing materials. Theophrastus dismisses practices and beliefs that spring from fear. Yet since Theophrastus *does* admit that prayer may on occasion be appropriate while gathering dangerous plants, which would imply that he thinks it entirely admissible to ask for divine *help* during a dangerous activity, it is clear that he is not bothered by "supernatural intervention" in the course of nature. *Propriety* is the issue, not naturalism or supernaturalism. In Theophrastus's world, humans should behave just as "properly" as the gods certainly do.

Theophrastus's Optimal World

Theophrastus's rejection of many popular beliefs and practices as "superstition" is at base a matter of ethics expressed as etiquette: superstitious beliefs are wrong because they cause people to act in ways that are socially inappropriate, embarrassing, and vulgar. The kinds of elaborate religious prophylactics employed by common people, moreover, are not only degrading; they are also unnecessary. People have nothing to fear from those forces and beings they attempt to placate. The world, including all the varied forces of divinity, is simply not as scary and dangerous as most people think it is.

We should not leave this study of Theophrastus without noting that he provided no real "evidence" that the world and its gods were as benign as he assumes. He just assumes it. And we should recognize that this is a remarkably optimistic—"polly-annish"?—view of the world. Theophrastus has no new evidence that would demonstrate that the gods are good. He has discovered nothing previously unknown about nature that could have *demonstrated* that unseen forces will not harm those who offend them. Therefore his confident presupposition of that "fact" should be seen for what it was: a new, counterintuitive, and remarkably optimistic *belief* about the world, a theological optimism that preaches faith in an optimal universe.

4

Dealing with Disease

The Hippocratics and the Divine

Though Theophrastus's writings contain our earliest evidence of the terms *deisidaimōn* and *deisidaimonia* used in a derogatory manner, he was evidently not the first to use them in this way. After all, he seems to assume that the readers of his *Character Sketches* will recognize them as insults, which suggests that in those cases he is not completely innovating. The sentiments he expresses in those contexts, in any case, are not new with him. As we will see in Chapter 5, Theophrastus must have learned much from Plato and Aristotle, his teachers, about the "new sensibility" advocated by philosophy toward traditional religious beliefs and practices. This chapter will demonstrate that other intellectuals, in this case medical writers, shared the same concerns and attacked popular notions about nature and the gods.

We cannot be certain when most of the Hippocratic writings were composed. Most scholars are convinced that attribution of any of them to the historical Hippocrates, who was a contemporary of Socrates in the fifth century BCE, cannot be demonstrated and is perhaps improbable. None of them provides firm clues as to authorship or date of composition. But scholars believe that the Hippocratic work *On the Sacred Disease* is one of the earlier works of the Hippocratic corpus; it probably predates Theophrastus's activities. If so, that may explain why the author, though sharing many of Theophrastus's criticisms of popular beliefs, does not use the term *deisidaimonia* to label them. Xenophon and Aristotle, both predecessors of Theophrastus, used *deisidaimonia* in a positive sense to refer to "piety" or normal religion (see Chapter 2). Apparently, the use of *deisidaimonia* in its negative sense had not become common by the time of the writing of *On the Sacred Disease*. The document, however, represents an early attempt by a Greek intellectual to criticize popular "misconceptions" about nature and offer an alternative vision of the divine. It constitutes an early salvo in the battle over superstition among the Greeks.

In modern readings of Hippocratic medicine, this little book has been considered revolutionary.[1] The author argues, contrary to what was no doubt the opinion of the vast majority of people in the Greek world, that certain diseases believed to be caused by a god or other superhuman being are actually no different from other diseases. The symptoms described look to us like some kind of epilepsy or fit and seem also to have been linked by the ancients to madness, at least of a temporary sort. The author describes convulsions, severe shaking, loss of normal consciousness and control over one's body, and foaming at the mouth. He also says that, after initial attacks, people with the disease are able to tell when they are about to have another fit. (We need not be concerned to diagnose the illness in modern terms; the author may well be referring to what modern medicine would take to be different specific diseases.) According to popular thought, the fits were caused by an attack from a superhuman being, a god or goddess or daimon. Along the way toward criticizing that belief,

the author provides us with other valuable information about ancient popular beliefs and practices and his own, more "scientific,"
opinions and teachings.[2]

In popular opinion the fits resulted from a god or daimon
"polluting" the body of the victim. The proper treatments, therefore, were ritualistic purifications and spoken remedies, such as
incantations, songs, and spells (*Sacred Disease* 1, 4, 21).[3] The language used for the onset of the disease is not perfectly clear.
Though it is often translated as "possession" by a daimon, it is
not certain from the Greek that people really thought of the
daimon as invading the body.[4] The Greek usually just says that
the god or daimon "arrives" (*aphēkei,* 3). Or the disease itself is
simply called "the daimon" (see §15). In any case, the divine being
is either the direct cause of the disease or the disease itself.

Besides "purifications and charms," other remedies are mentioned. In one instance the author mentions that healers would
take the "cleansing agents" (*ta tōn katharmōn:* written spells?
charms? or perhaps bloody materials themselves?) and hide them
in the ground, throw them into the sea, or carry them off into the
mountains "where no one will touch or step on them" (4).[5] The
idea is that the "cleansing agents" themselves (or, in an alternative
reading, the refuse left over after the cleansing, the stuff "cleaned
off") have now become dangerous pollutants, and any contact
with them will further spread the disease.

The author sometimes uses the term "magic" to describe some
popular remedies. And we have enough references in other ancient texts, some more "literary" and some actual magical spells
and recipes, to imagine what the author had in mind. Homer
knew of spells ("songs," *epaoidē*) that could staunch bleeding
(*Odyssey* 19.455ff). In Aristophanes' play *Wasps,* which may have
been composed roughly around the same time as *Sacred Disease,* a
son tries to cure his father from a "diseased" addiction to serving
on Athenian juries. Although this is comedy, the audience proba-

bly recognized the remedies as a combination of magical and more respectable religious therapies: ritual baths and purifications, "Corybantic rites" (ecstasy sometimes induced by music or dancing), and sleeping in an Asclepian sanctuary (*Wasps* 117–125). Plato mentions religious healers who make money curing rich people; they get their powers from the gods by means of sacrifices and incantations (*Republic* 364B). Scholars can point to recovered papyri and lead tablets from the fourth and third centuries BCE that contain spells by which diseases, sometimes depicted as "animal plagues," may be cured. The similarity to the *Sacred Disease* and its association (according to popular imagination) of different kinds of diseases with different animals and gods is notable.[6]

Besides "magic," however, the author mentions other, more "legitimate," remedies, such as sacrifices (presumably to the attacking deity, §4). He may be exaggerating here, but the author claims that popular opinion held that different kinds of fits and abnormalities were caused by different deities: if a man acts like a goat, bellows loudly, and shakes on his right side, he is afflicted by "the Mother of the Gods"; if his cries are higher and louder, people say he is acting like a horse, and blame Poseidon; if he defecates during his fit, they blame the goddess Enodia ("by the wayside"); if the excrement is runny, like that of birds, they say the fault is that of Apollo Nomios ("Pastoral" Apollo?); if he foams at the mouth and kicks, Ares is the cause; but if he has attacks of terror and delirium during the night, jumping out of bed and running outside, he is supposed to be under attack by the goddess Hecate (goddess of the underworld) or "heroes" (spirits of the dead, §4). With so many gods and goddesses to worry about, it is no wonder that people sought remedies from many quarters: sacrifice, prayer, magic, and "cleansings."

Our author provides hints about popular beliefs concerning such "cleansings." People seem sometimes to have feared that superhuman beings might attack indiscriminately. Gods and goddesses were known to be not entirely predictable. But healers apparently offered explanations for why some people were attacked and others not. The Hippocratic author, criticizing the view, mentions the belief that the afflicted persons may have incurred some kind of "blood guilt" (and thus the assumption by the healer that the "cleansing" must be done by using blood itself; see §4), or that they had become polluted in some other way (there were many such ways, such as coming into contact with a place or thing connected with a violent death), or that they had been bewitched, or had committed some other impious deed that had offended a deity. The remedy could be to placate the offended deity, "clean off" the pollution (understood, from a modern point of view, as a rather mechanical process), or drive away the attacking being by the use of superior force, as in magic (see also §21).

Popular healers apparently practiced preventive medicine, also ridiculed by our author. They taught their patients to avoid bathing and certain kinds of foods: they should avoid red mullet, black-tail fish, hammer-fish, and eel; they should not eat goat, venison, pork, dog, rooster, turtle-dove, buzzard, or other "strong" meats. Certain vegetables, such as mint, garlic, and onion, were forbidden since spicy food was considered bad for sick people. Over and above diet, the healers had other restrictions. They told their patients not to wear black, not to sleep on or wear anything made of goat skin, and not to place one hand or foot on top of the other (§2).

We have to guess why these treatments would have made sense to ancient practitioners and their patients. The goat skins may imply a connection with the "Mother of the gods," whom we have already seen connected in the text with goats. Fear of putting one hand or foot on top of another looks like the sort of folk belief whose origins may be no longer ascertainable, like fear of stepping on a crack today. The connections of certain foods in certain combinations with illness also occur in probably every culture, and usually adequate historical explanations are impossible to give. (I was told as a child that drinking milk with fish or Italian food would give someone worms, perhaps simply because my mother and people of her background found the combination, for whatever reason, disgusting or strange.) In any case, we certainly should reject the Hippocratic author's explanation for the existence of these treatments. He claims that they were *invented* by the "charlatans" in order to mask their own ignorance and possible failures behind a facade of esoteric knowledge and secret lore. But the "superstitious" treatments and beliefs no doubt made perfect sense to most of the people who practiced them. He rejects the beliefs not because they are self-evidently false, but because they do not fit *his* system of sensibility. So, if we want to understand why our author rejects them, we must understand his rejections and arguments as they relate to his own system of healing.

The Hippocratic Critique of Popular Notions

Rather than denying that divine forces have *anything* to do with disease and healing, the author of *On the Sacred Disease* actually claims that divine forces are involved in *all* diseases. The Hippocratic author insists that popular healers are wrong not because they believe that gods have something to do with disease, but because they believe the gods cause *this one particular* disease, the "sacred disease," whereas other diseases are caused by other factors. Popular opinion perhaps took the fits caused by the sacred disease to be particularly divine because they appeared suddenly and were especially frightening. Our author asserts, on the contrary, that there is nothing *especially* divine about the sacred disease.

But the author also says that the disease should be considered

no *less* divine than any other. In fact, the clearest statement about
the "divinity" of disease is reserved for the last, emphatic section
of the work. After pointing out that all diseases spring from envi-
ronmental forces—cold, sun, changing winds—he says, "These
things are divine, so it is not necessary to discriminate and consider this disease as more divine than the rest. All are divine and
all are human" (21). Given such a straightforward statement, it is
odd that so many modern interpreters have taken the writer to be
arguing, on the contrary, that the gods and "supernatural forces"
have nothing to do with disease.

But how do we deal with those instances in which the author
does seem to deny divine causation for the disease? At one point
he argues that popular healers contradict themselves: if eating
certain foods or using certain materials, such as goat skins, bring
on the disease and avoiding them gets rid of it, then those should
be recognized as the causes, and so "the god is not the cause, nor
are the purifications the remedy" (2). Later the author argues that
"if indeed the god is the cause" of the disease, the healers ought to
take the patient to a sanctuary, offer sacrifices, and ask the god for
healing (4). That they do not do so, he claims, shows that the
popular healers contradict themselves and only mask their own
ignorance and self-interest. Again, we need not accept this author's depiction of the situation. We know from other sources
that people *did* go to sanctuaries, offer sacrifices, and expect healing from the gods.[7] Our author is using every rhetorical trick in
the book to discredit his opponents, here using accusations of
self-contradiction. But the author himself seems actually to contradict himself. He says clearly that all diseases are divine, caused
by divine-natural forces; so how can he deny that divinity causes
disease?

The answer to this problem lies in recognizing the author's
main goal: to discredit an entire system of healing and substitute
for it his own. The popular system depended upon thinking

about the gods as personal agents with whom people had to deal just as they dealt with other human beings, who might become angry, who might be unpredictable, and who might at any moment attack someone for all sorts of reasons. The Hippocratic author believes that such a view of the gods is, more than anything, impious.[8] He rejects the idea that any *particular* disease is due to a *personal, direct* attack by a god bent on expressing anger or on harming particular persons. The gods, according to his system, still have much to do with disease, insofar as they have much to do with all of reality. But they do not *personally* or *directly* cause particular diseases in particular people. The Hippocratic writer denies personal divine agency for disease causation, but he retains a belief in impersonal divine forces active in nature, including diseases.

The Hippocratic author also rejects popular notions of pollution and argues against certain popular practices of purification. He especially objects to the use of (what to him seem) disgusting and vile substances (he explicitly mentions blood) in attempts to "purify" the sick person, as if the sickness were punishment for impiety. Instead of using disgusting materials or attempting to force the gods to heal by the coercive methods of magic, people "should do the opposite of such things: they should offer sacrifices and pray and bring such [unholy people] into the sanctuaries and appeal to the gods" (4). In other words, the author admits that there may be people who have rendered themselves unholy, but the problem should be rectified by the traditional religious activities of sacrifice and prayer in the recognized religious institutions. It is "unworthy," though, to believe that the gods would use a personal attack of illness to punish someone for an act of impiety. The gods purify; they do not pollute. "I do not consider it worthy [to believe] that the body of a human being would be polluted by a god, the most perishable by the most holy."

Note the opposition proposed by the author and the words he

places against one another. The word here for "most perishable"
(from *epikēros*) means "mortal," "subject to death." It refers to
that aspect of human existence, mortality, that the Greeks typically considered the main quality separating humans from gods.
It is linked here to the body *(sōma),* a favorite site in ancient
thought for differentiating human from divine. The word translated as "most holy" comes from the Greek *hagnos,* which also
means "pure," "undefiled," and is especially associated with divinities. For this author, the gods, as essentially clean, pure, immortal, and holy, *cannot* be the source for uncleanness, impurity,
mortality, or corruption.

But they *can* be the source for cleanliness, purity, and holiness.
As the Hippocratic writer continues,

> If it [that is, the body] should happen to be polluted or
> harmed in some way by something else [that is, by some-
> thing other than a god], it is cleansed and made holy by the
> god, not polluted. Indeed, it is the divine that most espe-
> cially cleanses us and makes us holy even in the cases of
> our worst sins and impieties. And we ourselves point out
> boundaries for the divine with regard to sanctuaries and
> holy areas, lest someone who is impure transgress them.
> And when we enter such areas, we sprinkle ourselves—not
> as if polluting ourselves by that action, but as purification
> [by washing away] of any pollution we may have previously
> incurred. (§4)

The author admits that his society delineated holy areas by mark-
ers. But *he* insists (most people in the ancient world would have
disagreed) that the real reason for demarcation was not that contact with sacred objects would render someone impure, but that a
holy area should be protected from inappropriate contact with
persons who were sinful and unclean because of previous impi-

eties. When any of us enters a holy area, he points out, we purify ourselves by the traditional religious rituals. That demonstrates that holy materials render us pure, not impure.

The Hippocratic author is making two main points here. In the first place, disease is not due to impurity that is transferred from one being to another. As several scholars have noted, Hippocratic writers in general advocated no conception of contagion or infection in the modern sense, and they rejected etiologies of disease that linked disease to an attack of impurity from one agent against another.[9] That is, though they knew of ancient concerns about contagion, they did not make such conceptions part of *their* system. In fact, they sometimes explicitly rejected them. Second, whatever kinds of impurity may exist in the world, they cannot be attributed to divine agents since it would be against the nature of divine beings to pollute, although it is not against their nature to purify.

The Hierarchy of Existence and Ethics

As has perhaps by now become obvious, this author's arguments against popular notions of pollution are primarily ethical and theological. Fundamentally, he charges his opponents with impiety: they do not have the correct theology. Popular healers and magicians are impious because they claim to control natural (that is, divine) forces. When they claim to be able to work wonders over nature, to pull down the moon, cause a solar eclipse, or bring rain or sunshine, they are claiming to be superior to the gods, who rightly have control over such forces. This is an argument from ontological hierarchy: humans, even healers and magicians, are lower in the grand scheme of things than divine forces. When people claim to manipulate those forces, they are claiming to be superior to them, which is impious and insulting to the gods.

Moreover, when popular opinion attributes disease and pollution to direct divine agency, it attributes shameful actions to divine beings. We should note the logic of the author's argument: if it would be shameful for a *man* to harm his neighbor out of anger or jealousy, how much more would it be shameful for a *god* to do so? Divinities are the "most pure." How could they, given their nature, stoop so low as to pollute the "most mortal" thing: a human body? Thus the Hippocratic author insists that there is—alongside the *ontological* hierarchy (that is, a hierarchy of being or existence)—also an *ethical* hierarchy in nature: it is impious to accuse the gods of doing such vile things because, as superior beings, they must also be morally superior. To suggest otherwise is to disrupt the divine-human hierarchy, thereby committing a sacrilege.

Hippocratic Religion

The points I am making about the role of religion in *On the Sacred Disease* also can be seen in other Hippocratic texts, though not to the same extent. The Hippocratic *Oath,* the most famous of ancient medical texts, explicitly invokes the gods. The oath begins with the physician swearing by the names of Apollo, Asclepius, Hygiea ("Health"), and Panacea ("All-heal"). The speaker calls on "all gods and goddesses" to bear witness to the oath. He promises to conduct his life and practice in a "pure and holy" *(hagnōs, hosiōs)* manner.[10] The author of the little work called *Law* (or translated elsewhere as *Canon*), in an attempt to differentiate true physicians from pretenders, speaks of the medical profession in terms of the "mysteries": he insists that "holy things" must be revealed only to "holy men" and that no one should be given all the secrets of the medical art until he has been "initiated." The texts give us no reason to explain away these sentiments as mere "vestiges" of the cultural trappings of religion. They probably express a genuine religious sensibility.

The author of *Regimen IV,* the fourth section of a longer Hippocratic work, explicitly addresses the significance of different kinds of dreams, some of which are admittedly inspired by the gods. Indeed, the author insists that dreams can often be interpreted by the physician to have diagnostic and prognostic significance. While the body is sleeping, the soul is awake and can then take stock of what is going on in the body without distractions from current sensations. The author notes that there are professional dream interpreters who specialize in such matters and often advise their clients about the prophetic significance of their dreams and tell them to pray to the gods. The Hippocratic author concedes that prayer in such cases is certainly a proper course to take, though he insists that patients should assume some responsibility themselves and depend on the gods merely to assist, not displace, human efforts (*Regimen* 4.87).

The author does *not* discourage patients from employing religious rites in an attempt to avert unwanted future events foretold in dreams; he simply encourages them to pursue Hippocratic medical therapies as well (4.88). The main point, he says, is that patients should learn how to interpret the signs given in their dreams so that they may pursue the appropriate regimens. The appearance of the sun, moon, sky, or stars in dreams, and the different conditions of their appearance, may indicate to patients what sort of bodily condition they possess at a given time. If one dreams of a bright, clear star falling out of its normal course and moving toward the east, that indicates that the patient will experience a clear and natural "separation" (4.89); "separation" is a technical Hippocratic term that refers to the separation of harmful materials from others in the body, a process that is necessary for recovery of health.

Mixed indiscriminately with such advice that looks "medical" and "scientific" to us moderns, however, are explicit recommendations to prayer. If patients receive "good" signs in their dreams, they should pray to the heavenly gods: the Sun, Zeus, Athena,

Hermes, and Apollo. If the signs are contrary, they should pray to the gods of the earth and the heroes, whose particular tasks are to avert evil (4.89). If a patient dreams that the earth is blackened or suffering from drought, that indicates a "dry" condition in the patient's body, in which case he should pursue "moistening" regimens *and* pray to Earth, Hermes, and the heroes (4.90). The author concludes the entire book on *Regimen* with a claim that he has presented the very best procedures by which human beings may maintain their health "with the gods' help" (4.93).[11]

Hippocratic medicine never presented itself as an epistemology "liberated" from religion the way Enlightenment science did. On the contrary, the Hippocratic physicians, along with other intellectuals of their day, proposed a new theology. Rather than separating nature from the divine, as happened in the modern world, they implicated divinity even more thoroughly in nature. The treatise *On Breath,* for instance, presents a "theology of air." Air, according to this author, is the "greatest ruler over everything in the universe," and is spoken of as contemporaries would a god.[12] This scientific theology was well enough known that Aristophanes could make fun of it in a play (*Clouds* 220ff). Similarly, the author of *Fleshes* presents "heat" as a divine being: it is immortal; it perceives, sees, hears, and knows all (§2). There is no good reason to take this language as "mere" personification. Rather, it reflects the same philosophical theology of *Sacred Disease:* the forces of nature—cold, sun, changing winds—are themselves divine.

My point here is not to deny that Hippocratic physicians sometimes placed themselves in competition with religious therapies. They were clearly attempting to mark off a bit of "turf" for themselves in the marketplace of healing therapies, and thus did differentiate themselves from certain cultic healing practices. One place where this sort of tension may be discerned is in the little treatise on *Diseases of Young Girls,* which incidentally provides an etiology for the "sacred disease" somewhat different from the one we have already encountered.

The author argues that the "sacred disease" strikes young virgins more often than other people not because of any divine attack but simply because they suffer from excessive blood. Their menstrual blood has built up in the body due to the fact that virgins have not yet been penetrated in sex, which according to common opinion would have opened up an egress for the menstrual blood or at least facilitated its passage.[13] The surplus blood rises up and suffocates the heart and diaphragm, causing numbness that expresses itself in a certain kind of madness. The remedy is for the girl to have sex with a man as soon as possible and get pregnant. The author does criticize priests for encouraging women to dedicate expensive clothing to Artemis upon recovery from the disease, hinting that the priests, for their own gain, deceive the women. These Hippocratic statements, though, cannot be taken as a rejection of religion; they instead represent a somewhat typical criticism of priestly promotion of excessive expenditure in religious practices and disapproval of the idea that the gods may be "bought off" to do good. The author certainly rejects the belief that Artemis or any other god has caused the disease. And he avoids giving Artemis the credit for the healing. He wants to assume that credit for himself. But to take his words as a rejection of religious observances completely—or as a general statement that divine forces have nothing to do with healing—is not warranted.

Often modern scholars have simply labeled some statements or aspects of these texts as vestiges of "superstitious" or "prescientific" prejudices "left over" but a bit out of place in the otherwise naturalistic or scientific Hippocratic system.[14] But such a characterization is due to an imposition of modern assumptions onto the ancient texts—assumptions about nature, the scientific study of it, and "religion" or the "supernatural." The idea that Hippo-

cratic medicine was a "secular" rejection of religious rites, even in
the field of religious healing, is another case in which the views of
the Enlightenment have been anachronistically read back into the
Greek world. By all indications, the Hippocratic writers shared
the basic religious sensibilities of their fellow intellectuals of classical Greece, and those were not "secular" in anything like the
modern sense.[15] The Hippocratic writers do not totally reject the
activity of the gods, the efficacy of dreams, or other "religious"
factors *because there was no reason for them to do so.* They object to
certain religious practices and beliefs, but not to religion in general or to techniques and mechanisms that *we* might think of as
"religious" or "supernatural" or "magical." They were advocating
a new "sensibility" about nature and the divine—a sensibility that
would eventually label its opposition "superstition." How philosophy, Plato and Aristotle in particular, elaborated and system-
atized that sensibility is the subject of the next chapter.

5
)

Solidifying a New Sensibility

Plato and Aristotle on the Optimal Universe

Plato never uses the word *deisidaimonia* in his surviving works. Aristotle's single use of the term is positive rather than negative: it refers simply to "piety" or "the appropriate attitude towards the gods and religion" (*Politics* 5.9.15 [1315a1]). This is no surprise if, as I have speculated, *deisidaimonia* came to be used pejoratively only around the time of Theophrastus, who wrote after the time of Plato (ca. 429–347 BCE) and Aristotle (384–322 BCE). Yet both Plato and Aristotle are important for my study because the new sensibility about the gods and nature that we have already encountered in Hippocratic sources is clearly evident in the writings of Plato and Aristotle as well. In fact, the centrality of Plato and Aristotle for ancient philosophy and science meant that their notions of nature and divine activity within it exerted tremendous influence on other intellectuals for the duration of the ancient world.

Disease in Myth and Popular Culture

In the first century CE, the Roman medical writer Celsus commented that "in the old days" people generally believed that diseases were due to the anger of the gods (*On Medicine* proem. 4). He seems to have been right. The *Iliad,* for example, famously begins with a scene in which Apollo becomes angry with Agamemnon, the leader of the Argives (Greeks), and thus inflicts the entire camp of Greek warriors with a plague. Agamemnon had taken a beautiful young woman as a captive, "spoils of war," for his own use. Her father, Chryses, a priest of Apollo, comes to the camp to beg for the return of his daughter, offering a ransom for her. Agamemnon mistreats the old man, insulting him and sending him away empty-handed. As punishment for this mistreatment and for Greek arrogance, Apollo attacks the camp with disease:

> The arrows rattled on the shoulders of the angry god as he moved; and his coming was like the night. Then he sat down apart from the ships and let fly an arrow; terrible was the twang of the silver bow. The mules he attacked first and the swift dogs, but then on men themselves he let fly his stinging arrows, and struck; and ever did the pyres of the dead burn thick. For nine days the missiles of the god ranged throughout the army. (*Iliad* 1.46–52; trans. A. T. Murray; rev. William F. Wyatt, Loeb)

Achilles suggests that the Greeks consult the soothsayer, Calchas, who informs them that Apollo sent the disease. The girl must be returned to her father without ransom and a hecatomb of oxen presented to him for sacrifice. The Greeks do so and further "purify" themselves, throw the "defilements" into the sea, and sacrifice to Apollo. The plague ceases.

Apollo is not the only god with a temper and a quiver full of diseases. Artemis is often depicted in the *Iliad* as killing or sending disease upon women, as Apollo does upon men.[1] Indeed, the gods in the *Iliad* seem much like the human characters in the narrative: impetuous, vain, jealous, greedy, and vengeful. The story of the *Iliad,* in fact, is often driven by the very "human" actions and emotions of the gods or the "pacts" made between gods and heroes of one side or the other.

To be sure, the gods are not the *only* cause of disease in Homer. When Odysseus encounters his dead mother in the underworld, he asks whether she died of Artemis's arrows or a "long sickness," suggesting that perhaps certain illnesses (chronic?) could be due to causes other than direct attacks from deities, and that "acute" or sudden diseases were those particularly attributable to the gods (*Odyssey* 11.171–173).[2] But we certainly cannot depict this as a differentiation between "natural" and "supernatural" causation. The gods are one *natural and social* force among others in the causation of disease. Elsewhere in the *Odyssey,* for example, the different possible causes of illness are indiscriminately mixed: even though the Cyclops was blinded by Odysseus, he is told by his relatives that it is an illness sent by Zeus (*Odyssey* 9.411ff).

None of these notions is peculiar to Homer. Hesiod also reflects popular assumptions when he depicts Zeus as the angry author of disease, sometimes afflicting an entire city for the misdeeds of only one person: "The son of Cronos lays great trouble upon the people, famine and plague together, so that the men perish away, and their women do not bear children, and their houses become few, through the contriving of Olympian Zeus" (*Works and Days* 238–245; trans. Hugh G. Evelyn-White).[3] Hesiod also furnishes us with the famous story of Pandora, the woman created by Zeus when he was angry at Prometheus for stealing fire and giving it to human beings. After the human Epimetheus accepts from Zeus the gift of a jar, Pandora herself opens the jar and by doing so releases diseases into the world. Hesiod says that diseases "spontaneously" *(automatai)* afflict human beings, but everyone knows that Zeus was the ultimate cause (*Works and Days* 100–104).

Although these examples come from texts composed much earlier than most of those analyzed in this book, they present a view of divine activity that continued into later times.[4] The assumption that gods and other superhuman beings (such as daimons) may be vengeful or jealous or cause disease was shared by most people around the ancient Mediterranean throughout antiquity.[5] These are the assumptions that intellectuals such as Hippocrates and Theophrastus were combatting—the assumptions that came to be labeled by some upper-class elites as "superstition."

Plato's Hierarchical Universe

Famously, Plato's means of combatting such views of the gods was to exclude all poets from his ideal city. In the *Republic,* Adeimantus, one of Socrates' dialogue partners, bemoans the fact that many people believe that the gods cause all sorts of misfortunes and sufferings for people, even for good, virtuous men.[6] Priests and diviners and all sorts of charlatans convince people, especially rich people, that they can bribe the gods to procure benefits and to persuade them to overlook human misdeeds, even those of dead ancestors. Popular religious leaders even offer the use of magic to help people compel the gods to harm their enemies. And they practice purifications and sacrifices so they will not suffer in the next world in spite of their vicious deeds in this one. Adeimantus complains that people find support for such practices in the poets, citing passages from Hesiod and Homer in particular (*Republic* 364B–365A). If we believe the poets, we might as well commit injustices and then sacrifice to compensate for our sins (365E–366A).

Socrates agrees with Adeimantus's complaint, further suggesting that the myths of the poets should not be taught to people but instead "buried in silence" (378A). The gentlemen agree that the gods are necessarily good and can do no evil (379A–D, 408C). Unlike popular opinion and the teachings of the poets, the gods are not the cause of everything, but only of the good (380C). The myths of the poets teach people otherwise. If the myths are communicated at all, therefore, it should be only to a select minority and under pledge of secrecy. The myths must not be taught because they would encourage immorality, such as people mistreating their parents, sons killing their fathers. The myths are unholy because they incite unholy behavior. So the poets, even Homer and Hesiod, must not be allowed in the city.

We should note that Socrates and his interlocutors agree as a starting point that the gods are purely good.[7] They don't need to prove it to one another because no one in the dialogues argues for the opposite opinion. They all *assume* that God must be the best of everything (as stated in 381B). Thus the myths are wrong for teaching false notions about divinities. But the bulk of the critique of the poets comes down to ethical issues: the poets ought to be rejected and silenced so that people can be taught to be moral. Correct views about divine forces are necessary for social order and public morality. Honoring gods and parents, the speakers concur, demands correct views about divine morality (386A).

Thus Plato's argument against popular notions about the gods and nature is primarily an ethical one. It also includes a strong element of social and cosmological hierarchy. In fact, in order to understand why popular "superstitions" bothered Plato so much, we must pay attention to his broader theories about the nature of nature. We must understand his universe as a social and cosmic hierarchy. Though Plato's cosmological and ethical ideas may be found in many of his works, I here concentrate on the *Timaeus,* which is generally acknowledged as his most important and historically influential cosmological treatise.

First, we must recognize that Plato again *begins* his argument with highly important *assumptions* that are nowhere proven. He seems to believe that one must begin from these presuppositions. Put simply, much of Plato's position can be expressed as interlocked propositions:

A. The cosmos is divine.
B. The divine is good.
C. Therefore the cosmos is good.

Thus Plato, early in the *Timaeus,* states that both the cosmos and the Demiurge (the divine being who constructed the universe out of chaos) are "beautiful" or "noble" *(kalos)* and "good" *(agathos).* To say otherwise would be simply impious and shameful. In fact, the cosmos is the *most* beautiful of things that have come into existence (this would, in Plato's system, exclude those entities that have always existed and therefore do not "come into existence"), and the Demiurge is the "best" *(aristos)* of all "causes" (29A). Again, we must admit that these statements provide the *starting point* for Plato's other arguments; they are themselves not demonstrated.

If the Demiurge is "good," however, he must then be completely devoid of envy *(phthonos,* 29E)—or of any evil for that matter. God (Plato sometimes simply calls the Demiurge "God" —*ho theos*) wanted everything to be good and nothing to be evil *as far as possible* (*kata dynamin,* 30A). He therefore made the universe (sometimes designated by the Greek term *kosmos,* sometimes, as here, by the term *ouranos,* which can also be translated "sky" or "heaven") perfectly proportional and self-sufficient. In fact, the universe is itself, for Plato, a "blessed god" (*eudaimōn theos,* 34B). The cosmos that we inhabit is a "visible, living" creature, the abode of other creatures. It is a "visible god" made in the image of the invisible. It is the greatest, best, most beautiful, most perfect of things made (92C).

It is also constructed throughout as a hierarchy. The highest beings in the created universe are the celestial gods, which include the stars, other heavenly bodies such as the sun and moon, and even the earth (40A–D). Apparently somewhat "lower" are the "other gods": Cronos, Rhea, Zeus, Hera, and others known from tradition. All these mentioned so far are the "immortals" (40D–41A). Below them exist "mortal" living creatures, those that exist in the air, those in the water, and those on land. The mortal beings were not made, as were the "immortals," with complete purity, but at a second or third degree of purity (41C–D). Above most of the other animals, but among the mortals nonetheless, are human beings, of two kinds. The better of the two is man *(anēr)*, the inferior is woman (42A).[8]

Human beings, though, may move up or down in the hierarchy. Those men who obey their superior "souls" avoid the consequences of violent passions and errors and thereby may become stars. Those men who pursue the baser passions and desires, on the other hand, may be reborn as women. If the person then sins even more, he/she may be reborn in a bestial form in the next life (42B). Thus the clear hierarchy (here put simply) consists of (1) divine stars, (2) men, (3) women, and (4) beasts.

Later in the *Timaeus* Plato elaborates this hierarchical scheme further, and in doing so informs us where daimons occur within it. First, we must note that for Plato the human body is also constructed as a hierarchy. The soul takes on different forms—imagined either as a tripartite soul or as three different but related souls—according to its nature and function, and the different "souls" (or "parts" of the soul) occupy different locations in the body. The most divine, rational soul is located in the head; a bit lower, in the chest, resides the part of the soul that is the source for emotional strength, such as courage (see 70A); the belly and genitals, even further down, contain the lowest part of the soul, that associated with passion and desire. The genitals, as lower members of the hierarchical body, are disobedient and unruly, led by desire rather than contemplation and self-control, which are represented by the head, so to speak, and the heavens. The head is thus male and the genitals female (whether of a man or woman; see 91B). God has given to each person a divine daimon who attempts to lead the highest portion of the human soul to virtue. This soul, aided by the divine daimon, exists at the top part of the body and tries to pull the person upward to heaven, the abode of the soul's true "family" or "kinfolk" (90A). People therefore move up or down in the cosmic hierarchy according to whether or not they heed their divine daimon, on the one hand, or the lower passions, on the other.

At this point Plato returns to the subject of reincarnation already broached and elaborates further, in a manner that somewhat "mythically" explains how different beings came into existence. Men who were cowards or acted unjustly became women in their next life; woman *came about* from cowardly or passionate men (91A). Birds came about from the souls of men who were relatively harmless but empty-headed and silly (91D). Four-footed beasts came about from men who could not learn from philosophy to contemplate the things above. Their upper bodies were dragged earthward, as their thoughts had been. They thus became beasts who could walk only on all fours (91E). Snakes ("footless, wriggling creatures") came from people who were most foolish, and water creatures from men who were the most thoughtless and stupid. They proved to be unworthy even to breathe pure air, so they were forced into the turbid depths to breathe muddy water (92A–B).

What is most important for my purposes about Plato's hierarchy is not simply that he assumes a hierarchy, but that he combines, indeed jumbles together, what we could consider *different* hierarchical scales without explicitly noting that he is doing so. But it is important for *us* to analyze the interrelations among these different hierarchical scales because they will provide the key for Plato's rejection of popular religious beliefs and practices, of "superstition." By taking apart the different hierarchies that he jumbles together, we can analyze Plato's assumptions; and this we may do by noting the different terms that invoke different kinds of hierarchical values.

First, there are simply the ontological terms that presuppose hierarchy. The cosmos, as noted above, is "great" *(megistos)*, "excellent" *(aristos)*, and "most perfect" *(teleōtatos,* 92C). The ontological hierarchy is matched by aesthetics: the cosmos is also "the beautiful" *(kallistos)*. These hierarchies are graphed spatially as well. The different regions of heaven, occupied by beings of differing status, provide a central concern for the *Timaeus,* but heaven may also play the role of the "highest" in comparison with earth and, lower, water; or with the triad "air/water/depths," extending to the "murky depths of water." And as we have seen, the body mimics the cosmic hierarchy, with head, spine (or trunk), and genitals in a descending hierarchy.

More telling, though, is the way Plato mixes up what we might differentiate as *intellectual* qualities and *moral* or *affective* qualities. Men, Plato writes, may be punished with a lower incarnation if they are "light-minded" *(kouphoi,* which we might translate as "air-heads"); simpletons *(di' euētheian,* 91D); foolish *(aphrōn; aphronestatos,* 92A); mindless *(anoētotatos)*; ignorant *(amathestatos;* cf. *amathia,* 92B); or "unable to obey reason" *(anhypēkoon tou logou,* 90B). But they may also be demoted for "moral" failings: if they are cowards *(deiloi)* or unjust *(adikōs,* 90E), for example. The lower parts of the body, the genitals, prove their inferiority by the fact that they are disobedient *(apeithes)* and self-willed *(autokrates)*. People led by the genitals are driven by desires *(di' epithymias)* and tend to be domineering (cf. *kratein,* 91B). The souls punished by being forced into the murky depths of water proved their inferiority not only by their stupidity, but also by their "impurity of soul" (cf. *akathartōs,*

92B). Throughout this section of the *Timaeus*, Plato mixes
together—apparently indiscriminately—intellectual and moral
terms of superior and inferior.

Note that there seems to be no consciousness that what could
be taken as several *different* hierarchies are being inextricably implicated with one another. From a modern point of view, it appears odd to *assume* a match between intellectual power and
moral rectitude. We do not automatically take "error" to be as
culpable as moral failure. This may, to be sure, reflect more a
modern peculiarity than an *ancient* one. In any case, in order to
understand Plato's logic about the morality of the gods, we must
put asunder what Plato has, perhaps unconsciously, joined together: the hierarchies of ontology, intellect, morality, aesthetics,
gender, and space. The important revolution in ancient thinking
that Plato here represents (I do not believe he invented it) is not
the assumption of hierarchy—that was everywhere in the ancient
world—but the assumption that the different hierarchical scales
match one another: that superior beings are superior with regard
to morality as well as intellect, power, and beauty. Ontological hierarchy is matched by axiological hierarchy.

The peculiarity of this intercalated hierarchical system is seldom noticed by modern readers, probably because the *theological*
aspect of it—that divinity is necessarily moral *and* ontologically
superior—is one that pervades our own assumptions about the
nature of the divine. We *assume* that God, if one exists, is good.
But the failure of modern readers to remark on the peculiarity of
this philosophical hierarchy should not be allowed to mask just
how odd the idea was. Before the Greek philosophers, no one in
Greek culture (or possibly in the ancient Mediterranean as a
whole) had been so bold as to assume that beings of superior status were by definition also morally superior. It was a profound
revolution in ancient thought, even if most scholars have not recognized it as such. And perhaps most surprising, it was never
proven; it was assumed.

On Harming One's Enemies: The New Ethics of the Gentleman

As we have seen, one of the main arguments of ancient intellectuals against the popular beliefs they labeled "superstition" was that gods and daimons, *as superior beings,* were also good and just. They insisted that people should not fear gods or daimons because such beings were superior not only with regard to power but also morality. This position flew in the face of almost unanimous ancient opinion, which assumed that gods and other superior beings need not be ethical. The philosophers were therefore advocating an idea that must have struck most people as counterintuitive.[9]

Another of the intuitive "truths" of the ancient Greek world was that people did and should "help their friends and harm their enemies," an ethic also expected of the gods.[10] Thus no one was surprised to see gods and goddesses in the *Iliad* fighting for their "favorites" and against the enemies of their "favorites." "The enemy of my friend is my enemy," according to traditional assumptions. And people expected the gods to act likewise. So Apollo fights for Aeneas and Hector but against Patroclus and Achilles; Athena helps Odysseus but tricks Hector.[11] The principle "help friends, harm enemies" was, in the words of Mary Whitlock Blundell, simply part of "traditional Greek morality."[12] But this is again an aspect of traditional morality and religion that came under attack from philosophers, with Socrates and Plato, apparently, leading the way.

Some scholars have noted that an explicit rejection of the traditional assumption that one should hurt one's enemies "is not found before Socrates, who argued that one should harm no one, even in retaliation."[13] But the Socratic and Platonic arguments against the principle became highly influential in later philosophy. They helped to provide a new ethic for discussing the proper behavior of the educated gentleman. And that ethic helped strengthen and bring cohesion to the philosophical definition of superstition and the attack upon it. Socrates' position is stated in various places, in the writings of both Plato and Xenophon.[14] But it is elaborated and placed in a broader context of philosophical ethics in Plato's long dialogue *Gorgias,* which will provide the source for my exposition of the principle.

The *Gorgias* may be read as Plato's own "apology," put in the mouth of Socrates, for pursuing a life of philosophical contemplation rather than politics. It ostensibly presents a debate between Socrates and Gorgias (perhaps the most famous sophist and teacher of rhetoric in Athens at the time), Polus, and Callicles (disciples of Gorgias) on the nature of rhetoric. Socrates begins by trying to get Gorgias and his pupils to define rhetoric and explain exactly what its benefits are. Socrates' position is that rhetoric is basically just "flattery of the masses" (463A–B) and ultimately of no use for inculcating virtue or true "happiness" (the Greek term, *eudaimonia,* is famously difficult to translate, but it refers to that "blessedness" or "ultimate well-being" considered the greatest good, certainly in most of Greek philosophy and probably in popular thought as well). Polus and Callicles defend rhetoric by arguing that it offers supreme power, because the power to persuade other human beings leads to unlimited power to have one's way and thus to protect oneself if necessary from harm threatened by other human beings (see, for example, 452E). Especially in a democratic city, the power to persuade is real power. Socrates argues, though, that rhetoric works only by making people *believe* something, not by teaching them the truth itself. Rhetoric produces belief, not knowledge (455A). He gets Gorgias to admit that rhetoric may be used for good or ill. If one is concerned to know what truth and justice are, rhetoric will be of no help. Thus the dialogue becomes, to a great extent, a debate on the nature of justice, good, and evil.

Space prohibits relating the long and complex argument contained in this complicated dialogue. For my purposes it will suffice to use the dialogue to highlight certain Socratic-Platonic slogans that come to be important for the ancient philosophical condemnation of superstition, slogans that influenced Greek philosophy thereafter. I distill them here from the convoluted meanderings of Socrates' argument in the *Gorgias* to the following: (1) "No one does evil willingly"; (2) "It is better to suffer wrong than to do wrong"; (3) "Only the good person is happy"; and (4) "The good man cannot be harmed."[15]

1. "No one does evil willingly." Polus had begun by praising rhetoric because it gives people power over other people. With that sort of power, one could do "whatever one wishes," whether that be helping one's friends or hurting one's enemies, taking other people's property or wreaking vengeance on those who have themselves attempted to harm one. Doing "whatever one wishes," therefore, is a great good provided by rhetoric. Socrates counters by arguing that "doing whatever one wishes" is not true power if the thing done is itself bad, and he backs up this point with his famous argument that "no one willingly chooses the bad" (466D–468C).

The argument goes like this: we do not wish for bad things themselves, even for bad things to happen to other people; rather, we ultimately just want the benefits that may accrue to ourselves. So cities execute people or expel them or confiscate their property *not* as ends in themselves but because they believe those actions will result in benefits for the city, say, by getting rid of a potential threat or perhaps by being able then to confiscate the punished person's property. Even when people do harm, Socrates claims, it is not the harm itself that they are ultimately after, but the benefit that may accrue as a consequence of the harm. People may submit to a painful medical operation, for example, but they are not truly "willing" the pain, only the benefit of health that may come about in spite of the pain. Thus all people wish for *benefit,* not *harm,* which is to say that they choose good and not evil, even when it may appear that they are choosing evil. And so, according to Socrates, it only *appears* that people choose to do evil. They are *actually* choosing some ultimate benefit (or something they perceive as a benefit) as the "end" for which the evil is only a means. "No one chooses evil."

2. *"It is better to suffer wrong than to do wrong."* According to popular opinion, one would surely rather inflict harm on someone else than be harmed. The benefit of being a tyrant, according to Polus and Callicles, was not only that the tyrant could "do as he wished," but also that he could protect himself from injustices while treating his enemies harshly with impunity. It strikes them as ridiculous (as it must have struck just about everyone) for Socrates to maintain that he would rather suffer evil done to him than commit evil himself. Socrates thus repeatedly defends his own belief that it is better to be wronged than to commit wrong (469B–C; 527B, passim).

Socrates first gets Polus and Callicles to admit that people agree that it is bad to be the victim of injustice, but that it is even more ignoble (shameful, disgraceful) to *commit* injustice (474C). A good man may in circumstances suffer an injustice himself, but if he commits an injustice he has proved himself to be an unjust man, and thus dishonorable. Socrates here substitutes the term *aischos* (shame, disgrace) for the word used up to this point for "evil" or "wrong" *(kakia).* After many turns in the dialogue, Socrates gets the others to agree that what is ignoble, shameful, disgraceful *(aischros)* is "bad" *(kakos).* Thus *aischros = kakos.* Therefore, if it is "worse" *(aischion;* more shameful) to commit an injustice than to suffer injustice, it is also "more evil" *(kakion)* and thus to be avoided. By playing on common notions of honor and shame, Socrates forces Polus to admit that it is worse to commit injustice than to suffer injustice. A man who knows what is *truly* in his own benefit (and thus truly wishes to do good by himself) will never commit an injustice against another person.

3. *"Only the good person is happy."* Polus and Callicles had expressed a "common sense" of Greek culture by assuming that the person with most social power, say the tyrant, was also the happiest: he could do whatever he wished; he had whatever he wanted; he could live as he pleased. They admitted that the tyrant must commit all sorts of injustices in order to maintain his grip on power, but that was the cost of maintaining his "happiness," his "well-being" *(eudaimonia).* Socrates argues, on the contrary, that an unjust, evil person cannot be truly happy or blessed. Only the good person is truly happy *(eudaimōn,* 470E). As a corollary to this claim, Socrates insists, again contrary to common opinion, that the evildoer will be better off if he is caught and punished for his deeds than if he escapes punishment unscathed. According to Socrates, escaping punishment for wrongdoing is worse than suffering punishment for it (474B).

Basically Socrates succeeds in arguing his position in this case by getting his interlocutors to equate the health of the body with the health of the soul: they admit that virtue is to the soul as health is to the body. Just as physicians inflict pain on a body to heal it of disease and render it whole, so judges inflict pain on a soul to heal it of vice and render it virtuous (477B). Therefore pain, when it leads to a more virtuous life, is "good" (478D). "Blessedness" or "well-being" *(eudaimonia)* is the absence of evil in the soul (478E). Most people don't recognize that a sick soul is worse than a sick body, which is why people have wrong opinions about what they should pursue and what they should avoid (479B–C). Though they know enough to go to a doctor when in corporeal pain, they are too ignorant to go to a philosopher to cure their souls. Nonetheless, vice is to the soul as sickness is to the body (504–505). One should therefore *welcome* punishment for vice, for true "health" is only possible for the virtuous person.

4. *"The good man cannot be harmed."* Polus and Callicles had attempted to persuade Socrates that a sufficient knowledge of rhetoric would enable him to protect himself from being harmed

by other persons. They repeatedly evoke images of Socrates or some other poor soul being dragged into court unjustly and taken advantage of by enemies (somewhat prophetically, of course, in Socrates' case). Socrates' answer lies in another of his famous paradoxical claims: that the truly virtuous man cannot ultimately be harmed (521C). In this case again, Socrates depends on the willingness of his interlocutors to compare soul to body. Since he has already gotten them to agree that vice is to the soul as disease is to the body, he next argues that doing wrong is worse than suffering harm to one's body because committing an injustice damages the soul, whereas suffering an injustice constitutes damage only to the body. The virtuous and wise man will prefer even a "noble death" to committing an injustice. Doing wrong harms the soul, but dying is merely the separation of the soul from the body (522E).

We should note that after all this argument in which he tries to convince his dialogue partners that virtue is *intrinsically* good and right, and vice is *intrinsically* bad, Socrates ends the discussion with an elaborate account of afterlife punishment and reward (523A–527A). It is almost as if Plato was none too sure that Socrates' arguments for virtue would stand on their own, so he supplements the arguments with a "myth" about judgment, punishment, and reward for souls in the afterlife. If for no other reason, people should avoid vice and embrace virtue in order to escape punishment after death.

The significance of these different Socratic-Platonic, counterintuitive slogans for the developing meaning of "superstition" are obvious. By universal assumption, the gods are supremely "blessed," "happy," and "well-off." The very *meaning* of divinity for most people was centered on the notion of *eudaimonia* that gods were assumed to enjoy and humans sought. According to the philosophers, though, *if* the gods are supremely blessed, they *must also* be supremely virtuous. Furthermore, just as the wise man will never do harm, even to his enemies and even in retaliation, so the gods never commit harm (except to administer appropriate punishment for the ultimate betterment of the person; Plato does entertain, remember, the notion of remedial punishment in the afterlife). Moreover, if the good man can never truly suffer harm (even death is merely the separation of the soul from the body), so the gods certainly cannot be harmed by mere humans. It is ridiculous, therefore, to think of the gods being hurt or discomfited by a dearth of sacrifices or human ministrations. If a wise man like Socrates need not fear harm, so much less the gods. In summary, as everyone accepted that the gods were supremely "blessed" and powerful, able to do whatever they liked, so the philosophers came to argue that the gods also were supremely virtuous, beneficent, and beyond harm from human activity. There was certainly no reason to fear them.

We should note, however, that the philosophers had no "evidence" that could have "proven" that the gods acted like Socrates, never suffering ultimate harm, never harming. The philosophers had not discovered some piece of reality that demonstrated that the gods were virtuous. The philosophical position was a projection of a new gentlemanly ethic onto the realm of the divine. It was a logical extension of a philosophical ethic for humans to the gods, which was so logical because it also partook of the logic of hierarchy we have analyzed in the previous section: those higher on the ontological scale must be higher on the ethical scale. Thus if virtuous men do not harm even their enemies, the gods must not do so either.

Aristotle on "the Mean"

Aristotle accepted these Socratic-Platonic views. Like Plato (and everyone else in the classical world), Aristotle assumes that "the divine" is part of nature. Aristotle shares Plato's hierarchical view of nature: divine beings, though still part of nature, are highest, shown by their greater honor or worth *(timos),* their freedom, and the fact that they neither come into being nor depart from being *(Parts of Animals* 1.5 [644b23–645a8]). Animals fall below that category: they come into being and die, and they are not divine. Human beings fall between divine beings and the lower animals because they share in divine essence (4.10 [686a25]). Nature, which does everything justly and fairly, respects the social hierarchy of all of reality: the more honorable parts of the body are given the more honorable places in the body (3.4 [665b2]; 3.3 [665a23]).

Since gods and heroes are superior to human beings *(Politics* 7.13.1 [1332b17–24]), they are also supremely happy and blessed *(eudaimōn, makarios,* 7.1.5 [1323b26]). For human beings, Aristotle agrees that virtue is necessary for happiness (7.8.2 [1328b36]; 7.12.3 [1332a8–11]).[16] And Aristotle agrees that the virtuous man will be cruel to no one, and fierce only toward those who commit injustice and need disciplining (7.6.3 [1328a9]). There are yet other themes relevant to the philosophical critique of superstition that receive greater elaboration in Aristotle, two of which I address in the remainder of this chapter: Aristotle's promotion of "the mean" between extremes and his teleology.

We have already seen how Theophrastus paints superstition as "excess" religion. *Deisidaimonia* is the "extreme" for which piety is "the mean," the appropriate "moderate." He learned well from Aristotle. Aristotle makes elaborate use, especially in his work *Nicomachean Ethics,* of the notion that all vices are extremes of behaviors or traits whose "virtue" lies between the two extremes of excess or deficiency.[17] It is no accident that Aristotle's language clearly recalls ancient medical theory, which portrayed health as a balance between two opposing tendencies. Too much of "the dry" or "the wet" or "the hot" or "the cold" makes a body sick. Hippocratic writers before Aristotle had taught that a balance of the different "humors" (often four, but there was no unanimity at this early period) of the body constituted the state of health, whereas an overabundance or predominance of a particular humor or substance constituted illness. Aristotle, the son of a physician, explicitly links his ethical theory to medical theories of balance and extremes.

As in medicine and the body, so for character—virtue or health is a middle position between two extremes: excess and deficiency. The man who is afraid of everything is a coward; the man who is not afraid of anything, including things he *ought* to be afraid of, is rash. The person who indulges every little desire is morally "sick" at one extreme; the person who will not allow himself to enjoy even decent and sensible pleasures is morally "sick" at the other extreme (*Nicomachean Ethics* 2.2.6–7 [1104a12–27]). One should feel neither too much nor too little anger (2.5.2 [1105b26–29]). As Aristotle puts it, "Ethical virtue is the mean. How so? It is the mean between two vices, one of too much, the other of too little. . . . It is moderation in both emotions and actions" (2.9.1 [1109a20–25]).

A large section of the *Nicomachean Ethics* reads as if it could have served as a model for Theophrastus's *Character Sketches*. Aristotle provides small character descriptions of different types of men. The virtuous man is generous; the man of vice is profligate on one side or stingy on the other. The virtuous is magnanimous; the man of vice is either arrogant or small-minded. The virtuous with regard to anger is gentle (he becomes angry at appropriate times and situations but remains in control); the man of vice is either irascible or spineless. The virtuous man is witty; a man with an excess of wit is a buffoon and one with a deficient amount is a killjoy. And on and on (2.7 [1107a28–1108b10]).

We may be inclined to raise the same question we confronted with Theophrastus, however: how is one to know so confidently *where* the middle is? Most people consider the middle to be wherever *they* are. Significantly, Aristotle recognizes that the middle or mean is relative: it may be different for different people. For some people, a certain amount of food suffices, but the same amount may be too little or too much for others (2.6.7 [1106a36–1106b5]). Thus also for ethics: compared to a coward, a brave man looks rash; and compared to a rash man, a brave man may seem cowardly. "Hence either extreme character tries to push the middle character towards the other extreme; a coward calls a brave man rash and a rash man calls him a coward" (2.8.3 [1108b23–26]; trans. H. Rackham). Aristotle realizes that we all tend to push the "middle" to be where we are.

The proper thing to seek, according to Aristotle, is the "mean" in relation to the particular person: "Virtue then is a settled disposition of the mind determining the choice of actions and emotions, consisting essentially in the observance of the mean relative to us, this being determined by principle, that is, as the sensible [*ho phronimos*] man would determine it" (2.6.15 [1106b36–1107a3]; Rackham's translation slightly modified). Of course, one could say that this just begs the question, since it doesn't tell us how to identify "the sensible man." Aristotle does provide another test for ascertaining what is "the middle" and what is "the extreme": pain. If we experience pain rather than pleasure when doing something, that is an indication that we should move toward the other pole; we have found that we are in an "extreme" of either excess or deficiency (2.9.4–5 [1109b2–8]; see also 2.3 [1104b4–1105a16] for the idea that pain and pleasure are what alter our behaviors).

It is hard to see, though, how this "test" would work in practice for many of the vices Aristotle discusses. For instance, it is virtuous to be a generous benefactor, spending from one's own pocket to benefit or entertain others. "Vulgar" men don't know how to strike the right balance: they either spend far too much, and thus come across looking like show-offs, or they spend too little and come across looking like skinflints. But the "vulgar man" is not able to *feel* when he is spending too much or too little. The person's own experience of "pain" or "pleasure," therefore, cannot here serve as a reliable indicator of when the person has spent too little or too much. In this case "pain" does not work well as a "test" for the mean. Rather, the situation demands a sense of "taste" or "etiquette," something that Aristotle experienced as second nature, but that someone else, especially someone of a different class, may have found inscrutable. Again we are left, therefore, with a "virtue" (moderation) for which it is impossible to make dependable prescriptions.

For Aristotle, though, virtue *is* something that has to be instilled into someone by training, discipline, and socialization (one of the main points of all of the *Nicomachean Ethics;* see 2.1[1103a14–1103b25], for example).[18] Thus Aristotle would not consider it a particularly damning criticism of his notion of the "mean" to point out that it is like social etiquette or taste, social graces taught and instilled in persons over time.[19] Just as one has to be socialized to know which fork is the appropriate one to use (to use a slight anachronism), so one has to be socialized to know how much is the right amount of money to spend for a particular social occasion—or what is the right amount of respect and awe one should demonstrate toward a god or daimon. The principle of the "mean," in any case, is not a reliable test for discerning virtue and vice in many cases apart from the requisite socialization.

The very fact that the mean cannot usually be prescribed but must be learned through socialization makes the notion even more serviceable for conservative ideological purposes. As Theophrastus's and Aristotle's writings on excess and deficiency themselves demonstrate, what counted as "appropriate" behavior had much to do with upper-class sensibilities. Notions of "moderation" or "the proper mean" could not function very well to prescribe ahead of time what would count as appropriate religious behavior and what would be condemned as "superstitious." But that simply gave the philosophers, as themselves higher-class gentlemen, more power to do the labeling.

Teleology: The Most Perfect World Possible

One of the things that most bothered ancient intellectuals about popular religious beliefs and practices is that they seemed to accept a rather unpredictable and capricious universe, and certainly one that was less than optimal. Gods and other superhuman forces could be expected to behave in certain ways, to be sure, but they were no more dependable, in the popular imagination, than most human beings were: they could become angry or jealous or spiteful at the drop of a hat. Greek philosophers developed a conception of the universe—and divine activities within it—that they could convince themselves was at least a bit more secure, predictable, and optimal. And the doctrine of natural teleology, elaborated to a great extent in Aristotelian philosophy, served to reinforce the view that nature was sensible, indeed as perfect as possible.[20]

The Greek word *telos* means "goal," "purpose," and "end." It can even be used to refer to a state of completion, maturity, or perfection.[21] Each of these terms supplies some of the sensibility of the ancient philosophical doctrine of teleology. Aristotle's work *Parts of Animals* contains his attempt to explain the nature and purpose of all the different parts of the bodies of animals, so it provides some of his clearest statements and arguments in support of natural teleology. The basic thesis is that "Nature does nothing in vain." As Aristotle states early in the book, "Nature makes everything for the sake of something (for some purpose)" (1.1 [641b12]). Everything created by Nature has a purpose, a reason for being, and Nature makes nothing superfluous (*periergon;* see 3.1 [661b24], 4.11 [691b4]).[22]

A good example of Aristotle's way of thinking can be seen

in his explanation for why human beings have hands. He cites Anaxagoras as teaching that man is the most intelligent of animals *because* he has hands (that is, man's hands enabled him to become the most intelligent). Aristotle thinks the causal explanation should go the other way around: Nature gave man hands *because* he was the most intelligent animal. The other animals would have been too stupid to know how to make the best use of hands, unlike man. "Hands are tools, and like a sensible person, Nature always distributes each thing to the being capable of using it" (4.10 [687a7–12]). The hand is an extremely versatile tool. Man, as the most intelligent, was the rational choice for which animal would get hands since he was smart enough to discover all the different uses to which a hand could be put. Aristotle concludes, "Since . . . Nature accomplishes the best given the existing possibilities, it is not that man is the most sensible of animals because he has hands, but that he has hands because he is the most sensible" (4.10 [687a15]).

The phrase, "the existing possibilities," is significant. According to most ancient theories about Nature and the possible, Nature is itself constrained by necessity. Nature itself cannot do just anything imaginable, but must work within the confines of material reality. And this is part of Aristotle's teleology also: Nature does everything as perfectly as possible *given the constraints of reality.* Aristotle explains, for instance, that the purpose of an ax (its "end," *telos,* goal, reason for being) is to split wood; in order to accomplish that purpose, an ax *must* be made out of a very hard material—either bronze or iron—that is harder than wood and can be worked to have a sharp edge. Someone could not make an ax out of just any kind of material. The ax must be made of hard metal *in order to serve its purpose* (*Parts of Animals* 1.1 [642a2–13]). In the same way, Nature has to work within the confines of reality to make things the *best possible* way given the constraints of reality and the desired ends.

Thus Aristotle admits that Nature is sometimes, as it were,

"thwarted" from accomplishing her more idealistic desires by the constraints of reality. For example, Nature prefers to locate the organ that rules sensation (for Aristotle, the heart) in just one place in an animal's body. "Nature wants [*bouletai*] to make the body a unity, and when she is able, she makes it a unity; if she is not able, she makes it a plurality." Thus in a centipede, which is extremely long, the "ruling part" occupies more than one place in the body, which is why a centipede is able to continue to live when cut up (4.5 [682a2–8]). Nature's desire was thwarted by the contingencies of materiality, in this case by the centipede.

An aspect of Aristotle's teleology that is related to this notion of the "constraints of necessity" is his assumption that Nature operates as a "zero-sum" economic system.[23] According to most ancient thought, normal economies are "zero-sum" economies: there was a fixed amount of wealth assumed to exist in any society, and if one person grew richer, another person or persons necessarily had to grow poorer. The "credit" accrued by one class necessarily had to mean a "debit" charged to the other class. In his *Politics,* for instance, Aristotle deprecates trade (the business of merchants); in his opinion it is not "according to nature" since it necessarily involves some people profiting at the expense of others (1.3.23 [1258b2]; see also 2.4.2 [1266b1]). This assumption explains why political conflicts in the ancient city were so often depicted as different classes fighting over an unchanging amount of wealth. Conflicts were thought to be caused either by the upper class attempting to get more and more wealth, which would further impoverish the lower class, or by the lower class attempting to "rob" the rich.

Ancient philosophy (and medicine, for that matter) interpreted all of Nature as operating on the same principle. Aristotle explains, for example, why animals with horns have fewer or smaller teeth than animals without horns: Nature tends to balance resources; the material that would normally have gone into making teeth has been redirected for the production of horns. The lack of teeth is compensation for their horns (*Parts of Animals* 3.2 [664a1]). Aristotle also explains, to cite another example, that birds of prey have relatively smaller bodies because they are furnished with large wings and strong instruments (beak, claws, nails) necessary for capturing their prey; their wings, beak, and claws are balanced out by their smaller bodies (4.12 [694a]). The zero-sum economic system is one of the constraints within which Nature must operate in her attempt to create the best world possible.

It is fascinating to see how these different principles that rule Aristotle's Nature—teleology, the constraints of necessity, zero-sum—come together in some of his explanations for why the world is as it is. Take Aristotle's explanation for why man has no tail (4.10 [689b2–25]). Unlike many other animals, man has, in place of a tail, fleshy buttocks and thighs, which provide protection and enable him to sit more easily. By this arrangement Nature took care of several problems with one simple solution. (1) Since man stands upright, he needs to carry more of his weight on the lower part of his body so that the upper body will be lighter and less likely to tip over; so Nature shifted some of the weight that most animals carry on their trunks and shoulders down to the lower half of man. (2) Second, his fleshy buttocks also allow man to sit, which is more necessary for him since he stands up straight and becomes fatigued faster standing than quadrupeds do. (3) Furthermore, the materials that *would* have gone into making a tail for man were used up in making the buttocks, thighs, and calves thicker: "the nourishment gets used up for the benefit of the buttocks and legs before it can get as far as the place for the tail" (trans. Rackham). (4) Finally, since the buttocks provide protection for the anus, there is no need for a tail, and Nature would not make something for which there was no need. Here we encounter a combination of several ideas that all unite to form Aristotelian teleology: everything in Nature has a purpose; Nature always provides what is needed; Nature provides only what is needed and nothing superfluous; and Nature has to work within a zero-sum economy.[24]

This teleology provided ancient intellectuals with a way to make sense of the potential chaos of the world. We should notice, though, that it was both ideologically conservative and rather optimistic in its view of reality. It is easy to see how it was conservative: if Nature has constructed everything in the best possible manner, any radical change in the structure of the world—such as a challenge to the natural and social hierarchy—will be disastrous, *if* it is possible at all. The philosophical teleology was optimistic because it insisted that the world was ultimately and essentially "good," in fact, the best that it possibly could be. Teleology is perfection within limits. The perfection must be simply believed. The limits must be accepted. Popular beliefs, "superstition," posited a less than perfect world—in fact a scary and dangerous world—and thus offended the philosophical sensibility.

Systematizing a Sensibility

Plato and Aristotle had much to do with solidifying ideas about the gods and nature that came to be assumed as *the* correct philosophical views by many different intellectuals of the ancient world, including those who adhered to different philosophical schools.[25] They taught that the ontological hierarchy of nature was matched by an ethical hierarchy: beings who were superior in nature and power were assumed to be superior ethically. This concept of matched ontological and ethical hierarchies was a completely new sensibility in the ancient world.

Plato and Aristotle, I believe, did not themselves completely invent the new sensibility. As I showed in the previous chapter, early Hippocratics apparently made the same assumptions in the treatise *On the Sacred Disease,* which may well predate Plato and Aristotle but in any case shows no clear influence from them. Plato's and Aristotle's achievement was to solidify the new ideas about nature and the gods and incorporate them into their philosophical systems.

And we should note how the different themes analyzed in this chapter fit together into a system. Added to the idea of the matched hierarchies was the Socratic teaching that popular opinion was also wrong in its assumption that one should "help one's friends and harm one's enemies." It now became a philosophical virtue to harm no one, not even one's enemies. But just as the "good man" alone is happy, and the "good man" will not harm, so it became accepted that the gods must behave likewise. The gods, everybody admitted, are happy; therefore they are good; therefore they harm no one; therefore the myths are wrong; therefore we need not fear the gods. "Fear of the gods" became an error and a philosophical vice. By the time of Theophrastus, it received the designation *deisidaimonia:* superstition.

Central Aristotelian notions also became part of the regular philosophical critique of popular religion. Aristotle's ideas about "moderation," "balance," and "the mean" became incorporated into the philosophical notion of superstition. Superstition was religion taken to extremes, religion out of control, religion that forgot the virtue of balance. As we have seen, this hardly furnished a prescription for knowing *where* the "extreme" or "excess" actually lay. One had to be properly socialized to have acquired the "taste" needed for knowing what was too little, what too much, and what just right. But that small problem did not bother Aristotle or the philosophers. *They* knew what amount of religious piety was right, even if the "masses" did not. So again, superstition became a vice invented and controlled by the philosophical class.

And finally, Aristotelian teleology provided important ammunition in certain attacks on superstition. It is true that some philosophical schools rejected teleology entirely. The Epicureans were well known throughout antiquity for rejecting teleology. In their view things were as they were because of accident, not foreplanning, providence, or the beneficence of "divine Nature." And the Skeptics would prefer to say that teleology is a doctrine about which we can have no certain knowledge. But as we will see later in this study, Aristotelian teleology came to exert a powerful influence on later criticisms of superstition. It fit with the generally "optimistic" view of nature advocated by the new philosophical sensibility. Philosophical teleology taught that the world that exists is the best possible world—that is, the world is as good as it possibly could be made even by a god, given the contraints of materiality (there will be more demonstration of this in the chapter below on Galen). It was therefore very optimistic about current reality and also very conservative ideologically. And it provided one more reason to reject popular religious notions as "superstitious." The moral ambiguities of superior beings taught by myths and assumed by the common people could not be true if "Divine Nature" had planned correctly and properly carried out her plan. The "optimal universe" taught by Aristotelian teleology fit with the notions already outlined above that the world is a good place because it *ought* to be a good place. To believe otherwise would come to be "superstition."

6

Diodorus Siculus and the
Failure of Philosophy

Diodorus Siculus presents both possibilities and problems for an investigation into ancient superstition. His huge *Library of History* would seem to be an obvious place to look for an ancient definition of superstition because it uses the word *deisidaimonia* (or some form of *deisidaim-*) many times in many different contexts, and contains countless stories about popular religious beliefs and practices, as well as some philosophical critiques of them. The work also presents problems in that Diodorus used all sorts of sources for its composition, many, it would seem, uncritically. The *Library of History* purports to be no less than a history of the world, written over a period of thirty years during the first century BCE. It incorporates material from other authors often now lost to us. And so the dilemma: when we encounter a use of *deisidaimonia*, whether in a positive, a negative, or a neutral sense, are we witnessing Diodorus's own point of view or that of some source he is simply quoting (not to say "plagiarizing")?

In this chapter I argue that the very complexities—indeed con-

tradictions—of Diodorus's presentations of *deisidaimonia* and ancient "superstition" actually render his work most valuable for
understanding ancient superstition: by parsing out the different
"voices" or points of view all jumbled together in Diodorus's *Library of History* we may be able to reconstruct the ancient debate
over superstition. We may even be able to gauge how successful
philosophers like Plato, Aristotle, and their successors were in solidifying their "new sensibility" about nature and the gods. This
chapter will show that the philosophers were unable fully to win
the day in their arguments against "superstition." Even other upper-class intellectuals, though they knew about the philosophical
arguments, were not truly won over by them. Diodorus is a case
in point.

Deisidaimonia in Diodorus

The traditional definition for *deisidaimonia,* "fear of gods or daimons," does make sense for some of the occurrences of the term
in Diodorus's *Library of History*—but only for some. Diodorus
relates, for example, typical stories of how an army or a people are
overcome by *deisidaimonia* and become debilitated in a fight.
The Carthaginians, he says, in their battle against Syracuse, became convinced that the gods were fighting against them; they
were thus seized by *deisidaimonia* and gave up the fight (14.77.4).
Similar scenes are often recounted. Soldiers hear about an ambiguous prophecy and are therefore afraid to go into battle
(19.108.2). Temple robbers experience *deisidaimonia* when they
become afraid that a god will avenge the theft by means of some
terrible punishment (27.4.8). It is often impossible to tell in these
contexts if Diodorus considers the fear to be the sort of cringing
vice condemned by the philosophers, but the term *deisidaimonia*
clearly refers here to fear of divine beings and what they might inflict on humans.

In many other contexts, though, English translations that render *deisidaimonia* as "superstition" and play up the aspect of fear may be misleading. Usually *deisidaimonia* in Diodorus's writing could just as easily be translated as "piety" or "proper respect" toward religious entities—and in fact this is the most common way Diodorus uses the term. Diodorus relates, for example, that the Celts will not even touch gold if it is "consecrated," even if it is lying around ready for the taking; and he attributes this to their *deisidaimonia* (5.27.4). He notes other people who will not steal valuable votive offerings because of *deisidaimonia* (5.63.1–3). Similarly, *deisidaimonia* concerning a sacred place leads people to be particularly careful about oaths taken there (11.89.5–6; see also 1.79.1). Admittedly, sometimes people's actions motivated by *deisidaimonia* seem to strike Diodorus as strange. He remarks on the Egyptians' piety toward cats, for instance, which led them to kill a Roman soldier because he had accidentally killed a cat (1.83.8). But he does not condemn or demean the belief. It may be tempting for modern scholars to translate all these occurrences as "superstition" and to assume that they refer to fear, but in each case, the word could just as well be translated as "respectful" or "pious": people in such cases behave with a properly religious attitude.

In fact, some uses of *deisidaimonia* in Diodorus clearly indicate that he usually takes the term more in the sense of "pious" than "superstitious." He relates how Egyptian kings used to wear animal skins and headdresses and burned incense made from fragrant plants, all in an attempt to impress their people and make them *deisidaimona* toward their rulers (1.62.4). Lest we too quickly translate this as "superstitious" and take it as an implied criticism, we must read further, where Diodorus continues by recounting how Egyptian priests conduct daily rituals in the presence of the king in order to fill *him* with *deisidaimonia*. The account goes on to say that the goal was to influence the king to conduct both his life and his reign in a "god-loving" manner (*theophilē*, 1.70.8). Here *deisidaimonia* and "god-loving" are apparently synonyms. If there is any connotation of fear, it is one more like awe and respect than craven cringing.

And then there are those cases in which Diodorus uses the term *deisidaimonia* apart from any connotation of fear at all. Indeed, it sometimes refers to the acceptance of a belief that rather brings confidence—albeit misplaced confidence. For instance, one day during the siege of Tyre when Alexander the Great was building a causeway to the city in order to capture it, a great monster sprang out of the sea and foundered on the causeway under construction. After a few moments it freed itself and swam away. Both sides, the Macedonians and the Tyrians, took the occurrence as an omen *in favor of themselves* (17.41.5–6). As Diodorus explains, "The marvelous occurrence led both sides into *deisidaimonia* since they each judged it to be a sign that Poseidon was about to help them" (17.41.6). As we know, eventually Alexander and the Macedonians won and the Tyrians lost. But for both parties, *deisidaimonia* refers to *confidence* due to what is taken to be a sign indicating divine aid. Even if *deisidaimonia* refers to *false* belief (the false belief that a freak occurrence is a good omen), the belief is reassuring, not threatening. *Deisidaimonia* does not here mean "fear of the gods," much less craven or exaggerated fear.

To cite another example: after the death of Alexander, one of Alexander's commanders, Eumenes, urged the other generals to cooperate in leading the large army. Attempting to overcome rivalry among the commanders, Eumenes invented a cult of Alexander, complete with new rituals. They made a throne, worshiped the "divine Alexander," and thereafter conducted their meetings as if Alexander were truly in their presence. Diodorus concludes, "As their *deisidaimonia* with respect to the king grew stronger, they were all filled with happy expectations, just as if some god were leading them" (18.61.3). *Deisidaimonia,* which here apparently refers neither to false belief (in Diodorus's view) nor to fear, inspired the generals with new joy, confidence, and a willingness to cooperate.[1] The term refers to religious reverence for Alexander, which is certainly not considered inappropriate by Diodorus. Like many "religious experiences," we may imagine, *deisidaimonia* fills the participants with confidence and a sense of communal well-being.

As noted above, Diodorus sometimes relates *deisidaimonia* to a *false* belief, and this may incline modern readers to think of it as equivalent to the modern "superstition." But that again would be one-sided and misleading. In relating the story of Medea, Diodorus claims that she was able to trick the king Pelias, his daughters, and the entire city into thinking that she was inspired. In addition to using drugs to alter her appearance, Medea constructs a statue of Artemis to overawe the people. Then she pretends to be inspired and possessed by the goddess. She thus casts the king and his daughters into *deisidaimonia.* Indeed, Diodorus notes that Medea is able to carry out her deception because of the *deisidaimonia* of the populace (4.51.1–3). They all come to believe "that the goddess has arrived making blessed [*eudaimona*] the household of the king." It should be noted that although the people have been tricked, the term *deisidaimonia* does not itself refer to the false belief. Rather, it refers to the religious disposition of people that *may* make them susceptible to deception, not to the deception itself. The word, therefore, refers most often in Diodorus neither to false belief in particular nor to an inappropriate fear of divine forces.

Thus here in the first century BCE, long after philosophers had begun using *deisidaimonia* in the negative sense of "superstition," Diodorus, a well-educated gentleman himself, still uses the term in a basically positive sense. This should perhaps not be surprising since Diodorus's sensibilities about religion incline toward the traditional and the popular, not the philosophical.

Diodorus's Religion

Precisely because Diodorus is *not* mounting any kind of critique of popular religion, his work may serve to illustrate typical religious beliefs and practices of the ancient Mediterranean. Every once in a while, we catch Diodorus in what may be described as a "philosophical" mood, as when, for instance, he comments that the myths about Hades are fictitious but morally useful for encouraging piety *(eusebeia)* and justice *(dikaiosynē)* among people (1.2.2). And Diodorus may have an opinion about misplaced piety here or there, as when he calls it "excessive piety" *(hyperbolēn eusebeias)* that motivated an Egyptian king to give up his throne in response to a dream from the god of Thebes (1.65.5). Generally, however, Diodorus's religious notions are run-of-the-mill.

For example, the Persian king Darius, the father of Xerxes, is praised for piety toward the gods and for honoring Egyptian sanctuaries, in explicit contrast to his predecessor Cambyses; Diodorus praises Darius for associating with the priests of Egypt and studying divine matters (1.95.4–5). Diodorus praises the Chaldeans for their "philosophizing," which includes astrology, the use of spells, augury, and prophecy in general (2.29.2–4). Divination by inspection of entrails is considered pious and true, along with the assumption that impiety, which here means disbelief in the gods, will be punished (6.6.3ff; see also 13.97.5–7). Diodorus accepts that the Delphic oracle was saved from Persian destruction by divine intervention (11.14.3–4). Indeed, Diodorus often relates stories suggesting that omens and prophecies are regularly vindicated by subsequent events (see, for example, 19.2.9; see also 13.97.5–7). Though, as we have seen, Diodorus knows that leaders, such as generals, kings, or priests, may fake omens or other religious events (see 20.11.2 for just one example among many), he never offers a critique of prophecy, divination, or omens, nor does he seem to allow such stories to shake his confidence in the phenomena in general. Basically, Diodorus has no problem with the normal, daily activities associated with popular religious belief and practice in his culture.

Moreover, when Diodorus condemns behavior associated with religion, it is usually of the sort that would have offended the sensibilities of popular religion. He regularly paints quite negative portraits of impiety or disrespect of the gods traditionally understood. It is impious, for example, to drag a man away from an altar to which he has fled for refuge (14.4.7). The practices most condemned by Diodorus are tomb destruction, temple-robbing, interfering with the Delphic oracle, and hubris that the gods find offensive—all quite traditional offenses in Greek popular imagination. And the gods themselves punish people directly for these misdeeds.

Indeed, Diodorus seems to relish passing on stories of the gods' excruciating punishment of those who have not respected the property of sanctuaries or tombs. A plague breaks out among Carthaginian troops because their general had destroyed tombs (13.86.1–3). Here Diodorus notes that the people are overtaken with *deisidaimonia,* but he seems to assume that they are perfectly justified in their fear: they *are* suffering divine retribution because of the impiety of their general. Another general, this time Himilcar, suffers for his impiety in plundering the temples of Demeter and Core, leading to a major turning point in the war to his own disadvantage (14.63). Dionysius, tyrant of Syracuse, is condemned for plundering shrines, which motivates the gods to join the battle against him (14.69.2–3). One may note that Dionysius seems to succeed in any case, which may indicate that one could get away with impieties for a time. But Diodorus later implies that Dionysius's final defeat, at the hands of the deity and in favor of the Carthaginians, may be attributable to divine revenge for his earlier looting of the temple (15.14.4; 15.16.3). Impieties toward the Delphic oracle regularly lead to disasters for the guilty: the Phocians are warned by earthquake and punished by fire because they tried to steal gold from the oracle and later attempted to take refuge at the shrine (16.56.5–8). In fact, several leaders who commit sacrilege against Delphi later come to awful ends: they fall off cliffs, are killed in battle or by terrible diseases, or end up in prostitution. Philip of Macedon, on the other hand, attains great success as reward for coming to Delphi's rescue (16.61–64). Thus, although Diodorus calls fears of divine retribution for temple-robbing *deisidaimonia,* it is for him a well-founded fear indeed (27.4.3). All of this accords with traditional, popular piety.

This is not to say that Diodorus is unaware of more "philosophical" or "scientific" interpretations of nature or the divine. In fact, when speaking about events of nature or history, Diodorus will sometimes offer two different explanations for an occurrence, one deriving from traditional religious assumptions and the other from philosophy or the "science" of his day. He gives his readers a menu of options from which they can choose the explanation they find most compelling. He comments, for example, on the birth of a seven-month fetus by noting that it is highly unusual "either because the gods do not will it or because it does not accord with nature" (1.23.4). When he describes the Athenian plague, he offers a humoral-balance etiology, much like the medical writers and "natural philosophers," but then relates, without condemnation, the purification rituals performed by the Athenians in an attempt to appease the gods and purify the city (12.58). He comments on a plague that overcame Carthaginian troops by suggesting that it could have been retribution from the gods for the Carthaginian plunder of the temples of Demeter and Core, but it could additionally have been caused by *miasma* (atmospheric pollution) affecting the breathing and bodies of the soldiers, a common medical explanation usually offered as a countertheory to that of divine causation (14.70.4). Diodorus knows that "pious people" *(hoi eusebōs diakeimenoi)* and "natural philosophers" *(physikoi)* may disagree about the causes of an earthquake and tidal wave, the former attributing it to divine causation, the latter offering other explanations (15.48.4; see also 15.50).[2]

In all of this, however, Diodorus does not really sound like a philosopher: he introduces different explanations and leaves it to his readers to "take their pick," which suggests that Diodorus is not himself entirely convinced by the philosophical critique of "superstition" and popular religious belief. This suggestion is strengthened by the many accounts in Diodorus in which he presents the gods as quite clearly harming people. Artemis is famous, he claims, for her vengeance against the impious (4.22.4). The gods are said to strike the Carthaginians with disaster, which the Carthaginians eventually avert by means of sacrifices (15.24.3). The gods strike a building in Sicily with lightning out of jealousy: they are offended because it is larger than any of the temples in the area (16.83.2). And the gods typically punish people for arrogance and hubris (see, for example, 20.13.3). Furthermore, Diodorus seems regularly to accept typical notions of religious pollution and purification (in addition to those mentioned above, see 3.58.2, 11.45.7–9), notions that had by his time been criticized and rejected by philosophical and medical writers. Therefore not only does Diodorus generally use the term *deisidaimonia* in a nonpejorative sense; he also accepts many views that by his time had already been condemned by other writers as "superstitious."

Diodorus and the Philosophical Critique of Superstition

It is therefore especially interesting to note the instances in Diodorus's text where *deisidaimonia* is openly criticized. Importantly, in each case philosophy is involved. Although these cases are few, they demonstrate that Diodorus is not unaware of ongoing attempts by philosophers to critique popular religious beliefs and attack "superstition."

According to Diodorus, until the third century BCE, Ethiopian kings had been under the control of the Ethiopian priesthood. The priests would even tell the kings when they should die, and the kings would submit, convinced by specious arguments of priestcraft, the kings' *logismoi* (thoughts, reasonings) being overpowered by *deisidaimonia*. King Ergamenes, however, disdained the command, entered the holy sanctuary that had been forbidden to kings, and killed the priests. It is important to notice the language used in this story. The previous kings had been fooled because of their "simple understanding" *(haplē dianoia)*; they accepted "ancient" traditions because they were not capable of critical thinking; they were thus overpowered by *deisidaimonia*. Ergamenes, however, had been shaped by Greek education *(hellēnikēs agōgēs)* and had studied philosophy. He therefore assumed the *phronēma* (state of mind) worthy of a king, and thereafter conducted matters according to his own will (*prohairesis*, 3.6.3). This is clearly a philosophical morality tale about how Greek education and philosophy can liberate anyone, even a barbaric Ethiopian, from *deisidaimonia* that keeps him shamefully controlled by priestcraft and potentially fatal ignorance.

A similar story occurs about the Theban general Epameinondas, who was attempting to rouse the Thebans to attack the invading Spartans. The people, especially the "older folk," were hesitant because of certain ill omens. (They took a blind herald's shoutings about some escaped slaves to be an omen prophesying their own enslavement.) Epameinondas advocated "nobility" and "justice" over attention to omens. He had been, we are told, "philosophically educated and [now] applied sensibly the principles of his education" (*paideia*, 15.52.6). Later, in order to convince the army to ignore the bad omens, he manufactured several good omens. He finally succeeded in liberating the soldiers from their *deisidaimonia* (even though he had to resort to deception) and convincing them to stand for battle "emboldened in their souls." Here, as was the case with the Ethiopian king, Greek philosophical education and "noble values" prevail over *deisidaimonia*, referring here to paralyzing belief in omens. Of course, Epameinondas, as an educated man, had to promote a false belief to rid the masses of their *deisidaimonia*. We may imagine that he resorted to "the Platonic lie" for the sake of philosophically educating the masses and governing properly. The term *deisidaimonia*, therefore, doesn't refer *simply* to fear about divine signs and omens; it rather refers here more generally to traditional, popular religious beliefs.

Stories about philosophy liberating people from *deisidaimonia* may have been used by Anaxarchus of Abdera, the philosopher who, according to Diodorus, convinced Alexander to enter the city of Babylon. The term *deisidaimonia* does not occur in this account, but it is nonetheless worth attention because it shows a philosopher attempting to educate a ruler to ignore popular religious fears and beliefs. Having been warned by the Chaldean astrologers that if he entered Babylon he would die, Alexander camped outside. But then Anaxarchus, a follower of the teachings of Democritus, convinced Alexander to ignore the astrologers. Alexander's change of heart is portrayed as the "healing" of the "soul" by philosophy, a well-known topos.[3] Up to this point, the story resembles the other two: philosophy brings liberation from bondage brought on by attention to omens and astrologers.

Actually, however, in this tale the astrologers prove to be right.

(Does this indicate that Diodorus is combining two sources: one a "philosophical morality tale," and the other a more "popular" one that teaches that even rulers shouldn't ignore the warnings of the gods?) According to Diodorus, after Alexander enters Babylon various portents presage his death. Indeed, Alexander dies, angry at the philosophers who had convinced him to ignore the warnings of the astrologers. As I have already pointed out, Diodorus himself takes omens, prophecies, and astrology quite seriously. So it is especially interesting when he passes on moral stories that portray philosophy as liberating people from *deisidaimonia,* which here refers to paying attention to astrologers, seers, and omen-readers.[4]

"Superstition" or "Practical Knowledge"?

The overall picture that emerges from Diodorus's rather confused and contradictory uses of *deisidaimonia* gradually becomes clear. Philosophers condemn *deisidaimonia,* and educated men like Diodorus know and can rehearse the arguments. Philosophers do not argue against cults of the gods in themselves or against belief in divine forces; they do not even argue against the idea that the gods might heal someone. But they do criticize any reliance on certain persons as special sources for knowledge of the divine: Chaldean astrologers, omen-readers, seers *(manteis).* And they explain that people shouldn't fear the gods. Importantly, however, although Diodorus *knows* the philosophical arguments against *deisidaimonia,* he does not completely accept them. Although Diodorus is an educated gentleman, he apparently is not an adherent of a philosophical school and is probably not philosophically trained himself. In fact, at times he may pass along accounts that could serve as attacks on philosophers. He complains about philosophers constantly disagreeing with one another (2.29.5–6) or hypocritically not living up to their professions of virtue

(9.9, 10.7.2–3).[5] In the end he is much more willing to accept popular religious beliefs and practices than to adhere rigidly to philosophical doctrine about "superstition."

Diodorus, in spite of the confusion and even contradictions in his presentation of *deisidaimonia* and popular religion, may serve us well in our quest to understand variant views of superstition. First, his work is evidence of the ongoing debate about superstition: what exactly is it, and why is it wrong? Second, Diodorus provides evidence for the *philosophical* location of the critique. It was philosophy, and those "sciences" under its influence, such as medicine, that furnished the home for the invention and definition of "superstition" and the negative meaning of *deisidaimonia*. Third, Diodorus provides evidence that the philosophers had not won the debate, even among other educated gentlemen, perhaps even of the upper classes.[6] Although philosophy had itself achieved a strong consensus, we cannot expect that others, even educated people, always took the same attitude toward "superstition" as did the philosophers. If the goal of philosophers in their invention of superstition was the reform of popular opinion and religious practice (and it may well not have been), then they were failing even to convince members of their own class and educational level.

If we may take Diodorus's complex and large *Library of History* as a source for reconstructing a portrait of Diodorus himself, we may imagine him as embodying something like a "practical knowledge" of nature and the gods. He is perfectly aware of the philosophical teachings on the nature of the universe and the gods. He knows that there are other explanations for disasters than the anger of the gods or the pollutions of daimons. But he has no intention of giving up the techniques for manipulating nature and superhuman beings that have been passed down dependably through the ages. One probably should not fear the gods *irrationally*, but who was able to prove that there might not be quite *rational* reasons for fearing the gods or daimons in certain circumstances? After all, everyone knew that human superiors enacted punishments for wrongdoing and sometimes even for petty slights. Who could prove that gods and daimons did not also? In order to make one's way in the world, precarious as human existence always was, it paid, Diodorus may have thought, to use whatever resources available. If those came from professional physicians or educated philosophers and observers of nature, fine. But one would be rash to forsake traditional resources for dealing with nature—resources such as sacrifices, appeasement of the gods, purifications from pollutions, and avoidance of impiety. The philosophers had their own opinions, of course, but Diodorus represents another option, even for the well-educated Greek: a life lived according to the principles of common sense and "practical knowledge"—about the gods, daimons, and the rest of nature.

7

Cracks in the Philosophical System

Plutarch and the Philosophy of Demons

If the writings of Diodorus demonstrate the difficulties philosophy faced in pushing its own view of superstition on the general populace, the writings of Plutarch demonstrate the problems philosophy faced in closing its own ranks. Plutarch, writing more than a century after Diodorus, had many things to say about superstition, most of them not surprising. What is surprising are the various—sometimes contradictory—things he said about daimons. After all, one of the central tenets of the philosophical critique of *deisidaimonia*—and a central theme of the invention of superstition—was the claim that fear of daimons was ridiculous because daimons did not harm. Plutarch knows such arguments, even rehearsing them himself. What is initially confusing—but may end up proving fruitful for my purposes—is the presence of diverse and even contradictory roles that Plutarch assigns to daimons. Plutarch comes dangerously close to what other philosophers would have labeled "superstition," mainly, ironically enough, in some of these comments about daimons—yet in doing so thereby provides us with evidence of philosophical debates about demonology, and thus evidence for the ongoing debate about superstition.

Plutarch on Superstition

Plutarch wrote a whole treatise devoted to an attack on superstition: *On Deisidaimonia*. It is impossible to read it without being reminded of Theophrastus's character sketch of the "Superstitious Man" from four centuries earlier. Plutarch mocks—no doubt with no small amount of exaggeration—many of the same sorts of behavior: consulting witches, attempting to purify oneself by magic or bathing in the sea, squatting all day on the ground. Much of what Plutarch calls superstition, he claims, comes from barbaric practices imported by gullible Greeks, and he lists in particular "smearing oneself with clay, wallowing in mud, washing oneself, falling facedown on the ground, shameful bowing, and absurd prostrations" (166A). Plutarch objects to using barbarian words and phrases in worship (166B). The superstitious man, Plutarch complains, will sit outside his house all day in sackcloth and rags, or even naked in muck, confessing numerous sins and misdeeds; he avoids certain foods or drink; he won't even walk down a lane if his *daimonion* has not permitted it; or he sits fearfully in his house all day having himself "fumigated" by some old woman (168D). Superstitious people believe that if they eat certain fish "the Syrian goddess" will gnaw through their shins, inflict them with sores, and melt their livers (170D). At its most extreme, superstition has led whole populations to sacrifice human beings, even children (171B–D). All of this is by now familiar to us: superstition is shameful behavior performed to propitiate divine beings; it is the importation of foreign, barbaric practices into more "staid" and "honorable" Greek culture; it is religion carried to extremes and motivated by fear of gods and daimons.

Plutarch's treatise, however, is more than a simple attack on superstition. It is actually a comparison (a *sygkrisis* in rhetorical jargon) of superstition and atheism. According to Plutarch, both atheism and superstition spring from ignorance about the true nature of the gods. But superstition is worse because it is wrong opinion compounded with emotion, namely fear, which is always more dangerous than wrong opinion alone (164E). Superstition is the mistaken idea that gods (including daimons) cause pain or harm (165B), a false idea that provokes unnecessary fear. In contrast with some emotions that may even have beneficial side-effects—arrogance, for example, may make someone bold or brave—fear renders people weak, powerless, and shameful. And the most enervating kind of fear is fear of the gods because the gods are everywhere, all the time, and inescapable (165C–D).

Plutarch provides several examples and arguments to demonstrate that fear of the gods is the worst kind of fear. If a man is afraid of another human being or even the state, he may escape, seeking refuge as a last resort in the temples of the gods. But if one fears the gods, to whom does one go for protection (166E)? When the atheist is ill, he considers that he may have eaten or drunk too much or become overtired. He looks for appropriate solutions in his life, location, or regimen. But when the superstitious man becomes ill he believes he is being "beaten by a god" or "attacked by a daimon." He throws the physician and philosopher—those who may actually have helped him a bit—out of the house and wallows in his divinely ordained suffering (168B–C). Some Jews, Plutarch notes, have been so superstitiously afraid to fight on the Sabbath that they have allowed themselves to be destroyed by their enemies (169C). Superstition renders human beings shamefully impotent.

Superstition also robs people of the joy they should derive from proper religious celebrations. Atheists may mock traditional religion and laugh at religious feasts and festivities, but they are none the worse off for that. The superstitious, on the other hand, cannot even enjoy religious festivals because they are afraid of committing some small mistake in a prayer or sacrifice and thereby incurring divine punishment. Superstitious people are so pitiful and despicable because they treat the gods—from whom they derive the greatest benefits—like bears or snakes or the most ferocious of beasts (169D–E). By their use of foreign, barbarian phrases and names, superstitious people dishonor traditional, ancestral, native piety (166B). Plutarch, very much a pious Greek himself, portrays superstition as "excessive piety" that actually takes all the joy out of religion (166E). It would be better to ignore the gods completely than to dishonor them by fearing them. After all, the gods aren't actually harmed by the unbelief of humans; they may even laugh at it. But the gods are dishonored when people attribute to them shameful passions and vicious behavior.

Plutarch's *On Superstition,* therefore, contrasts superstition with atheism, with superstition losing the competition. Plutarch's position must have seemed counterintuitive to most people, who doubtless would have assumed that *too much* attention to gods and daimons was better than *too little* and that being overly scrupulous was a "safer bet" for guarding against divine displeasure than denying the existence or care of the gods. Plutarch makes the typical philosophical move of criticizing popular opinion, in this case about religion, by paradoxically pushing what to most people must have seemed the obviously wrong position: that atheism was to be preferred to excessive religiosity. Plutarch's position is also typically philosophical in its argument that the best position is the "moderate" one, the "mean" between the excesses of atheism on the one hand and of superstition on the other. Atheism and superstition, the "extremes," should both be avoided by attending to religion properly observed, the "mean."

We have already and often encountered the philosophical argument that superstition is "excess" religion, even as early as

Theophrastus. What comes out more explicitly in Plutarch, however, is the other reason for the philosophical rejection of superstition: the philosophers' insistence that fear of gods and daimons is impious because it attributes shameful behavior and emotions to divine beings, who because they are superior to human beings cannot be inferior to them morally. Indeed, this is actually the more fundamental rationale underwriting the philosophical rejection of popular religious belief as "superstition." Simply claiming that certain religious behaviors are excessive does nothing to articulate an actual prescription for discerning whether something is superstitious ahead of time. For example, how would someone be able to tell—without Plutarch there to serve as the arbiter of good taste—that it was permissible to pray to a god, but that using a Syrian term to pray to a Syrian god was "excessive"? The claim, in other words, that "superstition" is "excessive religion" can in practice do little to differentiate superstition from religion: as we have seen even Aristotle admit, one person's "excess" is another's "moderation."

Plutarch's argument that superstition wrongly attributes harmful actions to divine beings provides a more reliable marker. And this aspect of the philosophical position, though present in other texts we have examined, comes out more clearly in Plutarch's treatise. Plutarch says that the mass of superstitious people despise the advice of "philosophers and political leaders," who have tried to teach them that the divine is characterized not by evil or dishonorable traits, but by "goodness, magnanimity, kindness, and helpfulness" (167E). To prove that the gods are offended more by superstition than atheism, Plutarch puts himself in their position:

Why, for my part, I should prefer that men should say about me that I have never been born at all, and there is no Plutarch, rather than that they should say, "Plutarch is an in-

constant fickle person, quick-tempered, vindictive over little
accidents, pained at trifles. If you invite others to dinner and
leave him out, or if you haven't the time and don't go to call
on him, or fail to speak to him when you see him, he will set
his teeth into your body and bite it through, or he will get
hold of your little child and beat him to death, or he will
turn the beast that he owns into your crops and spoil your
harvest." (169F–170A; trans. Frank Cole Babbitt, Loeb)

The now familiar logic of Plutarch's position is clear: if it is wrong
to attribute harmful, petty behavior to honorable men, *so much
the more* is it wrong to attribute it to gods and daimons.

It should be noted that Plutarch holds this position about both
gods *and daimons* in this treatise. It is this inclusion of daimons
with gods as *necessarily good* that seems to be contradicted in
other of Plutarch's writings and that has led to various scholarly attempts to make his position consistent. We must turn,
therefore, to a broader survey of demonology in Plutarch's writings.

Philosophical Demonology

The word *daimon* occurs in early Greek sources, and to some extent throughout antiquity, as simply another term for a god or
other divine being. Greek art and literature contain all sorts of
representations of what we could call "nature gods," for example
river daimons, often in the form of bulls or horses. We see various
horse-shaped daimons such as centaurs or *seilenoi* generally connected with water. There are Ionian horse daimons represented in
art, often monstrously combining various body parts: a man's
body with the legs and tail of a horse and a huge, erect phallus.[1]
The "Agathon (Good) Daimon," a deity linked to the home,
sanctuary, or other building, is often portrayed, in art as well

as texts, as a snake. This particular daimon came from under-ground, as snakes in general were thought to do, and was allowed to live under and in homes and sanctuaries as a protective and auspicious daimon.[2] In all these contexts, daimons are gods or some kind of divine being much like a god. Another popular way of thinking about daimons, though, was as the detritus of dead people. In Hesiod and much literature, daimons are simply the dead.[3] Since people could also think of the dead as having been "graduated" to a higher level, perhaps even to divine status, dai-mons were considered to be either straightforward gods or beings intermediate between gods and humans.

By Plutarch's day, many of these popular views had received philosophical elaboration, though others were rejected by philos-ophers. In his work *On the Daimonion of Socrates,* Plutarch pres-ents what had by his time become a traditional philosophical account of daimons, especially associated with Platonism. The treatise provides an account of the conspiracy against and execu-tion of the tyrants who ruled Thebes in 379 BCE with the support of Sparta. Embedded in the narrative are philosophical discus-sions about the reality and meaning of oracles. Along the way, a character in the dialogue tells about a stranger who had spent a night before a tomb, intending to remove the remains of the dead man interred there to Italy unless he received some indication from a *daimonion* during the night forbidding him. The story provokes a debate about whether or not belief in daimons who communicate messages constitutes superstition *(deisdidaimonia),* and one participant in the discussion brings up the famous *dai-monion* (the superhuman "guide") of Socrates in order to defend the belief (580C).

The different theories and statements about daimons in the treatise are too complicated to recount thoroughly here, but a general—and admittedly somewhat homogenized—account will serve my purposes. It is generally admitted that daimons are by nature superior beings. As superior entities, they communicate with humans by superior means. According to one theory, for instance, daimons communicate directly with the mind of a person, without making use of the coarser instruments of voice or air or body (588E–589B). Daimons have served men as guides during their lives, warning of dangers, assisting in decisions. Not only Socrates but also Lysis and Epameinondas have benefited from daimonic guidance (586A). One speaker suggests, however, that daimons do not communicate with all human beings, only the most superior. According to one theory, the words of daimons *(hoi tōn daimonōn logoi)* are so subtle that they pass unnoticed through the bodies of normal people, but when those words encounter a "holy and daimonic man" they echo in him and he thereby discerns their messages (589D). Indeed, daimons may communicate by signs with humanity in general, which explains the existence of oracles and other divine signals. But a rare few individuals receive more direct communication. Daimons do not help all people indiscriminately, but rather encourage and lead those humans who are already closest to attaining holiness (593C–F).

One of the characters in the dialogue offers a "myth" to help explain the nature and functions of daimons. The story concerns a vision or "soul journey" experienced by Timarchus, a young friend of Socrates' son. A voice explains to Timarchus what he encounters in his heavenly journey. The stars he sees are actually daimons, whose essence consists of the purest part of souls. Stars that move above in the heavens are the daimons of human beings who have understanding. Stars that move in regular, straight courses are the daimons/souls that are self-controlled and disciplined, whereas stars that wander around are those under the influence of the passions. The daimon is the force that attempts to educate the soul and lead it upward to more and more virtue (591B-592B). Plutarch has here presented a philosophical account, derived from Plato's *Timaeus* (see 90A), of the nature and activities of daimons. It should be noted that there is no mention of any possibility of evil, malignant, or vicious daimons. The entire treatise assumes that as daimons are *superior* beings, they are also *good* beings.

But that is not the whole story. In his dialogue *On the Obsolescence of Oracles,* Plutarch presents another debate about the nature of daimons.[4] One of the participants, Cleombrotus, admits that although Homer used the terms "gods" and "daimons" interchangeably, Hesiod differentiated four classes of beings: gods, daimons, heroes, and humans (415B). Daimons are thus intermediary entities between gods and men (415A, 416C); they serve as caretakers of sacred rites and mysteries and avenge evil among human beings (417A–B). Gods are completely good; they deal only in "the good," not in "good and evil." They are characterized by "moderation, adequacy, excess in nothing, complete self-sufficiency" (413E–F; trans. Babbitt). Daimons, on the other hand, exist at different levels of moral rectitude. "[A]s among men, so also among the daimons, there are different degrees of excellence, and in some there is a weak and dim remainder of the emotional and irrational, a survival, as it were, while in others this is excessive and hard to stifle" (417B; trans. Babbitt). Cleombrotus suggests that the disreputable stories people tell about gods, the myths that describe their sufferings and passions, are actually about daimons, not true gods. People have been compelled to perform shameful religious rites to placate not gods but "evil daimons" *(daimonoi phauloi).* Even human sacrifices had at one time been common because they were demanded by evil daimons, who were placated by human blood (417C–E).

In order to support his interpretation, Cleombrotus cites Xenocrates, a student of Plato and head of Plato's school, the Academy, from 339 to 314 BCE. Xenocrates taught, Cleombrotus says, that there was a correlation between three types of beings (gods, daimons, and humans) and three types of triangles (equilateral, isosceles, and scalene, respectively). Xenocrates' point was apparently to correlate beings with triangles in a descending hierarchy of symmetry and perfection: the equilateral triangle is perfect because all its sides are equal; the isosceles is less so because only two of its sides match; and the scalene is the least "perfect" because it contains three sides each of different length. In what follows, the "daimonic" category is broken down into good and bad daimons, with bad daimons given credit for excessive and fearful expressions of religiosity, including perhaps human sacrifice in the "old days" (417b–e).

Modern scholars disagree about how much of Cleombrotus's position goes back to Xenocrates. In may be that Xenocrates taught simply the theory about the triangles and the hierarchy of perfection, and that the claim that it was evil daimons who demanded human sacrifices is Cleombrotus's addition. In any case, Plutarch is here presenting a theory about daimons that enjoys at least a putative philosophical pedigree dating back to the successor of Plato in the Academy, and it admits that evil, harmful daimons may exist.

Significantly, though, this position is rejected by the other characters in the dialogue, who call Cleombrotus's views "inappropriate and outlandish hypotheses" (418d). Indeed, some modern scholars take Plutarch's own position to be expressed by Lamprias, Plutarch's brother and another participant in the discussion.[5] Lamprias doesn't mention any activity by evil daimons at all and provides more classically "scientific" explanations for the phenomena surrounding oracles. But Cleombrotus is not easily dismissed. Replying to Heracleon, another participant in the dialogue who had objected to his theory about evil daimons, Cleombrotus retorts that *if* Heracleon believes daimons are immortal and free from all emotions and evil, like the gods, he can show no difference between daimons and gods—so why believe that there are such different beings at all (418F–419A)? The objection goes to the heart of the debate: if daimons are morally inferior, why do we think they are superior beings, like gods? If they are superior beings like gods, how can they do evil? If they are, on the other hand, completely like gods, both immortal and morally excellent, why are they called by a different name?

It is tempting to take the argument of Cleombrotus in *On the Obsolescence of Oracles* to represent a minority philosophical position that is firmly rejected by Plutarch. As we saw, Plutarch's argument against "superstition" was predicated on the insistence that gods *and daimons* are not evil and do not harm. Moreover, other speakers in the dialogue reject Cleombrotus's theory. But Plutarch himself makes similar statements about evil daimons in other of his writings. His treatise *On Isis and Osiris,* for example, is written not as a dialogue but presumably in his own voice. Here, Plutarch attributes to Plato, Pythagoras, Xenocrates, and Chrysippus the view that daimons are mixed beings existing between gods and humans. As intermediaries, they deliver human prayers to the gods and purvey oracles and good gifts from gods to humans (361C). They are not *completely* like the gods, however, because they are susceptible to pleasure and pain, and they may produce both good and evil, both virtue and vice (*aretē, kakia,* 360E). Plutarch again mentions Xenocrates as having taught that the shameful things people sometimes do at the behest, they think, of gods—beatings, wailing, fasting, indecent language, and lewd joking—are actually done to placate daimons, who may be persuaded by such behavior not to do anything worse to humans (361B). Plutarch also ascribes the idea to Empedocles that daimons must suffer to be purified of their misdeeds. Good daimons, for their part, may be translated to become gods, as were Isis and Osiris (361C–E, 362E). Of course, the admission that *some* daimons are "good" means that there are at least some who are "bad."

A few other passages from Plutarch's philosophical writings make similar statements. A character in the dialogue *On the E at*

Delphi also says that the imperfect or destructive actions people popularly attribute to the gods are actually committed by
daimons, not gods (394A–C). The statement is made by Ammonius, not Plutarch (though Plutarch is a "character" in the dialogue as well), but Ammonius is given the last word. In *On the
Face That Appears in the Orb of the Moon,* a speaker, Sulla, recounts a myth describing the various activities of daimons. From
the moon, their normal home, they descend back to earth to administer oracles and the mysteries, to punish misdeeds of humans, and to save people at war or sea. If they conduct themselves fairly, all is well. But if they act unjustly or out of anger or
envy, they are punished by being relegated again to human bodies
on earth (944C–D). Sulla's myth allows for the possibility of evil
daimons, though that is certainly against their basic, superior
nature. And daimons who are unethical do not remain pure
daimons but are "demoted" to the lower existence of embodied
humans.

Though again it is uncertain the extent to which we should attribute all these views to Plutarch—they occur, after all, in a
"myth" recounted in the dialogue by someone else—there are certainly enough indications in Plutarch's writings to posit the possible existence of evil, harmful daimons. How do we make sense of
the contradiction? Plutarch's main argument against "superstition" was that it wrongfully attributed evil motivations and intentions to gods *and daimons.* But Plutarch himself elsewhere
seems to admit the possibility of evil daimons. If they actually exist, why shouldn't people worry about them?

Plutarch's Contradiction

Scholars have sometimes noted the problem and offered different
solutions. H. Armin Moellering argued that the "contradictions"
in Plutarch's presentations of *deisidaimonia* were due to a development over time in his ideas.[6] Morton Smith noted that Plu-

tarch, in the treatise *On Superstition,* condemns the sorts of beliefs he elsewhere seems to accept. Though Smith admitted that Plutarch *could* simply be inconsistent, he also suggested that *On Superstition* may be pseudonymous.[7] The best explanation that attempts to discern Plutarch's "true view" of daimons, however, is offered by Frederick Brenk. First, Brenk notes, "The expression 'gods and *daimones*' . . . is a traditional phrase both in and out of Plutarch to refer to the heavenly panoply, and need not necessarily be interpreted as including evil or other *daimones* of the Neoplatonic types, that is, intermediate spirits akin to angels and devils."[8] Brenk's point seems to be that when Plutarch refers to "gods and daimons" in *On Superstition* he is not thinking at this point about the possibility of *evil* daimons in particular. He is making the philosophical point that divine beings (gods and daimons) are good and therefore do not harm—*in general.*

Brenk notes that *most* of the references in Plutarch's writings that attribute harmful or deceptive actions to daimons come from his "biographical" works. For instance, Pelopidas is commanded in a dream to sacrifice a maiden in order to expiate the deaths of other young women (*Pelopidas* 21). He refuses, insisting that even if bloodthirsty daimons exist who would demand such a crime, they must be powerless and certainly should not be feared or obeyed. This is, of course, a classically philosophical answer to a popular belief in harmful daimons. In *Numa* 8.3–4b, Plutarch calls stories about visions of daimons "superstition." Since these sentiments are entirely "philosophical," what do we do when we encounter other cases in which Plutarch seems again to slip into contradiction?

In his "lives" comparing *Dion* and *Brutus,* for example, Plutarch suggests that both men were given premonitions of their impending deaths, presumably by some sort of heavenly being. Plutarch admits that some people would scorn such beliefs, attributing them simply to superstition (*deisidaimonia, Dion* 2.2). But he demurs from skepticism himself:

I'm not so sure that we ourselves may not have to accept
that most extraordinary account from the ancients, that foul
and harmful *daimonia,* envious of good men and opposed
to their actions, may bring about troubles and fears, shaking
and undermining their virtue, in order that those men may
fail to remain unfailingly noble and pure and thus attain a
better fate after their deaths than the *daimonia* themselves.
(2.3–4)

Admittedly, Plutarch seems hesitant to accept this "most extraordinary account from the ancients" ("we ourselves may . . . have to
accept . . ."). He passes it on nonetheless.

In his account of Julius Caesar, Plutarch notes the activities of
two daimons. The first guided Julius to success during his life and
pursued and executed his assassins after his death. The second appeared later to Brutus, proclaimed himself to be Brutus's "evil
daimon" *(daimōn kakos),* and informed him that the gods had
been displeased by the murder of Julius *(Julius Caesar* 69).[9]

Brenk surveys these accounts, admitting that they *appear* to
present a fundamental contradiction in Plutarch's thought. He
insists, though, that they are rare cases, used in literary, not philosophical, contexts. Mischievous daimons, we may thus imagine,
occur in Plutarch's more "literary" works much like machines of
the narrative: they move the story along and provide motivation.
Brenk insists that these instances should not be taken to mean
that Plutarch himself ascribed to a theory of evil daimons. As
Brenk concludes,

Plutarch generally represents such views as stimulating and
provocative rather than credible, while he himself prefers to
minimize the influence of evil spirits even if they should exist. . . . Thus Plutarch, though offering in the mouths of
some of the personages he created the substance of Neoplatonic demonology—a demonology which had its roots in

Xenocrates—remains faithful to the teaching of his divine master Plato in the *Timaeus* that the *daimon* is within us, the higher part of the soul, capable through virtuous living of attaining to the true apotheosis.[10]

Brenk may well be right. It would probably be a mistake to derive a considered philosophical position from the great variety of texts—and *kinds* of texts—represented by all of Plutarch's writings. But it may also be a mistake to attempt to discern Plutarch's "true intention" (especially in the *singular*) behind the varied expressions about daimons in his work—many of which occur on the lips of others. Brenk may himself, therefore, be overly minimizing Plutarch's contradictions.[11] After all, Plutarch sometimes appears to speak in his own voice when the text attributes imperfection or even evil to some daimons—as in his comments in the treatise *On Isis and Osiris* discussed above. Plutarch certainly allows the opinion to be attributed even to his philosophical heroes, such as Plato. The contradictions cannot be dispensed with as easily as Brenk suggests.

Fissures in Philosophy

Perhaps, though, we should move beyond reading Plutarch's texts as an indication of his mind and toward reading them as vestiges of his culture—both popular and philosophical. His varied representations of daimons, in that case, testify to the difficulty philosophy itself faced in solidifying its consensus about the necessary goodness of nature and the divine. Not only did philosophy fail to convince the rest of the population that superhuman beings can do no wrong; it also was having difficulty maintaining discipline among its own troops. Thus even philosophical characters such as Plutarch, Cleombrotus, Ammonius, and the venerable Xenocrates speculated that there *may* be at least *quasi*-divine beings (they never doubted, apparently, that daimons were superior to humans and partook of divinity *in some sense*) who might indeed be provoked by human actions to anger, envy, or selfishness. Some of them might even be imagined as harming humans, as leading men astray into dishonorable or self-destructive behavior.

It is not hard to imagine how this slippage in philosophical orthodoxy could have occurred. The optimal view of nature promoted by traditional philosophy—that nature is basically good because it *ought* to be good, that superior beings are excellent because they *ought* to be excellent—must have been a difficult faith to maintain in the face of all the messiness of nature in everyday experience. The admission, faint though it is, that *some* daimons may be evil is a crack in the confidence of an otherwise self-assured philosophical system.

Admittedly, these few philosophers never allowed that gods themselves might do wrong. To that extent, they were able to "hold the line" against popular "misunderstandings" about nature and the divine—that is, against "superstition." But the *logic* of their position was being dangerously undermined by the admission that some daimons might be evil. Daimons had generally been taken to be either the same as gods or very like them. Some philosophers had "demoted" daimons to a position just below the true gods. And then some philosophers had differentiated "good" daimons from "bad" daimons—allowing for evil only on the part of the latter. But once they had admitted that daimons, though superior to human beings, could be both good and bad, what was to prevent the same thing being said about gods? Plutarch seems to sense the problem, and thus his repeated insistence that gods can do no evil and that it is superstitious to fear gods *or daimons.* Yet in spite of himself, Plutarch has allowed a crack to open up in the system. The presence of evil daimons threatens to undermine the logic underwriting the philosophical critique of "fear of daimons." Apparently, at least *some* daimons were "scary" after all.

8

Galen on the Necessity of Nature and the Theology of Teleology

Unlike Plutarch, Galen embodies no inconsistencies when it comes to his confident belief in "good" deities and a benign nature. Also unlike Plutarch, Galen never explicitly addresses the problem of "superstition." His writings nonetheless furnish us with an important source for the study of the philosophical "sensibility" we have been examining. Writing several decades after Plutarch, Galen was also a careful student of philosophy—Plato and Aristotle especially—and he was the most prolific writer on medicine and "science" of the ancient world. He took notions we have already encountered—such as the idea that nature is both divine and constrained and the Aristotelian doctrine of teleology—and developed them in ways that help clarify the view of nature and the divine advocated by ancient intellectuals. By understanding that view, we can also understand what they found so offensive about "superstition"—including that of the Christians.

Galen was born in 129 CE, in Pergamum, a prosperous city in

Asia Minor (modern Bergama, Turkey). He studied and practiced medicine there and in different cities in the eastern Mediterranean, spending much of his life in Rome. He studied, he claims, with adherents of each of the major philosophical schools of the day—Platonic, Peripatetic, Stoic, and Epicurean—but he considered himself a loyal adherent of none, preferring to style himself an eclectic. He served for a while as the "family physician" to the emperor Marcus Aurelius and his son Commodus. Details of his death are unknown, but he seems to have died around 210. His many works provide valuable evidence for the scientific, philosophical, and religious sensibilities of a well-educated gentleman of the second century.[1]

Galen says very little explicitly about *deisidaimonia*. The actual term occurs only once in Galen's corpus, in a Stoic-like list of passions of the soul: "wrath, greed, *deisidaimonia*, various erotic desires of the body."[2] Here we learn nothing more than that Galen was familiar with the philosophical (originally Stoic) condemnation of *deisidaimonia* as a passion that disrupts the smooth functioning of the self and should be extirpated, like any other vice or weakness. Elsewhere Galen states that "barbarians and children" are ruled by their "temper" *(thymos)* rather than their "reason" *(logos),* so we may imagine that he would similarly condemn some popular notions as more suitable for barbarians and immature people, as philosophy had traditionally.[3]

Even when Galen does not use the term *deisidaimonia,* though, he provides other evidence that he would have assumed a traditional philosophical attitude toward "superstition." He condemns the predictions and prognoses of "charlatans and diviners" by insisting that they indulge in mere flattery; they lack real professional training; they go to extremes and excess in their predictions, exceeding proper scientific restraint by offering overly precise and exact predictions of how a disease will proceed (*On Examination* 1.9, 5.6; *On Prognosis* 1.6). Here we see themes we have seen before: superstition is the "other" to professional medicine; it represents the "excess" of which philosophical science is the "mean" or proper moderation.

As these few references indicate, most of Galen's criticisms are directed against rival medical theorists or practitioners or people with philosophical views he disagrees with, such as Epicureans. He seems to have felt little need to attack superstition or popular religion. Yet Galen did make a few comments about Jews and Christians that may provide clues as to what he thought about nonphilosophical religious beliefs, especially when we compare them to his own views about religion.

Galen on "the Followers of Moses"

Many years ago Richard Walzer collected and analyzed the few references in Galen's writings to Jews and Christians, most of which we may safely pass over for now.[4] One citation, though, merits attention because it takes us to the heart of Galen's philosophical theology and provides hints that Galen would probably have considered most Christians, had he bothered with them much at all, superstitious. In his long work *On the Usefulness of the Parts of the Body,* Galen discusses why eyelashes are constructed precisely as they are. Why are they of equal length and number? Why are they attached to cartilage rather than mere skin? Galen first castigates Epicureans, who would have said this all happened by accident, without forethought of the god. Galen says that even "Moses" offered a better answer because Moses at least attributed creation to divine foreknowledge and planning. But Galen also faults "Moses" (implying, of course, a criticism of "the followers of Moses," the Jews, and possibly also Christians)[5] because Moses seems to have taught that God created everything simply because he "wished it to be so." No, Galen insists, God himself (Galen here uses the Platonic term "Demiurge" for the creator god) was limited by the very constraints of necessity. Given the nature of matter and its limitations, the Demiurge *had to* make eyelashes the way they are. He *could not* have simply "willed" them to be of just any construction. Like Aristotle, Galen insists that even God is constrained by nature and matter. God could not have created man out of a stone in an instant, says Galen, even had he *wished* to do so.

This launches Galen into a comparison of those who follow Plato and the Greeks with those who follow Moses, to the detriment of the latter:

> This is where our opinion, and that of Plato and all others among the Greeks who correctly deal with the rationality of Nature, differs from that of Moses. For Moses, it is sufficient to say merely that God "willed" to order the universe in a certain way, and it was done. For he [Moses] thinks that everything is possible for God, even if he wanted to make a horse or a bull out of ashes. But we know that is not the case. We say, on the contrary, that certain things are impossible by nature. God does not even attempt those things, but from what is possible, he chooses the best to come about.[6]

Galen seems to know that Jews and Christians are fond of claiming that God can do the impossible, even if that means going "against nature." This strikes Galen in the first place as ridiculous: of course God cannot do the impossible; calling something impossible means that it is simply not possible! But the Jewish and Christian position surely also struck Galen as impious: for Galen, nature is itself divine and exists in its best possible form; to suggest that God might act *against nature* would be to suggest that nature is not already as perfect as it can be, and that would strike Galen as impious. Galen would consider most Christians superstitious because they had, in his opinion, both false and impious views about nature and the divine. In order to understand how fundamental this disagreement was, we must analyze Galen's religious views as they relate to his scientific and philosophical system.

Galen's Religion

In many ways Galen's beliefs about the gods are those of a typical philosophically educated gentleman of his day.[7] Admittedly, one encountered Epicureans who denied any divine interaction with humans; they rejected divination, any belief in prophecy, all stories of divine healings or answers to prayers. And then there were the Skeptics, who believed that humans simply could not know anything about the gods, even whether or not they existed. Such men would not insist that the gods never interact with humans; they would merely say that not enough evidence exists to establish the fact. They taught general suspension of belief, not actual atheism. But the majority of philosophically educated people in Galen's time, it seems, adopted some sort of Platonism, or Stoicism, or eclectic blend of different philosophical teachings—all of which accepted the official, traditional religions while interpreting them so that they fit the views of nature and the gods held by the philosophers.

This—the "mainstream" philosophical position—is precisely Galen's position. Thus we find no intention on his part to reject the cult of Asclepius, the god of healing. He mentions that his predecessors conducted recitals in the sanctuary of Asclepius, and he finds no fault with them on that account.[8] Throughout his writings Galen manifests a devotion to Asclepius that we have no reason to suspect was mere pretense or formality. Galen even professes himself a "servant of Asclepius" ever since the god healed him of an abscess that would otherwise have killed him (*My Own*

Books 2 [K 19.19]). Galen seems also to have accepted the cults of
other gods, including the cult of the divine emperor; he mentions, without demurral or criticism, the deification of Lucius by
Marcus Aurelius (*My Own Books* 2 [K 19.18]). Galen never hints
at any rejection of the official and traditional cults of Greece and
Rome.

In general Galen completely accepts the reality of divination.
Though he recognizes that some claims to divination or prophetic activity are charlatanry, he nonetheless believes that real
cases do occur. He even claims to have received "mantic" prophecies himself and to have benefited from divinatory experiences.[9]
Galen accepts the Pythian Apollo's proclamation of the wisdom
of Socrates and the divinity of Lycurgus. The same god, Galen
tells us, prevented a murderer from entering a temple by rebuk-
ing the man out loud. Galen believes in the traditional gods, their
roles as benefactors of humankind, and divine intervention in
human affairs.[10]

Naturally Galen does not have praise for *everyone* who claims
to be a diviner. He mentions, for example, that some people pos-
ing as diviners are charlatans in it only for the money; they get
their business by means of flattery.[11] And Galen is perfectly willing to criticize diviners when they infringe on his own turf or
when his own practice is labeled as divination by his enemies. He
argues that diviners, when they have the nerve to interfere with
medical practice, tend to be too exact in their predictions. They
pretend to know *exactly* what the disease is going to do regardless
of treatment (*On Examination* 5.6). When Galen himself is accused of practicing divination rather than medicine, he points
out that his prognoses provide a *general* prediction of what the
disease will do *if* a certain treatment is administered. In fact,
Galen, as we would expect given the importance of "moderation"
and the "mean" in his thought, depicts his prognosis as "the middle way" between total ignorance on the one hand and the overly

specific, overly confident predictions of diviners on the other. The diviners, in Galen's rhetoric, represent an "extreme of prediction."

Taking into account both Galen's general acceptance of divination along with his criticism of certain diviners, it is clear that he has no problem accepting communication between divine and human beings and even divine "interference" in human affairs. His statements that might be taken to suggest otherwise occur in contexts in which he is attempting to distinguish his own medical practice from other "healers" or from diviners.

For the ancient world, dreams may be taken as a subset of divination in general (one that occurs on a more personal and private level), and Galen has much to say about their divinatory significance.[12] Galen's father was instructed in a dream by the god Asclepius to educate Galen in medicine. Galen is proud of the event, relating it in his writings more than once.[13] It may have been in a dream (Galen does not say) that Asclepius announced that Galen should not accompany Marcus Aurelius on his German campaign, another event Galen relates more than once.[14] Galen matter-of-factly remarks that people may be instructed in medical treatment by dreams, and he was inspired in dreams to pursue treatments even for his own illnesses.[15] In another context Galen informs us that he had planned to omit an account of certain of his theories about the eye and vision from his work *On the Usefulness of the Parts* because he feared that the material would be too technical and difficult for general readers to comprehend, but "some divinity" (maybe Asclepius, though in this context Galen explicitly mentions only Nature) commanded him *three times* to include the material in his book. Of course, Galen the Pious obeyed (*Usefulness of the Parts* 10.12, 14 [Helmreich 2.93, 107]).

Galen even wrote on how to use patients' dreams to aid medical diagnosis. If patients dream of fire, they are probably suffering from an excess of yellow bile. Dreams of smoke indicate black bile. Snow or ice indicates phlegm. In a short text that survives in the Galenic corpus, *On Diagnosis in Dreams* (its authenticity has been questioned), we are provided with a theory explaining why the self is able to diagnose itself in dream states: the psychic substance or faculty retreats from the surface into the inner recesses of the body during sleep. There it is able to observe the internal stuff of the body, such as the state of humors, an overabundance of feces or other waste, and so on. The psychic discovery expresses itself in the images of the patient's dreams.[16]

Galen, a philosopher as well as physician, naturally interprets religion and popular beliefs by means of philosophy. He does not wholly reject the literary account in which Medea uses a magical potion to cause a robe given to her ex-husband's new bride to burst into flames; he just explains that she must have used a combination of highly combustible materials, as common magicians do in their tricks (*On Mixtures* 3.2 [K 1.658]). Galen mentions the typical belief, common among philosophers as well as the masses apparently, that some of the gods, in this case Asclepius and Dionysus, had started out as mortals but had been graduated to the level of divinities (*Exhortation to Study the Arts* 9 [K 1.22]). Galen makes typical philosophical statements about sacrifice and cultic rituals: without rejecting sacrifices or offerings, he mentions that "understanding" is better than sacrifice, and that it is much more impious to misrepresent the physiological hierarchy of nature than to fail to make offerings or burn incense (*Usefulness of the Parts* 3.10 [H 1.177]). These are, of course, typical sentiments found throughout ancient cultures and especially in philosophical circles. They imply no rejection at all of the traditional cult, merely a reorientation of perspective on cult as related to ethics.

Another of the common philosophical assumptions that we have already encountered, the doctrine of the hierarchy of nature, is also reflected in Galen's philosophical theology. Human beings occupy a position between animals below and gods above; they partake of the natures of both, sharing flesh, blood, and passions with animals and rationality with the gods. Different human beings also fall at different positions in the hierarchy. Men are, of course, generally closer to the divine than women. Men involved in manual labor are lower than those involved in labor of the mind. Thus some humans are "more divine" than others—especially, perhaps, the emperors, but including men such as mathematicians. We should certainly imagine that physicians, though "servants of Nature," are relatively high on the human hierarchy.[17] As the principle of physiological hierarchy is an important factor in Galen's science, so the principle of divine hierarchy is central for his theology. And that theology is not just an appendage of his science, but furnishes the very fabric of its rationality.

Divine Nature

This brings us to perhaps the most central aspect of Galen's theology, one that in some ways separates it from popular religious sentiments but also renders it a good example of the broader philosophical theology of his time: his portrayal of Nature as a divine personality. Scholars are divided over the extent to which Galen really does hypostatize nature into a divine person. Is his talk about Nature and "her" intentions or actions a mere personification of an abstract and nonpersonal force? Or does he conceive of Nature as a real, personal, divine being? We have to limit ourselves to an analysis of Galen's language and rhetoric, admitting that from this distance it is impossible to see inside his head. What is clear is that, whether Galen thinks of Nature as a personal god (or goddess) or an impersonal force, it clearly plays the central role in his theology: either "Nature" or "nature" is the supreme divine force that fashioned the world and continues to direct its mechanisms.

It is hard to avoid the impression that Nature for Galen is personal. He speaks of Nature as "well educated" *(eupaideutos)*. She has "thoughts" and "intentions." She makes plans and executes them.[18] And "Nature" may be interchangeable with "god," suggesting that perhaps Nature is a person at least to the extent that Asclepius is. Galen quotes Plato, for instance, to show that "god" placed air and water between earth and fire, but in the rest of the passage he refers to the agent as "Nature" (*Usefulness of the Parts* 8.9 [H 1.478]). As we have seen, Galen sometimes calls this force the *Demiourgos,* the "Demiurge" or "Creator"—a masculine term —as in Plato's philosophical theology.[19] I would argue that this alteration between masculine and feminine poses no hindrance to thinking of the divine force as a personal being. The highest divine beings in an ancient philosophical system would often necessarily be androgynous.

Galen himself addresses the issue at least once. He discusses the philosophical debate about whether Nature is "a wise and powerful god" or rather "some sort of soul apart from that of a god." He admits that he went to philosophy for the answer to this dilemma, but that philosophy could provide none. We limited human beings simply do not have the resources to discern the actual nature or substance of the divine. So this is one of those questions—like the precise substance of the soul, or whether there is more than one universe—for which Galen believes we can have no certain knowledge. About the particulars of the nature of god, Galen thinks, we must remain agnostic.

But not completely agnostic. Galen does criticize some theological opinions about the nature of divinity. For one thing, he entirely rejects any teaching that the divine force either does not exist or has nothing to do with the world. Epicureanism, with its belief that the gods do not run the universe and have no concerns for humankind, is impious and disproven for Galen by the teleological structure of the universe and all its inhabitants (see the analysis of his teleology below). On the other side, Galen rejects the philosophical belief that the divine force is absolutely and everywhere immanent in nature. Galen rehearses the philosophical doctrine of the "world soul," the idea that the divine force penetrates and diffuses all of nature, every crack and cranny, every bit of material, in a complete and full manner, and that the same "world soul" is responsible for everything in the universe entirely. But he rejects this doctrine on ethical and "pious" grounds. Galen considers it completely inappropriate to contend that the divine has anything to do with "scorpions and venomous spiders, mice and mosquitoes, vipers and worms, helminths and ascarides."

Here we confront the assumption that the ontological hierarchy of nature (how different things occupy different positions of "being" in nature) must be matched by an *ethical* hierarchy (things higher on the scale of being must be more ethical). Galen cannot believe that his beloved divine Nature created things that are evil and despicable. No, she must have done the best she could with what she had. The bad things of the world must be chalked up to necessary limitations of reality, not to the intentions of the perfect and divine Nature (*The Construction of the Embryo* 6 [K 4.688–701]).

Galenic Teleology

Galen's belief that Nature represents the best possible reality given the contraints of necessity fits in with another aspect of Galen's theology and science: his teleology. "Nature does nothing in vain." Galen takes over the notion to a great extent from Aristotle and shares it with many of his contemporaries among intellectuals. Everything that exists was planned and executed so that its form is the most perfect imaginable for its intended purpose.

As Aristotle had addressed teleology in his work on the *Parts of Animals,* so Galen also felt that the best way to demonstrate the truth of natural teleology was by careful analysis of the different parts of the body, its organs, members, and instruments. Thus those works in which Galen addresses what we would call anatomy and autopsy, especially his long work *On the Usefulness of the Parts of the Body,* were written, as he himself admits, most of all to prove that every part of the body is perfectly formed and arranged to fulfill its preordained purpose or function.[20]

Galen explains why he begins this work with an analysis of the hand (rather than, say, the brain, head, eye, or heart, as one might expect would be more important human parts). One must know, he says, the proper action for something before its teleological purpose and construction can be understood. It may not be obvious, in the beginning, what veins, arteries, tendons, nerves, etc., do in the body; but what hands do is obvious: they *grasp.* Since their function is so obvious, people can readily perceive how perfectly they have been constructed *for grasping.* Hands have a fleshy palm, which cushions the thing grasped while still protecting the delicate bone structure; the back of the hand is bony, serving as the framework for the mechanism; hands have opposing thumbs, so important for human grasping; all the digits have no more and no less than three bones—also perfect for grasping, according to Galen. The hand is a good starting place because its proper purpose is clear to anyone, who can then be shown how its structure is perfectly made to fulfill its purpose or function. Then Galen can move on to the more obscure cases of perfect corporeal teleology (1.16 [H 1.32–33]).

Later in the work Galen addresses why Nature placed sutures ("cracks") in the skull. In the first place, they allow egress for the noxious vapors that, according to ancient medical theory, inevitably build up in the head. The vapors would lead to disease if trapped inside the skull, but they can pass through skin, and so the sutures allow them out of the skull and keep them from polluting the brain. In the second place, Nature gave the skull su-

tures in forethought for wounds to the head. Without sutures a
blow to the head might cause a fracture that would spread all
across the skull, from one side to the other. But as it is, when a
fracture encounters a suture, it stops spreading, like fire at a
firebreak. The sutures were placed strategically at places on the
skull so that a wound would damage only part of the skull and
not the whole (9.17 [H 2.49–50]).

But how can Galen insist so adamantly that Nature does everything perfectly when there are so many obvious imperfections?
Diseases, after all, do happen. Why did Nature not create the
body so that it remains in a perfect state? Why do things go awry?
Galen is ready for such an impious (in his view) objection. In the
first place, he argues that such "mistakes" (a person born with six
fingers, for example) are so rare that they should not be used to
disparage Nature. Any artist who made one mistake out of 1,000
or 10,000 attempts would be considered supremely great. And if
an artist made only one truly perfect object in his whole life, we
would still consider him practically divine. But Nature makes
most of her objects perfectly suited for their function. And her
mistakes, when compared to her perfections, are rare indeed. So
we should be ashamed if we fault her for the very few and paltry
imperfections (*Usefulness of the Parts* 17.1 [H 2.444]).

Galen's second answer to the problem appeals to the principle
we have already encountered: Nature does the best given the
contraints of necessity and "the possible."[21] Nature cannot do the
impossible, precisely because it is impossible. Nature could not
have created a centaur, Galen explains, because a horse and a human being are too different to allow a combination of their natures. How should we imagine one being born? A creature so
large would not be able to grow in a woman's womb. And a mare
could not be inseminated by a man: besides the fact that the
equine womb would reject as foreign to its nature any human semen, the male penis is simply too short to penetrate sufficiently.

How do we imagine the nourishment of such a monstrous combination to have taken place? Would the horse part be nourished by raw grasses and coarse grains while the human part be nourished by cooked foods? In that case the beast would require two mouths and two stomachs. And if that were the case, it would also require two chests, and thus two hearts. Galen leads his readers through a *reductio ad absurdum* (*Usefulness of the Parts* 3.1 [H 1.124–123]). Nature made no centaurs because such a being is logically and physically impossible.

In the same way, Nature made the human body as perfectly as possible *given the contraints of reality.* Pain and mortality are necessary aspects of human nature given that the human body is made up of the stuff of lower materiality (much more subject to change) rather than divine substance (which permits stability). Nature *could not* have made a creature out of menstrual blood and semen—low, disgusting materials to be sure—that could have enjoyed the existence of the higher beings like the sun, moon, and stars (3.10 [H 1.175]). As Galen concludes,

> Certainly, had it been possible she would have arranged all of reality without anything base. But as it is, no technique exists that *could* have accomplished the works of creation and still render matter exempt from all evil—even if matter were all made up of the hardest substance imaginable and altogether unalterable. The only option was to fashion a cosmos that is actually possible [that is, rather than someone's "fantasy cosmos"]. For different things admit of different forms of matter. Doubtless, we and the stars did not come about from the same substance. Therefore, we should not wish for the same inability to suffer [as they enjoy]. We should not blame Nature if we know of some small imperfection in the face of myriads of useful things. As it is, we indict Nature and charge her with malpractice, as if it were

possible to avoid some tiny imperfection without disturbing and throwing into chaos the vast majority of her fine accomplishments! (5.4 [H 1.260])

By admitting but downplaying reality's imperfections, Galen defends his doctrine proclaiming the teleological excellence of reality and the purposeful forethought of Nature.

The Ideology of Teleology

We must not leave this analysis of Galen's teleological theology without noting how ideologically conservative it was. Teleology, if understood as any concentration on a "logic of the end," need not be conservative. After all, early Jewish and Christian apocalypticism, with its attempts to discern the meanings of the present by attending to "the end of the world as we know it," often functioned as an implicit critique of "the ways things are" and an explicit critique of Roman imperial rule. Some radical Christians and Jews used an apocalyptic worldview, with its predictions of an imminent destruction of Roman power and the establishment of a Kingdom of God—in which according to some visions "the last will be first"—to challenge the status quo and the powers that be. Some "logics of the end," therefore, could be put to counter-conservative or even revolutionary use.

But the teleology of Galen's system, like that of Aristotle who so influenced him, is thoroughly conservative. If things in the world all exist as they do because that is the best possible way for them to exist, there should be little incentive to attempt to change things. Aristotle's argument on the "naturalness" of slavery is just the most famous example of the conservative function of his teleology: some people's purpose is to serve, and that of others to be served; the true and proper "end" for some men is to be masters and for others to be slaves (*Politics* 1.2.8). Some are born to rule and others to be ruled. If Nature really does arrange everything perfectly, then things *as they are* are perfectly arranged. A more consistently conservative ideological notion could hardly be invented. Galen embodies that ideology. And his teleology helps explain why he would have found much "nonphilosophical" religion, including many Christians, to be "superstitious."

Christians viewed nature not as divine itself, though certainly divinely created, but as flawed, and they viewed God as perfectly capable of transcending the "normal" ("natural") system and altering its usual functions and procedures. They had no hesitancy in claiming that God could do the "impossible," even were that to go against whatever they may have considered the "laws of nature." God would have been above any such laws. For Galen and many of his fellow scientists, Nature itself *was* divine, indeed perhaps the most important and supreme divine entity. The "possible," therefore, referred to the limits of imaginable possibility *given the reality of Nature itself.* Galen objects to Jews and Christians because they do not recognize that things *are* the way they are because they *must* be the way they are. God cannot do the impossible. God is contained in Nature.

Galen would have considered most Christians superstitious because they would have held, from his point of view, false *and* impious opinions about Nature.[22] By acting as if God stood outside the contraints of Nature, Christians were simply ridiculous. But by implying that God could *go against* Nature, Christians were implying that Nature could be improved, that it was flawed. And that offended Galen's sense of piety.

9

Roman *Superstitio* and Roman Power

In this book I concentrate principally on Greek sources—for good reasons. The ancient notions of superstition I am delineating owe more to ancient philosophy than any other one institution, and ancient philosophy was originally a Greek product later imported into Roman culture. Latin terms related to the critique of religion were influenced by Greek terms with a long tradition in the earlier philosophical critique of popular ideas about the gods and nature. Furthermore, I began by asking why Christianity was perceived as "superstitious," and almost all the earliest literature pertaining directly to Christianity, whether written by Christians or by others about them, was written in Greek. But this chapter will shift our focus to Latin sources and Roman culture because the meaning of the Latin *superstitio* differed in important ways from the Greek *deisidaimonia,* and those differences help shed light on various meanings of superstition in a Roman context. More particularly, some special Roman connotations of *superstitio* help explain the Roman perception of Christianity as a dangerous superstition. As I will here illustrate, Roman *superstitio* differed somewhat from Greek *deisidaimonia* in the Roman emphasis on the *political threat* posed by superstition to the Roman state and people, and that difference provides a key for understanding the Roman perception of Christianity as a superstition.

Early Meaning and Philosophical Influence

Like *deisidaimonia, superstitio* was originally a positive or neutral term. In the Latin of the playwright Plautus (254–184 BCE), *superstitiosus* (the adjectival form) seems to refer simply to a soothsayer, a prophet, or someone who knows hidden things. For example, in one comedy, a girl who uncannily knows what is in a closed box is called *superstitiosa* (*Rudens* 1139), and in a couple of other instances the word occurs in phrases that could be translated as something like "The man's clairvoyant!" (*Curculio* 397; *Amphitryon* 323). We may also find a similar, nonjudgmental occurrence of the term in the writings of the philosopher Seneca, but outside a philosophical setting. In Seneca's play *Thyestes, superstitio* seems to refer to a quite understandable horror of the underworld, meaning something like "spookiness" (677–679). This should not be taken to indicate that the Romans found anything strange or spooky about prophecy or divination in general. Traditional Roman religion depended on omens, divination, and all sorts of prophetic activity, but in those cases the activity fell under the category of *religio. Superstitio* was reserved for strange, nontraditional activities of a similar nature. In these early uses, though, *superstitio* seems to operate without the strongly negative connotations of later uses of the term.

Michele Salzman has shown that in legal texts from a much later period, *superstitio* could still be used in a nonpejorative sense.[1] In *Digest* 12.2.5.1, transmitted by Ulpian (early third century CE) and attributed to Antoninus Pius (Emperor 138–161 CE), *superstitio* refers simply to someone's personal religious beliefs on which he or she may take an oath: "an oath sworn according to one's own [*propria*] *superstitio* is valid." And in *Digest* 50.2.3 the term refers to Jewish religion with no obvious disparaging meaning. Thus, like the Greek *deisidaimonia, superstitio* originally was used without any necessarily negative meaning, and it may occur even in later texts, though rarely, without the negative connotations that normally attend it.

Roman writers, however, were eventually influenced by Greek philosophy, and *superstitio* came under the influence of the Greek *deisidaimonia*.[2] As with *deisidaimonia,* under philosophical critique *superstitio* came to carry a pejorative meaning. And again, fear is the salient feature most often associated. Seneca, for instance, rehearses the by-now traditional Stoic rhetoric that paints *superstitio* as fear, as shameful; it represents the opposite extreme from atheism, also considered wrong by the Stoics.[3] *Superstitio* is a disease or passion, in particular the passion of fear, that philosophy is able to cure.[4] This philosophical topos is so familiar that even authors not very well educated in philosophy, such as Pliny the Elder, echo it as a truism: of all animals, he says, only human beings suffer from such avoidable evils as grief, luxury, ambition, avarice, inordinate lust for living, fears about burial and the afterlife, and *superstitio* (*Natural History* 7.1.5).

But fear is not always involved in the philosophical criticism of *superstitio,* and in some contexts it is not the most important aspect. Cicero, for example, uses the word to refer merely to false belief about the gods, in particular, believing myths about the gods' exploits. *Superstitio* is belief that the gods actually suffer from the same frailties as humans, that they are passionate and have emotions, that they fall in love, get angry, become sad, and fight with one another (*On the Nature of the Gods* 2.28.70). The myths may be interpreted symbolically to signify aspects of nature, and it is rational to provide "natural" interpretations for the myths. Unfortunately, most people fall into *superstitio* by taking them literally (3.39.92).

As was the case with the Greek philosophical treatment of *deisidaimonia,* so Latin writers contrast *superstitio* with true religion *(religio). Superstitio* is *religio* carried to extremes (Cicero, *Nature of the Gods* 1.42.117, 2.28.71). It is *religio* without understanding (Seneca, *Moral Epistles* 95.35). In fact, in making that argument, Seneca reveals that the *nature of an action* is not what makes the behavior *superstitio* or *religio,* but rather the *attitude of the actor.* The same act of piety performed by a philosopher may be *religio,* but *superstitio* when performed by those without philosophical understanding.

This sort of ambiguity made it possible for philosophers to label the beliefs of even other philosophers as *superstitio.* In fact, Cicero's entire dialogue *On Divination* presents an argument between Cicero's brother, who represents the Stoic doctrines about the gods and divination, and Cicero himself, who represents the doubts of the Skeptics. Cicero labels even the Stoic theory of divination *superstitio,* as he does the Stoic acceptance of "fate" (2.19, 81, 83, 86). Elsewhere in Cicero's writings, Skeptics label as *superstitio* the Stoic multiplication of the gods or their claim that the gods are all-powerful (*Nature of the Gods* 3.52, 3.92). Thus many popular beliefs about the gods, even when interpreted "rationally" by other philosophers, could be branded *superstitio.*

In nonphilosophical writings as well, *superstitio* could refer to things other than "fear." Cicero uses *superstitio* in a speech to refer to what people would consider normal religious observations such as sacrifices and prayers. What makes the practices here *superstitio,* however, is that the practitioner is a mother who is calling on the gods to *harm* her son (*Pro Cluentio* 68.194). What would be considered *religio* has become *superstitio* because of the evil motive of the practitioner. The gods should never be invoked to harm someone, especially one's own son! *Superstitio* is *religio* used for base ends.

Moreover, in line with a traditional Roman criticism of luxury or excess, *superstitio* is sometimes "too much religion" or religion that has been fussed over too much, as we have already seen to be the case with *deisidaimonia* and the philosophical criticism of superstition. Pliny the Elder, for example, condemns burning costly incense as *superstitio* (*Natural History* 22.56.118). This occurs in a context in which Pliny is criticizing different examples of luxury and excess, including the use of compound drugs when simpler ones "from nature" would do, and importing expensive drugs when the true Roman should be able to get along with local remedies. Compound drugs are attacked as foreign and artificial, produced because of the greed and ingenuity of human beings. *Superstitio* here is implicated in the conventional Roman rhetoric of "simplicity."

Roman writers do not all agree about the use of *superstitio* to refer to magic. Some of them, it is true, seem ready to label any sort of magic *superstitio*.[5] But others, though they reject magic and magicians, do not do so by employing the term *superstitio*. Pliny the Elder, for instance, vociferously and at length condemns magicians, even while passing along magical remedies and prophylactics, but he does not call magic *superstitio*.[6] This seems to be because magic, in Pliny's mind, is a combination of several different fields of knowledge; it is not just a perversion of religion (which *would* place it in the category of *superstitio*), but also of medicine and astrology. According to Pliny, magic grew partly out of the *superstitio* of Orpheus, but also out of legitimate medicine. He even calls magic a *scientia*, a kind of knowledge (30.2.7, 8). Pliny considers *superstitio* wrong, for one thing, because it is false belief: it posits false cause-and-effect relations. But Pliny never argues that magic is wrong simply because it is false. Indeed, since Pliny believes that the machinations of magicians are often efficacious, he provides recipes or therapies people may use to counteract their assaults (see, for example, 28.23.85–86). Pliny attacks magicians on moral grounds as enemies of humanity.

Magic is wrong not because it is ineffective or because it is *superstitio,* but because it is the use of nature to hurt people.[7] The term *superstitio* in Pliny, on the other hand, is limited to false beliefs connected particularly with religion.

Thus we can trace a history of *superstitio* in Latin writings that mimics the history of *deisidaimonia* in Greek, and the tropes we have already discerned in the philosophical invention of superstition recur also in the Latin sources. *Superstitio* is offensive to the philosophers and those under their influence because it refers to fear and passion, the unnecessary emotions that disrupt the self-sufficiency and calm of the true noble gentleman. *Superstitio* is *religio* taken to excess. *Superstitio* is the gullible attribution of literal truth to the offensive myths about the gods and heroes, which are offensive because they attribute impious and shameful actions to those superior beings. *Superstitio* thus represents a disruption of the hierarchy of nature and virtue assumed by philosophy to provide the structure of the universe and society. And, continuing in the theme of the "shameful," *superstitio* is *religio* or something that looks like *religio* used for base or even evil purposes. To this extent *superstitio* is the Latin equivalent of the Greek *deisidaimonia,* imported and translated for Roman audiences from Greek philosophy.

Superstitio as Anti-Roman

Yet there is another connotation to *superstitio* that sets it apart somewhat from the Greek *deisidaimonia.* As we have seen, *deisidaimonia* seems often to have been used, apart from philosophical contexts, to refer simply to piety or traditional Greek beliefs and practices. To be sure, philosophical criticism of *deisidaimonia* sometimes did imply that the offending practices had been imported from foreign sources or represented "strange" and "new" religions, but the idea that *deisidaimonia* constituted a serious *po-*

litical threat to the Greek polis or people is rarely seen in the Greek sources. If anything, most people assumed rather that the *philosophers'* teachings about the gods posed a danger to the state and the normal functioning of nature. *Deisidaimonia* could have been perceived as the respect due to unseen forces and necessary for the common good. In Latin sources, on the other hand, *superstitio* regularly carries connotations of political danger. This political meaning of *superstitio* significantly affects its use as a label for groups such as the early Christians.

The political danger implied by *superstitio* is connected in many contexts with the use of *superstitio* to represent *foreign* religion. It is unclear whether one of these themes—*superstitio* as political threat or *superstitio* as foreign—preceded and influenced the other. Were certain practices considered dangerous to the state because they were quintessentially those of foreign enemies of Rome? Or were potentially insurrectionist practices, such as fortune-telling or magic, later connected to foreigners as *also* anti-Roman? Different scholars have advanced one or the other explanation.

According to Michele Salzman, for example, the terms *superstitio* and *superstitiosus* were probably "used to refer to divination, soothsaying and divinatory practices associated with religions originating outside Italy. (Divinatory practices and divination within the framework of Roman religion are not included in the term.)"[8] Though Salzman notes that *superstitio* could also refer to "non-orthodox Roman practices with more or less disparaging associations" (174), she implies that its original reference was to "alien" practices. If that is the case, we may imagine that *superstitio* originally referred simply to "strange" and "alien" religion that was taken to be politically anti-Roman because of its association with foreigners.

Though he is not explicit on the issue, L. F. Janssen seems to assume that the evolution of *superstitio* happened the other way around. Accepting an etymology suggested by Emile Benveniste, Janssen argues that *superstitio* originally referred to certain practices such as divination and magic that were used by people in an attempt to promote their own *private* interests instead of—or even at the cost of—*public* interests. *Pietas* referred to the proper "care of the gods" that made up *religio,* the traditional religions of Rome. Janssen notes, "Every Roman citizen believed Rome's everlasting life and growth was fully guaranteed by the gods, who had patronized the birth of the city of Rome. . . . As long as Rome's citizens would not fail in showing *pietas* to the gods and displaying *virtus* [courage] in the defense of their city, Rome would stand forever."[9] *Superstitio* referred to the pursuit of private religious practices for purely selfish interests, and thus the negative connotations of *superstitio:* "[I]n the opinion of the Romans there was no good in fostering one's own interests before the *res publica.* Even their beloved children were a secondary consideration compared with the salvation of the state" (140). *Superstitio,* therefore, meant "saving the individual at the cost of the commonwealth" (150). Janssen thus seems to assume that the meaning of *superstitio* as "foreign religion" was secondary: foreign practices were labeled *superstitio* because they so often were taken to be politically threatening and used by people who bypassed traditional religion by recourse to alien techniques to get what they wanted.

However we imagine the origin of the combination, by the first century BCE we often find *superstitio* as a reference to the religious practices of non-Romans and as a reference to religious practices seen to be a threat to the Roman "common good"—and both often in the same context. *Superstitio* poses a danger to the Roman state *(res publica Romana),* to the Roman people *(populus Romanus),* and to the Roman name or rule *(nomen* or *imperium populi Romani).* Indeed, *superstitio* had come to refer most particularly to activities imported into Roman society from the outside, to prophetic, divinatory procedures that looked non-Roman precisely because they seem to have been borrowed from Egyptians, Druids, Chaldeans, or some other foreign people.[10] "Magic" was suspicious, for one reason, because it came from elsewhere (at least in the caricatures of Roman writers), as is indicated by the very borrowing of the term *magus,* in Eastern usage originally meaning simply a "wise man." "Magic" was also suspicious because it could so easily be turned against the public good and toward private advantage.

So *superstitio* in the literature of the Roman upper class came to refer most particularly to the depraved, strange, spooky, and dishonorable religions of other peoples (see, for example, Livy 10.39.2). Furthermore, conservative Roman writers saw foreign practices, especially prophetic ones, as preying on people's fears. In the grip of fear, it was thought, even some Romans would go beyond the proper bounds of Roman religion and have recourse to foreign powers, believing that something "more" was needed. Such people succumbed to the temptation to excess, in this case, a fear-motivated excess that was labeled *superstitio.*[11]

Before we too quickly condemn the famous xenophobia of conservative Roman writers, we should attempt to view the situation from their point of view. After all, from the beginning of Roman expansionist policies, Rome's enemies had drawn power from their own traditional religions. Livy seems to shudder when he recounts the tale of how Rome's great enemy Hannibal, at the tender age of nine years, was caused by his father to ascend a Carthaginian altar, place his hands solemnly on the offerings to the gods, and swear eternal enmity against the Roman people (Livy 21.1.4–5).

In his *Histories,* Tacitus relates a prophecy advertised by the Druids that Britain would succeed in resisting Roman rule. Referring to a fire in Rome, the prophecy stated, "Long ago the city was captured by Gauls, but the [Roman] imperium remained be-

cause the seat [temple] of Jove remained whole; but now this fatal
fire is a sign from heaven of divine wrath, portending the possession of all human things by the peoples beyond the Alps" (*Histories* 4.54). Druid anti-Roman prophecy, in other words, predicted that Roman supremacy would pass to the peoples north of
the Alps, that is, to Gauls and Druids. In what may be seen as a
"dismissal," but one that betrays nonetheless a posture of defen-
siveness, Tacitus calls the prophecy an "empty *superstitio.*" According to the Roman writers, the ferocity of those stubborn
Druids was fueled by means of mysterious spiritual powers, powers derived from their native *superstitio.* Tacitus portrays German
prophets similarly. He tells of a young German woman named
Veleda who, like other women credited by the Germans with divine powers of divination, they held in great esteem. She was especially powerful, Tacitus says, because she had prophesied that
the Germans would succeed and destroy the Roman legions (*Histories* 4.61). For Tacitus, this is all *superstitio.*

The use of indigenous religious traditions to oppose Rome,
moreover, was not simply a paranoid fiction imagined by Roman
rulers or Latin historians. We have much Jewish apocalyptic literature (for example, the books of Daniel, 1 *Enoch,* 4 *Ezra*) that,
though originally used as opposition to Greek hegemony, was
later turned against the Romans, called the "Kittim" in the Dead
Sea Scrolls.[12] From the beginning and throughout much of
Rome's history, the religious traditions of peoples subdued by the
Romans were used against Roman rule. *Superstitio,* in the sense
simply of other people's religion, was usually taken by definition
to be opposed to Roman imperium. Thus, as is easy to demonstrate from Roman legal texts, *superstitio* could be used to cover
all sorts of religious practices, including suspicious divination,
foreign rituals, and magic, that were perceived as maleficent and
threatening to Roman society and the state.[13] And when Romans
adopted such strange practices themselves—usually, it was under-

stood, for selfish rather than communal and state interests—they constituted an internal threat, "fellow travelers" of Roman enemies within the body politic.

It is therefore clear that when Pliny the Younger, Tacitus, and Seutonius, as examined in Chapter 1 above, worried about the *superstitio* of Christianity they were reflecting not just the philosophical criticism of superstition, which tended to see it as shameful and ridiculous but not necessarily of great importance politically. Rather, these Roman writers also were introducing into the picture the particularly Roman fear of *superstitio* as politically subversive and socially dangerous, as a threat to Rome itself. As Janssen has noted, "Consequently, the Romans did not apply to Christianity a qualification they had merely borrowed from Greek philosophy—such a course cannot explain their (esp. Tacitus') extremely sharp condemnation of this phenomenon—they indeed considered it as a downright injury to their most solemn institutions."[14] By lumping Christianity with all those other foreign "superstitions," Roman leaders and intellectuals were signaling their perception of it as a threat to Roman power.

Christianity and Roman Imperial Power

It is not hard to understand why these authors perceived Christianity as a social and political threat to Roman imperium. Simply the knowledge that Christians followed, worshipped, and heroized a Jew who had been executed in Judea on the charge of treason—for that is precisely the meaning of the inscription "King of the Jews" that was reportedly placed on Jesus' cross—would be enough to raise suspicions against them.

The Roman rulers of the ancient world knew, moreover, that Christianity had grown out of Judaism, from the soil of Judea. Christianity began as an apocalyptic Jewish sect. Jewish apocalyptic condemnations of the Romans, sometimes, as we have seen, coded as the "Kittim," were enthusiastically adopted by some early Christians. Had any Roman governor bothered to read the book of Revelation (though I feel sure none did), he would have immediately discerned in it anti-Roman political propaganda. Even a rather obtuse Roman aristocrat could have recognized that John's references to "Babylon," "sitting on seven hills," the daimonic ruler of the entire world, the "beast" and "whore," were thinly veiled references to Rome (see Rev. 17). How could a Roman nobleman, assured as he was that the rule of the inhabited world was his by right of superiority, conquest, and past achievement in civilizing its barbarians, have *not* taken offense at the jubilations of early Christian apocalyptic?

> Babylon the Great has fallen, has fallen
> And has become the home of daimons
> And a jailhouse for every filthy bird
> And a jailhouse for every filthy and hated beast.
> For every nation has drunk the wine of the fury of her
>   whoredom,
> And the kings of the earth have all had sex with her,
> And the businessmen of the earth have grown rich
> From the power of her decadence. (Rev. 18:2–3)

Even in "code," such an unreasonable (as it would seem to the Roman) condemnation of the *pax Romana* would be treason and rebellion, just like the anti-Roman predictions of the Druids, Gauls, or German prophets.

And we need not imagine that early Christian writers themselves would have recognized insurrection as implicit in their writings. The Apostle Paul, for instance, from whose pen we have the earliest extant Christian writings, may himself have been a Roman citizen.[15] He probably did not think of himself as anti-Roman. And our imagined Roman reader may indeed have felt a

bit reassured had he known the thirteenth chapter of Paul's letter
to the Christians at Rome, where Paul tells Roman Christians to
"submit to every ruling authority." "Authorities"—and here the
Roman would doubtless have thought of the Roman senate and
people as well as the emperor—are, Paul admits, ordained by
God. They wield the sword as servants of God, and are therefore
a threat only to those who do evil. Honor, Paul urges, should be
rendered to the honorable. A clearer acknowledgment of the
reigning system of Roman imperial power could hardly be requested.

But what if our Roman read further in Paul's letters, let's say
to 1 Corinthians, where Paul assures his readers that God will
"shame" the rich, powerful, and noble by bringing them down
and elevating the poor and ignoble (1 Cor. 1:26–28)? What if he
had read Paul's promise that the "rulers of this age" are "doomed
to perish" (1 Cor. 2:6), or that the world's rulers were mad to have
crucified "the Lord of glory" (1 Cor. 2:8)? It is true, as some modern exegetes insist, that Paul *may* have had in mind more the
daimons that he believed ruled the world and were liable for the
execution of Jesus rather than Pontius Pilate and Tiberius.[16] But
can we be sure? And would such nice distinctions have been evident to a Roman investigator?

Even an early Christian work that seems intent on depicting
Christianity as politically innocuous and nonthreatening cannot
completely suppress the rebellious connotations of Christianity's
apocalypticism. I speak here of the Gospel of Luke and its companion piece, the Acts of the Apostles. Both Luke and Acts repeatedly insist that the Roman rulers have nothing to fear from
Christianity itself. Roman governor after Roman governor in the
narrative pronounce on the innocence of the movement (Acts
18:12–15; 19:40; 23:29; 25:18–19; 26:31–32; 28:18). Any apparent
troubles with it are the result of jealousies and antagonisms of
other Jews. As Festus remarks to the Jewish king Agrippa, the dis-

putes between Paul and Jewish representatives from Jerusalem are merely a matter "of their own *deisidaimonia*" (Acts 25:19). As we saw in Chapter 1, it is not clear whether we are to read Festus's comment as saying that Christianity was a "superstition" or simply part of Jewish "religion." In either case, it is certainly not the intention of Luke-Acts to depict Christianity as anything but politically innocuous.

But what then would our Roman reader do if he encountered Luke 21, in which occur apocalyptic predictions about the destruction of Jerusalem? He certainly would have recognized that these were predictions by Jesus of the capture of Jerusalem by the Roman legions under Vespasian and Titus:

> When you see Jerusalem surrounded by troops, then know that its depopulation has arrived. At that time everyone in Judea should escape to the mountains, and everyone in its midst should get out; and those in the surrounding regions [of Jerusalem] must not enter into it. For these are the days of retribution, in which everything that is written will be fulfilled. . . . There will be great distress upon the land and wrath on this people, and they will fall by the bite [*stoma*] of the sword, and they will be taken away as captives to all the nations. And Jerusalem will be trampled down by the nations, until the time of the nations has come to its completion. (Luke 21:20–24)

In spite of the role prophesied for the Roman legions here, who could have helped but notice that the great Roman army has no more purpose in the grand scheme of things than to serve as a "holding force," to trample down Jerusalem, until the "time of the nations" is fulfilled and some cosmic "son of man" swoops in with the powers of the heavens to establish an ultimate empire, presumably on the ashes of Roman imperium?

I should make myself clear: I am not claiming that Paul and the author of Luke and Acts—or most early Christian authors for that matter—were intentionally anti-Roman or revolutionary when they wrote such things. I am saying that such sentiments would have been rightly perceived by a Roman governor as seditious by any of the normal criteria indicating anti-Roman *superstitio*. When combined with the Christian refusal to honor the emperor by making sacrifice to his image or genius, and with the famous Christian rejection of all the national and protective gods and goddesses of all peoples, such writings could scarcely have avoided suspicion of insurrection. Even if they never intended to mount an organized revolt on their own against Roman rule, by disseminating such writings Christians were indeed liable to accusations of *superstitio* by Roman authorities.

Thus the particularly Roman understanding of *superstitio* as constituting a political threat provided one strategy by which Christianity could be attacked as superstition. The more "philosophical" attack of Christianity as shameful, impious, and ridiculous would provide another strategy. And a second-century intellectual named Celsus would mount that attack on the "superstition" of Christianity, as we see in the next chapter.

10

Celsus and the Attack on Christianity

We know next to nothing about the man who penned the earliest sustained criticism of Christianity.[1] Celsus was an intellectual, obviously educated in the philosophy of his day. In the second century he published *True Doctrine (alēthēs logos),* an attack on Christianity.[2] Though the work does not survive, much of it is quoted by the Christian exegete and theologian, Origen, in his *Against Celsus,* written in the third century. Most modern scholars believe that by reading Origen's defense carefully we can make out the basic contours of Celsus's critique.[3]

Although Celsus never explicitly calls Christianity *deisidaimonia,* at least not in the quotations of his work transmitted by Origen, the way he criticizes the Christian movement and its doctrines follows philosophical tropes for criticizing popular beliefs. In other words, Celsus appropriates what had by his time become traditional philosophical critiques of aspects of Greek and "barbarian" religion, designated usually as *deisidaimonia,* and turns them against Christianity.[4] The logic of cosmic-ethical hierarchy I have traced in earlier Greek writers provided the structure for Celsus's attack on what he took to be the "impiety" of Christianity. By analyzing his attack on Christianity, we learn more not only about the ancient scientific criticism of superstition, but also why Christianity so offended its educated detractors.

Christian Scripture as Mythology

Celsus knows, in the first place, that Christianity grew out of Judaism, considered Jewish scripture to be its own holy writings, and claimed to be the divinely sanctioned continuation—even, in most Christian accounts, supersession—of Judaism. So he attacks Christianity by critically examining the stories contained in Jewish scripture, now for Christians the "Old Testament." And Celsus finds critical tools ready to hand in the well-known philosophical critiques of Greek and Roman mythology. He remarks, for instance, that the creation myths and various fables in Genesis are incredible and silly, though Origen claims that Celsus did not explain *why* they were silly or what about them struck him as particularly incredible.[5] And Celsus, as any good ancient philologian could have done, is able to point out contradictions and inconsistencies in the biblical accounts. The most obvious, apparently, were the contradictions between the teaching of Moses on the one hand and Jesus on the other. Noting, for instance, that Moses had promised wealth and power to the Israelites, but that Jesus had praised poverty and the rejection of power, Celsus asks, "So who was right?" Celsus can point to Jesus' instruction to "turn the other cheek" as displacing Moses' teachings about "an eye for an eye" (see Matt. 5:38–39), and demand, "Who is lying? Moses or Jesus? Or did the Father, when he was sending Jesus, forget the instruction he had previously given to Moses? Or did he change his mind, come to despise his own laws, and then send his messenger to accomplish opposite ends?" (*Contra Celsum* 7.18).

More telling, though, are Celsus's criticisms of Christian scripture by pointing out that the Old Testament depicted God and
Jewish heroes as shameful and immoral. The Bible is full of
anthropomorphisms concerning God. Did God really need a day
of rest after creating the world? Are we to believe that God got
tired after a measly six days of work (6.61)? The scriptures repeatedly speak of God's "arm," or "hand," or "back," or various other
body parts, in themselves ridiculous and impious suggestions
(7.34). In fact, to have God say that he created man in "his image" is an insult to the divine: God does not have a human form
and so could not have created man in "his image" (6.63)! Even
worse are those many passages that depict God as subject to passions, especially anger: if it is shameful for a man to give way
to his passions and wrath, how much more the God of the universe (4.71, 73)? Note again the philosophical argument "from the
lesser to the greater": behavior inappropriate for a gentleman is
that much more inappropriate for a god. Celsus thus also points to
narratives that imply that God himself was responsible for the
creation of evil in the world. After all, if God did create *everything*
out of nothing, as Jews and Christians claim and as the Bible was
supposed to teach, God must also be responsible for whatever evil
exists in that creation (6.54). To Celsus, the notion is impious
and immoral.

Of course, Celsus did not have far to look in the Bible to find
stories about the Jewish patriarchs that seem to provide examples of immoral behavior. The shocking behavior of Lot and his
daughters, mixing even incest with drunkenness, comes in for explicit condemnation, along with the enmity and trickery between
the brothers Esau and Jacob, or the mistreatment of Joseph by his
brothers, even to the extent of being sold by them into slavery!
And who would want to hold up the history of Joseph himself for
emulation? Celsus apparently considers it completely inappropri-

ate that a slave was highly promoted and heralded as the ancestor of the people of Israel (4.43–46).

Celsus rejects attempts by Jewish and Christian intellectuals to explain away such embarrassing biblical narratives by figurative interpretation. The allegorical interpretations, Celsus argues, "are far more shameful and preposterous than the myths, since they connect with some amazing and utterly senseless folly ideas which cannot by any means be made to fit" (4.51; see also 4.38–50). No, the best parts of the Bible contain material stolen from the Greeks and other peoples. The narrative about Noah and the flood, for instance, plagiarizes the Greek myth of Deucalion (4.11, 41). The good and decent ideas in the Bible and Christianity predate Christianity and Judaism and have been better expressed by the Greeks—without, it should be noted, the grandiose boasts that such things were revealed directly by a god or a son of god (6.1). What is good in the Bible came from other peoples; what is bad is shameful and immoral indeed.

Jesus as an Unlikely "Divine Man"

Celsus seems not to have treated the writings of the New Testament (more precisely, those early Christian writings that many years later came to make up the New Testament) in the same way. That is, he criticized the narratives and teachings of the Old Testament by appropriating traditional philosophical critiques of myths in general, but when he turns to the accounts about Jesus, he appropriates the sort of invective and literary criticism turned against individual persons and biographical or hagiographical accounts of them. He criticizes the Gospel portraits of Jesus by invoking upper-class notions of status, propriety, and ethics.

In the first place, Celsus rejects Christian claims that the Jewish prophecies pointed to Jesus. He uses Jewish arguments against them, pointing to Jewish disputants who insist that the prophecies referred to other events or persons, even to the Jewish nation itself, rather than to Jesus (1.57). "The prophecies," he insists, "could be applied to thousands of others more plausibly than to Jesus" (2.28).

More important, though, Celsus deprecates Jesus himself, his origins, life, and shameful death, to demonstrate that all claims to his divinity are worse than ridiculous; they are despicable and reprehensible—they are, indeed, immoral. The births of gods and great men are expected to be announced and trumpeted, by miracles if possible. Jesus' origins, on the other hand, were completely obscure and, if anything, embarrassingly humble. Jesus invented the story that he was born of a virgin, Celsus insists. "He was born in a Judean village and of a poor country girl, a working woman. . . . Her husband, who was a manual laborer who practiced a craft, kicked her out after she had been accused of committing adultery. . . . After being thrown out by her husband and while she was wandering around in disgrace, she gave birth to Jesus in secret" (1.28). Celsus cites what may by his time have already been a Jewish accusation against Jesus that his mother had been impregnated by a Roman soldier with the name or nickname of Panthera (panther).[6] Celsus scoffs at the idea that Mary had genealogies as illustrious as those given Jesus in the Gospels, as if such an obscure girl could be descended from kings (1.32)!

Jesus' life was also dishonest and immoral. He collected around himself a motley crew of disreputable characters—tax collectors and sailors—and they procured their livelihood by disgraceful means (1.62, 2.46). In fact, Jesus was never able to command a following of much more than ten or eleven such men. Celsus admits that Jesus may have performed a few miracles, but only as a common magician. After all, Jesus had spent his early life in Egypt, and while there had hired himself out as a manual laborer. He used his sojourn in Egypt to learn magic (1.38). So even if he did perform a few tricks, they were no more than those done by any marketplace magician, who for a few coins can make things appear and disappear. If you pay them a bit extra, they will even divulge the secrets of their tricks. They are not sons of gods, but, if anything, possessed by evil daimons (1.68). Rather than proclaiming Jesus' divinity by pointing to his wonders, Christians should be ashamed to worship a common sorcerer (see also 1.6, 1.71).

Jesus' body was clearly not divine. Celsus notices that the Gospel writers depict Jesus as predicting his upcoming death (any common criminal, he says, could have predicted that the law would eventually catch up with him!), but Jesus still seems anxious about attempts on his life. Celsus points out, sensibly enough, that if Jesus' body were really divine he would not have been concerned about being killed, since he *could not* have been killed—his body was not of the divine sort after all (1.66). Furthermore, Celsus notes that Jesus ate and drank, even animal flesh. Jesus ate the Passover, which Celsus recognizes would have included the flesh of sheep. Celsus assumes, as would most people of his culture, that food, especially animal flesh, is corruptible matter, made up of "filth." After all, the body that is composed of meat is also the body that defecates. If Jesus really did eat such matter, as the Gospels admit, then he must not have been a god, or else the Christian god is "shit-eating" (*skatophagein*, 7.13).

The crucifixion comes in for special disdain by Celsus. Generally speaking, Celsus points out that, even according to the Gospels, Jesus convinced practically no one during his life of the truth of his claims. He lived and died in shame (2.39). His followers ultimately deserted him as even the cohorts of a robber chieftain would certainly not do (2.12). During all the time of his arrest, trial, torture, and crucifixion, his god did nothing to help him and he was unable to help himself (1.54). At the end he cried and wailed—hardly the behavior of even a nobleman or philosopher, much less a god (2.24). Furthermore, the people who tortured and killed Jesus never suffered anything terrible afterwards, unlike the fate that would surely befall the murderers of a divine being (2.34, 8.41). Certainly, a man who was arrested and crucified in such disgrace simply cannot have been the "pure and holy Logos" of the universe (2.31).

As for the resurrection, Celsus makes short shrift of such stories. Celsus points out that Mary Magdalene, according to some of the Gospels at any rate, was the first to claim to have seen the resurrected Jesus. According to the Gospel of John, she was weeping in the garden at the time. Celsus sneers that the resurrection stories are due to the fantasies of a hysterical woman. Or perhaps the other accounts were produced by dullards who were just looking for a chance to appear important. Or perhaps simpleminded persons under the influence of a sorceror thought they had seen Jesus after his death. In any case, the resurrection stories prove nothing; they could have been produced by any number of factors, none of which necessarily had anything to do with divinity (2.55–60).

Celsus's treatment of the Gospel accounts of Jesus' life, death, and resurrection is an excellent example of ancient rhetorical and historical criticism. Celsus's diatribes may strike modern readers as vitriolic, but that was the tone regularly employed in ancient intellectual debate. Following the conventions of ancient rhetoric, Celsus consistently interprets Christian traditions in the worst possible light and turns Christian "biographies" of Jesus against their own claims. He criticizes Jesus on the basis of status and morality, the primary means of personal invective learned even by adolescents in their early schooling.

Damning Doctrines

But Celsus did not stop with attacking the myths of the Old Testament and the life of Jesus. He also turned his scorn on central

Christian doctrines. And in this regard the doctrines of the incarnation and the resurrection of the body especially drew his ire. With regard to the incarnation, Celsus coupled his other criticisms with a favorite Greek complaint against Christianity: that it was new and barbaric. Greek intellectuals of the second century (and other times as well) honored antiquity and classicism. Whatever was novel was suspect. Greeks did not always respect Jews, but they grudgingly admitted that Judaism was an ancient ethnic religion and thus merited some respect. They also knew that Christianity *claimed* to be the contemporary, proper expression of ancient Judaism. Christians claimed Jewish scripture as their own and defended their own religion by pointing to its antiquity in Judaism. But most people recognized that Christians, or the vast majority of them, did not keep the Sabbath or avoid foods spurned by the Jews, like pork. Nor were Christian men circumcised. Though Greeks and Romans typically, it seems, thought of the self-mutilation of circumcision as particularly barbaric, they could overlook this barbarism among the Jews since it was an ancient ethnic tradition and an important aspect of their religion. But in that case Christians proved their own *independence* from Judaism by their rejection of circumcision.

One of the ways Celsus expresses this ancient fetishism of "the old" is his questioning of the "recent" appearance of God in Jesus. If Jesus is *the* incarnation of the divine, why did it take him so long to appear in human history? Why at that time rather than earlier? Did God simply not care about the vast numbers of humanity that lived before the recent appearance of "God" in Judea? This last point also reflects the Greek and Roman disbelief that God, should he decide to live among humanity, would do so in a hole-in-the-corner place like tiny and insignificant Judea. Why did this "incarnation" manifest itself only to the Jews, and not to the Romans, the rulers of the earth, or to the Greeks, the custodians of culture and learning? Thus a most important critique mounted against the Christian doctrine of the incarnation was that it claimed that the God of the entire universe had appeared only quite recently and in a small, insignificant corner among an unimportant people (see 4.7–8, 6.78).

Moreover, if the supreme God has appeared in the fleshly body of Jesus of Nazareth, then the divine has suffered change from the better to the worse. Celsus argues that the incarnation implies that God experienced *change,* which is impious to attribute to divinity. Divinity is perfect, so any change (especially change into flesh!) must be from perfection to less than perfection, from good to bad, from beautiful to shameful, from happiness to misfortune, from what is best to what is wicked: "It is the nature of a mortal being to undergo change and remoulding, whereas it is the nature of an immortal being to remain the same without alteration. Accordingly, God could not be capable of undergoing this change" (4.14; trans. Henry Chadwick). If, on the other hand, the appearance of Jesus was only an *apparent* change on the part of God, then God has deceived people, and that is just as bad (4.18).[7] According to Celsus, daimons may descend and come to earth, appearing in bodily form to humans, but true gods would not do so (5.2).

Furthermore, Christians claim that Jesus did not simply descend from heaven to live among humans, but was actually born from a woman's womb. And why, Celsus demands, would the Supreme God have "breathed" his "spirit" *(pneuma)* "into the womb of a woman?" (In common assumptions and according to ancient science, semen is a powerful pneumatic substance containing the essence of the person.) As Celsus sneers, God knows how to make human bodies through other means than normal childbirth: "And he could have fashioned a body for this guy without poking his own pneuma into such filth" (6.73).

In the end the issue for Celsus, as we should by now expect, was one of status. If indeed a divine being wishes to appear to humans, surely he or she will do so in beauty. But Jesus, as even the

Christian scriptures attest, was ugly (6.75).[8] He ate filth (7.13–14). He acted like a slave, suffering servile torture and crucifixion (7.14). From Celsus's hierarchical point of view, any teaching that God could be revealed in such a man was "wicked and impious"—the typical themes of the philosophical critique of "superstition."

The doctrine of the resurrection comes in for similar critique. Celsus insists, for one thing, that the Christian doctrine of the eschatological resurrection of the body is actually an ignorant misunderstanding of the classical belief in reincarnation (7.32), which was itself acceptable in the opinions of some due to the influence of Pythagoreanism. But the Christian doctrine is crude and offensive. Against the doctrine of the resurrection of Christ, Celsus argues that "God would not have received back the spirit which he gave after it had been defiled by the nature of the body" (6.72). Here again, Celsus's criticism is based on his assumption of the spirit-body hierarchy that is matched, though in sometimes complicated ways, by a divine-human hierarchy. To get the sense of Celsus's disgust when confronted with the Christian doctrine of the resurrection of the body, especially in its context of Christian apocalyptic teachings, it is worth reproducing a lengthy quotation Origen has provided from Celsus:

> It is foolish of them also to suppose that, when God applies the fire (like a cook!), all the rest of mankind will be thoroughly roasted and that they alone will survive, not merely those who are alive at the time but those also long dead who will rise up from the earth possessing the same bodies as before. This is simply the hope of worms. For what sort of human soul would have any further desire for a body that has rotted? The fact that this doctrine is not shared by some of you [Jews] and by some Christians shows its utter repulsiveness, and that it is both revolting and impossible. For what

sort of body, after being entirely corrupted, could return to
its original nature and that same condition which it had before it was dissolved? As they have nothing to say in reply,
they escape to a most outrageous refuge by saying that "anything is possible to God." But, indeed neither can God do
what is shameful nor does He desire what is contrary to nature. If you were to desire something abominable in your
wickedness, not even God would be able to do this, and you
ought not to believe at all that your desire will be fulfilled.
For God is not the author of sinful desire or of disorderly
confusion, but of what is naturally just and right. For the
soul He might be able to provide an everlasting life; but as
Heraclitus says, "corpses ought to be thrown away as worse
than dung." As for the flesh, which is full of things which it
is not even nice to mention, God would neither desire nor
be able to make it everlasting contrary to reason. For He
Himself is the reason of everything that exists; therefore He
is not able to do anything contrary to reason or to His own
character. (5.14; trans. Chadwick)

We see here again the linking of the necessity of nature, the im-
plication of the divine *in* nature, the hierarchical structure of
nature, and the dependence on cultural notions of honor and
shame.

The overwhelming issues in the quotation are hierarchy and
propriety. It is "impossible" for God to raise up bodies *not* because it would involve "supernatural" intervention into "natural
cause and effect" but because it would be contrary to the natural
hierarchy of the universe for God to make the low, disgusting,
rottenness of flesh and blood the eternal home of the higher soul
or spirit. God cannot act against his own nature or against the nature of Nature. And one aspect of that Nature is its structure as a
hierarchical system of honor and shame. It is "impossible" for
God to raise bodies, therefore, because it is "shameful," and God,

as the most honorable being, *cannot* do the dishonorable. Indeed, the entire Christian apocalyptic narrative makes God look like a mere "cook"! Celsus's phrase about Christian doctrine turning the supreme being into a common cook must have bothered Origen; he repeats the epithet, with his counterarguments, several times (5.14–15).

For Celsus, though, the vulgar Christian doctrine of the resurrection of the body fits the low status of Christians themselves. The disruption of the corporeal hierarchy implied in the doctrine of the resurrection correlates with the disruption of social hierarchy signified by the fact that it is low-class, uneducated, vulgar people who grasp onto such teaching. And Celsus recognizes the implied threat to the hierarchy of society: "It is not respectable even to have this discussion with people who believe such a thing and are themselves so attached to the body. For they are the type of people who are unsophisticated in other ways as well—and are dirty and wholly without rationality and carrying within themselves the disease of sedition" (8.49; for other accusations by Celsus that the Christians are seditious, see 3.5, 8.2).

Finally, we should note Celsus's opinion that the Christian belief in the existence of Satan is also unethical and impious. To say that God is opposed by some sort of evil being of nearly equal power is blasphemous. The supremely powerful and good God would never allow the existence of such an opponent to his good will and beneficence. Celsus does admit the *possibility* of the existence of evil daimons (as I examine below), though the notion plays no large role in his grand scheme of things. But to elevate some particular "devil," or "Satan" as the Christian and Jewish scriptures call him, to such a high level as to be able to challenge God is the vain illusion and deceit of a sorcerer, someone out to trick common people through fear of powerful but wicked divine beings (6.42). The idea of Satan is unphilosophical, indecent, and insulting to the power and goodness of God (see also 8.11).

In sum, Celsus rejects these Christian doctrines sometimes

just because they seem to him incredible. But most of the time, we can tell that they seem incredible because they disrupt the cosmic-ontological-ethical hierarchy assumed as reality by Greek and Roman philosophy and science.

Philosophical versus Christian Demonology

It is precisely his commitment to that cosmic-ontological-ethical hierarchy that caused Celsus to take offense at another central difference between his own view of the world and that presupposed by Christianity: the nature and roles of daimons. Celsus lived not long after the time of Plutarch and was also influenced by various philosophical schools, including the Platonism of his day. Similar to Plutarch, for instance, Celsus believes that there are four classes of superhuman beings: god, angels, daimons, and heroes (*Contra Celsum* 7.68). Gods, contrary to popular opinion, do not descend to earth, but daimons do (5.2). In fact, daimons are the administrators of all things on earth—food, wine, fruits, water, air. Christians, Celsus argues, are ridiculous if they think they can avoid contact with daimons, unless they distance themselves from life entirely. Every time they eat, drink, or breathe they are associating with daimons. For Celsus, one cannot take part in the world and its products without trafficking in the daimonic (8.28).

Since daimons are the "governors" of all good things that we need in order to live, it is only right that we express our appreciation to them by offering sacrifices and prayers and, moreover, that we do so in order to ensure their continued good will (8.33). As far as disease goes, Celsus believes that different daimons are assigned to govern different parts of the body, and we may honor them in order to ensure health, good luck, and deliverance from disease or pain (8.58). The assumption here seems to be that though daimons may not actually cause disease, they may be encouraged by worship to heal human beings. Celsus criticizes Christians for refusing to participate in common, public festivals and rites. If idols are "nothing," as some Christian rhetoric proclaims (see 1 Cor. 8:4), why not participate in festivals? No harm can come from "nothings." If the powers behind the images, on the other hand, are daimons, then, according to Celsus, there is still no problem with festivals, "since these [that is, daimons] too are clearly the property of God, so we ought to trust them and accord them their proper rituals according to custom and pray to them so that they may be kind" (*Contra Celsum* 8.24). Celsus takes the traditional gods, therefore, to be basically benign daimons.

But as that quotation implies, if sacrifice and prayer *may* make daimons more likely to be "kind" to humans, may the same beings become less kind if ignored? May daimons or other superhuman beings, that is, actually be evil and harm humans? Celsus never comes right out and says so explicitly in the quotations we possess. (And he probably did not at all. Since Origen's intention is to argue that *all* daimons are evil and malicious, he probably would have grabbed onto any such explicit admission by Celsus.) We have already noted above that Celsus seems to have suggested that Jesus had an evil daimon. Moreover, Celsus compares powers "both in the air and on earth" to "regents and governors or officers" who may conceivably commit some harm if slighted (8.35). He doesn't explicitly call them "daimons," but that is probably what he meant. And in one place Celsus links "earthly daimons" to rather questionable religious rites: "For perhaps we ought not to disbelieve wise men who say that most of the earthly daimons are absorbed with created things, and are riveted to blood and burnt-offerings and magical enchantments, and are bound to other things of this sort, and can do nothing better than healing the body and predicting the coming fortune of man and cities, and that all their knowledge and power concerns merely mortal activities" (8.60; trans. Chadwick). Here "earthly daimons" (as opposed to "airy" or "heavenly" daimons?) are rather low-level administrators who are implicated in blood sacrifice and even magic. Celsus does not call them "evil," but given the usual reputation of magic as misanthropic and harmful, their involvement in it does cast some suspicion on their moral status.

Significantly, Origen jumps on these expressions to criticize Celsus and his "daimons." To Celsus's admission that some daimons, like human administrators, may commit harm if slighted, Origen counters with traditional moral-philosophical stories about virtuous men who refuse to return harm for harm (8.35), a point, as noted above, made in Plato's writings. As we will see in the following chapters, Origen, as will Eusebius after him, uses Greek and Roman philosophy to besmudge Greek and Roman philosophers and their theology.

But in the end, though Celsus hints at some acceptance of a notion of harmful daimons, he, like Plutarch, prefers the more traditional philosophical position. Daimons do not, after all, "need" the stuff of sacrifices: "It is better to be of the opinion that daimons are not needy or lack anything but that they simply take joy in those who behave toward them in a pious manner" (8.63). Celsus works hard to retain a respectable philosophical point of view: he seems to know that some people, even perhaps some intellectuals, concede the existence of at least potentially harmful daimons, but he prefers the more traditional philosophical view that daimons are superior, and therefore benevolent, beings.[9] Christians are superstitious, for one thing, because they attribute evil intents and practices to daimons, the classic fault of *deisidaimonia.*

Christians as "Low Class"

Finally, we should note that Celsus extends his critique of Christianity to include Christians themselves and Christianity as a social movement. Repeatedly, Celsus depicts, in scathing terms, Christians as low-class, uneducated, stupid yokels (1.27; 3.18, 44, 50, 52, 55, 59, passim). He complains that they are anti-intellectual because they insist that Christian teachings need not be defended in the court of common reason or philosophy but must be accepted on "faith alone" (6.10–11). And Christians are clearly immoral, as is proven in the first place by their practice of magical arts. They perform exorcisms and wonders by learning the names of daimons and appropriating the power of incantations (1.6; 6.14, 40–41). They manipulate the gullible and uneducated by their impious stories about the punishments God is eager to inflict on humanity (4.10). But of course all such deceits and manipulations are necessary because Christianity, rather than representing an ancient and respectable religion of a particular people, is a newly invented, false system advocated by a ragtag bunch of misfits who have forsaken the proper and peaceful religions of their own peoples and stolen the religion of the Jews (see 3.14; 5.33, 65).

The Logic of the Philosophical Position

It is unclear how much of an impact Celsus's attack on Christianity had or even how many Christians knew about it. Origen himself seems not to have known about Celsus or his book until they were brought to his attention by his patron, Ambrose of Alexandria.[10] I imagine, however, that other educated Greeks would have taken *True Doctrine*, if they bothered to read it, as a thorough and intelligent criticism of Christianity. It employed common rhetorical strategies of ancient debate. Eventually, as far as we know, all copies of the work were lost—perhaps destroyed by Christians. But Celsus's attack was not unique. True, it may have been the first such attack on Christianity mounted by an educated Greek or Roman, but it was not the last.[11] And its strategies were simply those that philosophy had already used, to a great ex-

tent, in its critiques of traditional religion, cult, and popular beliefs. Though he may not have used the term itself (we cannot be
sure he did not), Celsus attacked Christianity as a superstition, as
deisidaimonia. In Celsus's attack on Christianity we can trace the
lines—by now familiar to us—of the ancient philosophical criticism of "superstition."

And if we are fair, we must admit that to a great extent Celsus,
and those later Greek and Roman writers who also attacked
Christianity as superstition, were right. That is, if we accept their
presuppositions about the nature of the universe, which included
the nature of the divine, we can understand how they could not
have helped but perceive Christianity as liable to the philosophical critique of *deisidaimonia.* By the lights of Greek philosophy,
Christians were for the most part guilty as charged. Christianity
was new and barbaric. It arose on the soil of Palestine and was, in
the beginning, foreign to classical Greek religion. It portrayed a
wrathful, scary god, and thus openly taught that God ought to be
feared. In what is probably the earliest extant letter he sent to one
of his recently founded churches, Paul writes that his Greek converts had "turned from idols to be slaves *(douleuein)* of the living
and true God and to await his son from the heavens, whom he
raised from the dead, Jesus, who will save us from the wrath that
is coming" (1 Thess. 1:9–10). From its beginnings, apparently,
Christian preaching had depended on an apocalyptic promise of
destruction by an angry and jealous god. From a philosophical
point of view, the Christian God was someone who apparently
couldn't control his temper. He looked like Galen's mother, who
got so mad at her servants that she bit them in rage (see *Passions
of the Soul* 8 [K 5.40–41]).

Throughout the philosophical critique of *deisidaimonia,* as we
have seen so clearly in Celsus's attack on Christianity, an important issue was the maintenance of the hierarchies of nature. The
resurrection of the body was ridiculed not because it represented

supernatural interference in natural cause and effect, but because it disrupted the given physiological hierarchy. Why would the divine portion of a human being *want* to reinhabit a rotten, disgusting corpse composed of despicable substances such as blood, semen, menstrual fluids, and pus? Myths of divine incarnations similarly contradicted physiological hierarchy. How disgusting to imagine that an immortal being would submit to incarnation, especially, as Celsus repeatedly emphasizes, in the body of an obscure, lower-class, ugly Jew! The Christian notion that a divine being had suffered the pain and shame of crucifixion also came in for constant attack by Greek and Roman authors. True, some noble, beautiful, wise human might in some cases be elevated to divine status. The problem was not in any conjunction of divine and human—the problem with Christianity was that it worshipped a renegade Jew who had been whipped, tortured, and crucified like a slave. And this was so threatening to upper-class Greeks and Romans because it constituted a challenge to the hierarchy of the cosmos and thus of society.

Another recurring aspect of the philosophical critique of *deisidaimonia,* which makes less of an appearance in the surviving fragments of Celsus than in the writings of other critics of Christianity, was the notion that proper religious observances should be balanced and moderate. As Galen says, even excess in love is a disease.[12] Tellingly, Marcus Aurelius explicitly criticizes Christians in the second century for their "excess," including their excess of devotion that propels them to self-sacrifice.[13] One expression of the philosophical concern with moderation and the avoidance of excess or deficiency was the ancient upper-class goal of self-sufficiency, *autarkeia.* Greek philosophy of all schools claimed to be able to teach men (women were a different matter for *most* of ancient philosophy) to live without dependence on anyone or anything. The truly wise man lacked nothing. Whether financially or emotionally, the upper-class gentleman aspired to self-sufficiency.

From the beginning, Christian authors share none of this philosophical attachment to moderation and self-sufficiency (at least not until the writings of such as Clement of Alexandria in the late second century). Paul glories in his depictions of his own dependence on God, Christ, and even other Christians. When it is to his purpose, however, Paul emphasizes his self-sufficiency in phrases that recall those of philosophers. In a letter to the Philippians thanking them for a gift, for instance, he notes that whereas he appreciates their gift, he doesn't really *need* it since he is *autarkēs*, "self-sufficient" (Phil. 4:11). But elsewhere Paul readily admits his total *dependence* on God and explicitly rejects the idea that any human being can be self-sufficient: "*Not* that we are sufficient [*hikanoi*] of ourselves so that we could consider anything as really ours; rather our sufficiency comes from God" (2 Cor. 3:5–6).[14] And the other side of the philosophical coin expressed by "self-sufficiency," the denigration of any kind of "excess," runs counter to much early Christian sensibility. Early Christian apocalyptic promises of both future glory and future suffering, for example, play on the tropes of excess. It is hard to imagine the earliest Christians advocating a moderation of love, faith, or commitment, as the rhetoric and imagery of the many martyrologies attest. Early Christianity was a religion of excess, and it taught the impossibility of self-sufficiency, all of which rendered it superstition in the eyes of educated Greeks and Romans.

Finally, we should admit that by the lights of ancient philosophy Christianity proved to be superstitious in its demonology, as Celsus made clear. One of the most socially obvious aspects of Christianity was its role as a cult that offered healing from diseases understood, most often, as caused by daimonic attacks.[15] Christianity's reputation as a wonder-working, and especially healing and exorcising, movement is attested even by its enemies, as Celsus himself has demonstrated. This "social service" provided by Christianity may have increased its attraction to the ordinary inhabitant of the Greco-Roman world, since most people accepted the traditional belief that daimons, though superior in power and nature to humans, could be morally inferior and often did cause disease. The philosophical-medical systems, though, had unanimously rejected daimonic causation of disease because it was understood that the ontological hierarchy of nature must be matched by a corresponding ethical hierarchy: those superior on the ontological scale *must* be superior ethically. Otherwise, the hierarchy that underwrote all of ancient philosophical morality and science would collapse—or so it seemed. By accepting the popular notion that most diseases were caused by daimons, and then by promising deliverance from disease by the expelling of daimons by a superior power, Christianity proved itself to be superstitious: *deisidaimonia.* Thus, for many reasons, ancient authors quite understandably condemned Christianity as superstition. How one Christian intellectual responded will be the subject of the next chapter.

11

Origen and the Defense of Christianity

Origen has long been hailed as one of early Christianity's most brilliant and learned intellectuals. He lived from about 184 to about 254 CE, working mostly as a Christian teacher and scholar. Educated in Alexandria in ancient philosophy as well as Christian literature and theology, he lived much of his life in Caesarea in Palestine, writing great works of biblical commentary, theology, and Christian instruction.[1] His defense of Christianity against Celsus, known simply as the *Contra Celsum (Against Celsus),* was a strong, subtle, and sophisticated apology for Christianity in the ancient world, even if it may sound less convincing for a modern audience.[2] Its strength derived from Origen's ability to draw on his extensive familiarity with ancient philosophy and literature both to defend Christianity and to attack traditional Greek religion.[3] In another sense, Origen's apology was so powerful because he was able to nudge Christian doctrines closer to the sensibilities of ancient Greek philosophy: he interpreted scripture and Christian beliefs so that they *could be seen* as less offensive to a Greek intellectual audience. But Origen is important for my purposes more because he represents a new intellectual sensibility about nature and the divine, a sensibility forged in the crucible of his struggle to make sense of both Christianity and ancient philosophy and of his struggle to make Christianity more "respectable" to its "cultured despisers" of the third century. In his interpretation of Christianity, Origen either creates or reflects (according to how much originality we decide to assign him) a significant shift in ancient sensibilities about nature, the divine, and thus "superstition."

Countering Celsus

A complete rehearsal of the many ways Origen answers Celsus's varied criticisms would practically reproduce the text of *Against Celsus,* so I will limit myself for the most part to Origen's answers that further my own study of ancient superstition. It should be noted, however, that Origen considers himself able to dispense with many of Celsus's barbs with little trouble. He often notes, for instance, that Celsus simply has his "facts" wrong. Celsus, Origen claims, sometimes misquotes the scriptures to their detriment, or he overlooks passages or interpretations that would clear up the problems he highlights. One of Origen's favorite responses is to insist that Celsus is confusing "true" Christians with "heretics," whom Origen would prefer to disassociate from Christianity entirely, or with Jews, whom Origen is perfectly willing to agree were often in error. Partly, this exchange indicates the distance in time between Celsus's writing and Origen's: for an outsider like Celsus, writing in the second century, the differences among different early Christian groups, which Origen in the third century would prefer to think of as differences between "true" Christians and "heretics," would have appeared inconsequential if discernible at all. Origen, at any rate, is willing to agree with some of Celsus's criticisms because they refer to beliefs that Origen himself rejects as heretical—such as the "Docetic" teaching that Jesus only "appeared" to die and be human, or the use by some Christians (Gnostics? the term is debatable these days) of elaborate myths thought to derive from Egyptian religion and mysticism. All such instances Origen simply dismisses as a case of mistaken identity: Celsus is attacking others besides "true Christians."

Another defense that comes fairly easily to Origen plays on the ancient notion, commonly accepted by just about everyone, that "success proves truth," or as we in the modern world might put it, the proof of the pudding is in the eating.[4] Celsus himself has wielded this weapon against Christianity: Jesus must not have been divine because he was unable to defeat his opponents or even to save his life. The Christian god must not be real or powerful because he either cannot or will not protect his followers from torture and destruction. Rather than challenging the assumptions that underwrite such rhetoric, Origen simply turns it around on Celsus. In fact, Origen uses the "success" theme to turn what Celsus thought were Christianity's deficits into its assets. Did Celsus take the newness of Christianity to be a fault? Origen answers that the remarkable spread of Christianity *in such a short time* is an obvious sign of divine approval, even miraculous support (1.26–31). Did Celsus mock the ignorance and lack of sophistication of the Christian apostles? Origen answers that the astounding success of their preaching *in spite of their complete lack of education* must be proof that they were doing God's work (1.62). Did Celsus scoff that Christianity is everywhere spoken against? Origen answers that the divinity of Jesus is proved by the very fact that his message has become so successful *in spite of opposition* from all, "kings, governors, the Roman Senate, rulers everywhere, and the people" (2.79). By the middle of the third century, Christianity had made remarkable inroads in Greek and

Roman society; its presence could be seen in practically every city of the Empire; it numbered even higher-class people among its ranks. So Origen repeatedly points to the success of Christianity as proof of its divine origins.[5]

Another way to defend Christianity against the charge of novelty was to stress its links to Judaism via Jewish scriptures. And to counter Celsus's accusations that everything of value in Jewish or Christian scripture was "stolen" from Greek philosophy or literature, Origen is able to cite authorities, including *Greek* intellectuals, who had borne witness to the greater antiquity of the Jewish traditions when compared to the Greek. By Origen's day, there was a long-standing consensus among Greek writers that the Hebrews represented an ancient tradition. Jewish writers like Philo had long ago argued, and Greek writers like Hermippus and Hecataeus had long ago admitted, that the Greeks got much of their learning from nations to the south and east, including the Hebrews (1.14–16).[6] Origen is able to call on a shared intellectual agreement that Moses predated Greek philosophy, even Homer (see 1.18–22; 4.21; 7.28, 30, passim). By claiming Jewish scripture and heritage as their own, Christians were able to counter accusations that their religion was recent or innovative; they were able to assert for themselves a lineage more ancient than the Greeks and Romans, a pedigree prior to Homer's.

In an even more clever move, though, Origen answers Celsus's charge that Christianity taught people to forsake their ancestral religious practices and beliefs for something novel and untrue to their ethnic origins. Origen brilliantly points out that Greek philosophers had made entire careers attempting to teach people *to forsake* traditional practices and beliefs of their ancestral religions (5.35). When philosophers taught that the traditional myths were ungodly and impious, they were advocating a rejection of tradition. When philosophers taught people not to think about sacrifices in the "crude" way they had previously, as attempts to "buy" the good favor of the gods, they were challenging long-standing assumptions.[7] When philosophers interpreted myths allegorically as representing the forces of "nature," they certainly offended traditionalists. But just as philosophers taught all these things in order to lead people away from "superstition" to higher understanding and virtue, so Christianity, Origen insists, teaches people to forsake their traditional ethnic religions in order to lead them to truer understandings of reality and greater virtue. Celsus should fault this "novelty" of Christianity no more than he would the "novelty" of philosophical theology.

Christianity as Philosophy

We have thus already encountered one of Origen's primary strategies for defending Christianity: comparing it to philosophy.[8] In fact, Origen presents Christianity *as* philosophy—as the ultimately true philosophy. By Origen's day, philosophy's main task —more than its attentions to geometry, cosmology, and the "nature of nature"—was the teaching of "virtue." And that is the main accomplishment Origen repeatedly credits to Christianity. He admits, for instance, that Christians accept the facticity of the miraculous healings attributed to Jesus in the Gospels, and that those miracles furnish one reason people have accepted Jesus as divine. But he emphasizes even more the miracles Jesus performed—and continues to perform—on people's characters: "For continually, the eyes of those blind of soul are opened; the ears of those deaf to words of virtue enthusiastically hear about God and the happy life available from him; many who were lame of foot in their 'inner' person, as the scriptures say, have now been cured by the Logos and do not merely leap, but leap 'as a stag' [Isaiah 35:6], an animal that is an enemy of snakes and stronger than any poison of vipers" (2.48; see also 2.79). One of the most important missions accomplished by Jesus and his followers has been to teach virtue, the recognized task of ancient philosophy.

As we have seen, one of Celsus's attacks on Christianity centered on the characters of the apostles and early leaders of Christianity. They were mere "sailors" and lowlifes, and they eagerly proclaimed their own sins. Origen easily appropriates philosophical conversion stories, though, to counter the accusation: like other philosophies, Christianity has changed the lives of previously wicked people. Socrates had converted Phaedo, taking him straight out of a "house of ill repute." Xenocrates used his philosophical instruction to turn his student Polemo from a dissolute life to one of virtue (1.64; for other philosophical conversion stories, see 3.66–69). Furthermore, such stories are something of a rarity among Greek philosophies, Origen claims, whereas they are much more numerous among Christians, demonstrating not that Christians are *currently* licentious, but that Christianity is a superior philosophy in that it has had the same effect on many more people.

Celsus had also criticized Christianity by pointing out its divisions, with all sorts of contradictory claims being made by different Christian groups. To meet this criticism, Origen simply points to the several different schools of philosophy, each claiming to represent the truth. Heresies and differences among Christians do not impugn the truth of Christianity any more than different *haereseis* (which basically means "schools" or "options" in Greek) disprove the usefulness of philosophy (2.27, 3.12). And to Celsus's scoffing at the death and poverty of Jesus and his followers, which in Celsus's opinion prove false any claim to his divinity or virtue, Origen points to the similar circumstances of famous philosophers. Jesus went to his death willingly and with foreknowledge, *like Socrates* (2.17). He endured "poverty, the cross, and the plotting of evil men" as had Democritus, Crates, and Diogenes, the fathers of Cynicism (2.40). Origen depicts Jesus' death not as shameful, but as noble, drawing on a long literary tradition of the "noble death," especially that endured by philosophers (7.17, 56).[9] Jesus' influence in this capacity has been felt

long after his death, Origen insists: the sufferings of the apostles
and Christians up to Origen's own day are "noble deaths" endured for the sake of virtue and philanthropy (see, for example,
2.34, 45).

More than simply comparing Christianity to philosophy,
though, Origen adopts philosophical doctrines and tropes to defend Christianity against Celsus's attacks. Celsus had mocked the
Christian notion, for instance, that "man" is the highest creature
and the purpose for which the rest of creation exists. To counter
the criticism, Origen calls on Stoic teachings that had already
taught that "man" was the "end" (*telos:* goal, purpose, end) of "nature" (4.74). In response to Celsus's derision of the myths and
stories of Jewish scripture, Origen is able to offer quite philosophical-sounding allegorical interpretations of the same stories.
In fact, much of Book 4 of *Against Celsus* provides one allegorical
reading of the Bible after another. Allegorical interpretation, after
all, had been invented by Greek literary critics and philosophers
as a means of interpreting Greek myths, including Homer, so
that they could be taken as containing higher truths in spite of
their narration of abominable acts committed by divine beings.

In precisely the same manner, Origen interprets the most offensive parts of the Bible as teaching higher philosophical doctrines. The "massacre of one's enemies" that God seems to urge in
the Bible actually refers to the power that the righteous man ex-
erts over all things; the destruction of "the sinners upon the
earth" actually refers to the destruction of the "carnal mind";
when the Psalm speaks of crushing the infants of one's enemies
against rocks, we are to understand the "infants" as a reference to
"confused thoughts which evil has planted and caused to grow up
in the soul" (7.22; see Psalm 137:8–9). Origen was a master of allegorical interpretation, which he borrowed from Greek philosophy and used to interpret otherwise embarrassing passages in
Christian scripture, just as Greek intellectuals had done with
Homer and Hesiod.

Origen's defense of Christianity is full of philosophical commonplaces, easily appropriated by someone with his intelligence and education to defend Christian doctrines and practices. The apparently "barbaric" Christian apocalyptic predictions of a fiery end of the world Origen likens to philosophical doctrines of a "conflagration" that was thought to bring about a future (and recurring, in most accounts) "purifying" of the earth (5.15). Christian worship, with its lack of physical, especially "blood," sacrifices, is called by Origen "rational and smokeless sacrifice" (7.1). Origen notes that Christians believe that fellowship with the divine makes someone divine, a common philosophical theme (3.28). And against Celsus's accusations that Christians practice magic, Origen makes the philosophical-sounding counterpoint that Christianity is not magic because it is moral (1.68). The list could go on; Origen's appropriation of philosophical themes and language to defend Christianity pervades his book.

Furthermore, Origen uses philosophical commonplaces to impugn Celsus's own position, making Celsus appear *less* philosophical than the Christianity he attacks. Origen adopts previous Epicurean and Skeptic criticisms of the reality of oracles. Greek intellectuals had already argued that the oracles seemed to reward people regardless of their moral worth; the oracles often gave contradictory or uselessly obscure messages; and the oracles could themselves advocate unethical behavior—all of which should be taken to disprove their divine origins (see 3.25).[10] Origen appropriates a Platonic-sounding criticism of popular religion when he insists that idolatry is the worship of the *visible* and the *external* rather than the invisible and eternal (7.44). The worship of images, therefore, signifies *lack* of wisdom (6.14). And Origen casts the classic accusation of inconsistency against Celsus and his fellow Greek philosophers because, although they *recognize* that the images of the gods are not real gods but only objects, they nonetheless continue to worship them and even pretend to pray to them, mainly just to please "the masses." They know better, having been instructed by philosophy about the true nature of the gods, so their continued obeisance to images is insincere, truly an unphilosophical action (5.43, 6.4, 7.66).

Last but not least, we should note the many ways Origen attacks Greek myths precisely as Celsus had attacked Jewish and Christian stories from the Bible (1.17–18, 4.48, 8.66). Recalling that Plato had excluded all the traditional myths and poets from his ideal republic (4.50), Origen simply rehearses the traditional philosophical criticisms of the immorality of the gods as depicted in myths to impugn Greek religion entirely, insisting all along the way that Greek intellectuals cannot "save" the accounts by allegorical interpretation (3.22). Origen is at great pains to deny to Greek intellectuals the method of interpretation that he had already borrowed from them: the allegorical interpretation of authoritative texts. In all of this, though, Origen is simply turning the tables: he uses traditional Greek philosophy to attack Greek religion and culture and to portray, on the other hand, Christianity as the true philosophy.

Philosophy for "the Masses"

Throughout the ancient world, philosophy was a social force that directly affected a small proportion of the population. Only a tiny fraction of the inhabitants of ancient Greece and Rome, not to mention members of other ethnic groups, actually studied philosophy. And the teachings of philosophy had even an indirect influence on the lives of most people very little if at all. Though we occasionally come across a woman, a slave, or a manual laborer who had received philosophical education, by and large philosophy was an elite practice in the ancient world, confined mainly to upper-class, high-status men. This reality stands in some contrast, though, to the occasional pretensions of philosophy to have the education of humanity as its goal. Philosophy often claimed to be able to teach anyone to live the life of virtue and self-control. Yet apart from a few Cynics, few men who busied themselves with the study and teaching of philosophy took it upon themselves to launch any real attempt to make philosophers of the general populace.

This fact supplied Origen with a means for making Christianity special, even by the general norms of philosophy, for Origen claimed not only that Christianity was a philosophy, but that it was the best philosophy available because, for one thing, it was "philosophy for the masses"; it was the only "philosophical system" that had succeeded in reaching people of all social locations. In response, for instance, to Celsus's complaint that Christians were often asked to "believe" without critical thinking ("Do not ask questions; just believe!"), Origen says that *were* it possible for everyone to have the leisure, capability, and inclination to study, as if they were entering a philosophical school, Christian teachers *would* require such study of their followers. "But that is not feasible, because few people are eager to devote themselves to rational discourse, partly due to the constraints of normal living and partly due to human weakness. So what better method for improving the mass of people could be discovered than that given by Jesus to the nations?" (1.9). Most people both *cannot* and *will not* put themselves through the expensive, time-consuming, demanding rigors of a philosophical curriculum. Christianity accepts such "seekers," converting them from a life of vice to one of virtue without the necessity of traditional philosophical education. Furthermore, many of the particulars of philosophical training, such as advanced doctrines, geometry, astronomy, metaphysics, and arcane learning, are not so necessary for the virtuous life. So Christianity concentrates on the latter. Christianity is, like the famous claim made by Cynics for their method, a "shortcut to virtue" (3.50).

Thus Origen never denies the accusation made by Celsus that

Christian teachers seek out "women, adolescent boys, slaves, stupid men, whomever!" Rather, he makes it Christianity's virtue, reminding his readers that there had indeed been a few philosophers willing to teach a slave here or there (3.54). But Christianity has gone much further, teaching "not only the bright, but also the foolish, and again not only the Greeks but also barbarians" (6.1). Christianity is the truly universal philosophy that has turned no one away from its discipline of virtue and happiness. Indeed, Origen defends the coarse Greek style of the Bible, which Celsus had carped about and which was discernible to any well-educated Greek, by noting that the scriptures were providentially delivered in a style and manner that could be understood by the simple *so that* the virtues there taught could be available to the widest possible audience. Unlike most Greek schools, Christianity offers a philosophy that saves *everyone* from "superstition" and leads even women and children to virtue, away from theaters and dancing (3.56). The varied statuses of its converts demonstrate not its weaknesses but its strengths.

This last citation shows that Origen and Celsus, even when not using the word, are indeed fighting about what counts as "superstition." To the insinuation that Christianity is superstition, Origen responds that the traditional cults of the Greeks, as had been shown by generations of philosophers, are "superstition"— the craven worship of and service to daimons. Origen takes all of the worship of images as unphilosophical superstition. Thus the Greeks and all other peoples around the Mediterranean are implicated in the vice. "Superstition" becomes all "idolatry." Christian writers would label even Judaism as "superstition," because of its advocacy of sacrificial cult and practices such as circumcision, keeping the Sabbath, and dietary restrictions. Thus Origen holds Christianity up as the universal philosophy for all people, the philosophy for the uneducated as well as the educated, the philosophy for barbarians as well as Greeks, the only philosophy that

truly liberates humanity from the vice of superstition. It is true
that Origen here must use a somewhat different meaning of
deisidaimonia than that assumed by Celsus, albeit a meaning that
Origen has borrowed from apologists before him.[11] Now *deisidaimonia,* instead of referring simply to *fear* of gods or daimons, refers to all polytheism and worship of images entirely—to all of
what would later be called "paganism." But Origen has anchored
this relatively novel use of *deisidaimonia* to the familiar philosophical construction and criticism of superstition.

Tropes of Hierarchy

We have seen that in spite of the disagreements between Celsus
and Origen—for example, over how to interpret Christian scriptures and Greek myths or over the precise meaning of *deisidaimonia*—they are in much agreement about basic assumptions.
Both are committed to the tenets of philosophy. Both see religion's primary duty as educating toward virtue. Both want to
avoid the vice of superstition. In fact, many of their agreements
are due to the fact that they both share a basic understanding of
the universe as constructed as an ontological hierarchy, and they
both work to maintain rather than disrupt that hierarchy of being. As we saw in the previous chapter, much of what bothered
Celsus about Christianity was his perception that it offended the
hierarchy of the universe. Jesus seemed too "low class" in his life
and death to merit divine accolades. The Christian doctrines of
the incarnation and the resurrection of the body carelessly and of-
fensively combined things of high status—divinity, the soul, the
mind—with things of low status—a woman's womb, the flesh,
the corruption of matter. The vulgarity of Christians themselves
clashed with their claims to a special possession of truth and divine inspiration. Perhaps Origen *could have* challenged the hierarchical assumptions implicit in Celsus's critique, but most of the

time he does not. With Celsus, Origen assumes that the universe should be viewed hierarchically. He just interprets Christianity to fit that hierarchy better.

Celsus had accepted the philosophical view of his day that gods, daimons, perhaps heroes, and human beings occupied positions of descending rank. He took daimons to be beings intermediate between true gods and humans. Origen basically agrees, though the role of daimons, as I explore further below, will be up for debate. In any case, Origen assumes a cosmic hierarchy in which God occupies the highest position, and angels, human beings, and beasts rank below, in that order. Origen is willing to grant, though only for a moment, that his category of "angels" may overlap somewhat with what Celsus means by "daimons" (4.24). The intermediary role Plato, Plutarch, and Celsus had assigned to daimons, for instance, is assigned by Origen to angels (5.4). But the basic hierarchy is the same for Celsus and Origen. In another context Origen reveals that he would also be willing to taxonomize the different beings of the heavens into a heavenly hierarchy of "angels, thrones, principalities, and powers" (4.29). In *Against Celsus,* Origen does not speculate much on the natures and activities of these different beings, but his assumption of the basic cosmic hierarchy is clear. Furthermore, Celsus and Origen share the assumption that there is also an *ethical* hierarchy in the universe: they both assume that God is the supreme being and that as such he is also supremely good. But this belief necessitates some explanation for the presence of evil, and it is in their differing accounts of the reality and origin of evil that we see significant disagreements about the nature of the universe and the divine.

Much of the discussion about the nature of evil revolves around the question of the origin of evil: since it is agreed that God is completely good, where did evil come from? Celsus's answer sounds much like that of Galen encountered earlier—what we call "evil" is actually the constraints of necessity and matter, and due simply to the divine's having made reality in the best state possible given the necessary constraints of the material God had to work with. As Celsus puts it:

> The origin of evils is not something easy to understand for someone who has not studied philosophy. It is sufficient for most people to be told simply that evils are not from God. Rather, they are implicated in matter, and they reside in the nature of mortals. From the beginning to the end, the period of mortals reflects the same reality, and according to determined cycles, necessarily the same things also occur, past, present, and future.[12]

Celsus's view of evil is that it is simply a necessity of reality. "Evil" just refers to the pain humans experience when they confront the limitations of existence; they can no more avoid "evil" than they can matter: "Nature itself makes all people experience evil; evils are part of necessity and have no other place to go" (8.55).

In important ways Origen agrees. Contrary to the hasty claims made by "simpler" Christians, Origen is hesitant to say that "God can do anything." In response to Celsus's mockery of Christians who go around claiming that God can do the impossible, which strikes Celsus as simply ridiculous, Origen admits that *in a sense* God cannot, of course, do literally *anything*. Origen agrees that God cannot go against his very nature. It is not a theological statement, but simply a nonsense statement, to say something like "God is able not to be God." Just as something sweet cannot be *not* sweet and still be something sweet, and light cannot be darkness and still be light, so God, as God, cannot do wrong *and still be God*. "For the ability to commit injustice is opposite to his divinity and every power related to it" (3.70). Nor can God do anything shameful (5.23). To say "God can do evil" says nothing about God's power because it is not a statement about reality but an inherently illogical statement, a nonsense statement.

Origen agrees, therefore, that *in a sense* God is himself constrained by nature—his *own* nature. Thus, if Celsus wants to claim that God cannot do anything "contrary to nature," Origen will agree, as long as one stipulates that by "contrary to nature" one means "evil." On the other hand, if "contrary to nature" simply means "contrary to what we generally observe to be the way nature works," Origen will insist that God may indeed surprise us with miraculous deeds. In those cases, though, Origen prefers to say that God has "transcended" nature rather than acted "contrary to nature" (5.23). Thus the tricky question of "can God do the impossible?" is nuanced by Origen to allow for the surprising activities of the Christian God, who may wish to resurrect bodies, but also to maintain the rationality of an ethically hierarchical universe: God, as God, cannot do evil.

Origen also agrees with Celsus (and thus in this sense also with other Greek intellectuals) that things people commonly *think of* as "evil" are not true evil but simply represent the constraints of reality. Some pain and suffering is the result, we may say, of our coming up against the boundaries or hard edges of existence. Origen likens this to the way a carpenter, in order to produce a piece of furniture, will necessarily leave shavings on the floor, or the way builders cannot help allowing dirt to settle on the stones and plaster of a house on which they are working (6.55). Such things are simply the necessary and unfortunate byproducts of creation. So also, those parts of the Bible that *seem* to attribute the creation of evil to God need to be read more sophisticatedly. God is not really the creator of evil, even if the constraints of reality make it seem to people that he is.

Thus Origen meets many of Celsus's objections to Christian teachings by first accepting Celsus's assumptions about hierarchy and the divine and then interpreting Christian beliefs to make sense *within* that hierarchy. Celsus had complained, for example, that Jesus didn't *act like* what a Greek would expect of a god: his speech was uneducated and simple. Origen explains that Jesus, though divine, condescended to the level of the people. Jesus, as any good rhetorician would, always accommodated his speech to be appropriate for his audience (2.39). Jesus spoke in Hebrew, Origen says, in order to communicate with the common people, so we should not expect the Gospel accounts of his speech to conform to high Greek literary style (7.59).[13] Jesus didn't speak like a philosopher because such language would not have been understood. Rather, God used Jesus to communicate with educated and uneducated alike: "ordinary men and simple women and slaves, and, in general, of people who have been helped by none but by Jesus alone to live a better life, so far as they can, and to accept doctrines about God such as they had the capacity to receive" (7.41; trans. Chadwick). The life of Jesus is construed not to challenge the assumptions of the status of the divine but to represent rather its benevolent condescension.

Celsus had also argued against the doctrine of the incarnation by noting that it implied change, and it is the nature of the divine not to change. In fact, the incarnation implied change from the better to the worse, from divinity to humanity. Here again, Origen introduces his theme of divine condescension. Origen denies Celsus's charge that in becoming man God changed "from good to bad, from beautiful to shameful, from happiness to misfortune, and from best to most evil" (4.14). Origen admits that "the immortal divine Word" did assume a human body and soul and thus did significantly humble himself.[14] But Origen interprets this as divine condescension for the sake of mercy and love, in order to elevate those to whom Christ ministered (4.15). Furthermore, Origen denies that the divine changed its *essence* when the Word became flesh; rather the divine soul became mixed with the human body, "willingly descending into human mortality for the benefit of the human race" (4.18). The divine essence of Jesus assumed a body for its use, as in Greek thought divine powers often use bodies of male and even female prophets—without necessitating any assumption that the divine itself *is* "body" (1.70). Likewise, the body of Jesus was not *itself* divine, but constituted the *use* of a body by the divine (2.9). In the same way, in response to Celsus's criticism that Christians claim that the divine itself suffered and died in Jesus, Origen agrees that God cannot suffer or die: it was not the divine being in Jesus but his "human aspect" that suffered and died (7.16). The "changes" that Celsus finds offensive are interpreted by Origen as divine condescension. The hierarchy of divinity assumed by Celsus is for the most part kept in place by Origen.[15]

The coupling of hierarchy and divine condescension is used by Origen also to explain how God can be portrayed at times as inflicting suffering and even cosmic evils on humanity. Since God cannot be the author of actual evil, how do we interpret accounts of divine judgment? We should first note that both Celsus and Origen accept the idea that God will punish injustice and evildoers. In this case the suffering endured by some people *is* due to divine causation, but it is the proper retribution for wickedness, a sense of divine retribution shared by Celsus and Origen (see 3.16, 4.10). And it is remedial. Some pain and suffering, therefore, has been created by God for the sake of disciplining people to virtue, like the discipline of fathers, schoolmasters, or physicians: "For he creates corporeal or external evils to cleanse and educate those who will not be educated by speech and wholesome teaching" (6.56; see also 3.75).

This motivation even explains why the scriptures say so much about the "wrath" of God and seem to provoke fear among people about God's punishment (4.71–72). In this case, Origen insists, we are not dealing really with the vice of "superstition" *(deisidaimonia),* but with the heuristic use of fear to motivate simpler people, who are less capable of more elevated motivation, to live virtuously (see 5.15–20). In fact, Origen uses a version of the Platonic "golden lie," the idea that superiors may need to deceive simpler people somewhat for their own good. Origen suggests that *on occasion* even "superstition"—*fear* of the divine—may be necessary for the moral betterment of the masses (3.78–79; for more on the "golden lie," see 4.19). Stories about the "wrath of God" or teaching that instills fear into the masses may not be ultimately true, according to Origen, but are instances of the necessity of divine condescension for the education of simpler people.

None of this talk about condescension, about "the Word" descending to the level of the lowly, should be interpreted to mean that Origen was a democrat or a social revolutionary. Origen was no romanticist when it came to "the masses." He notes, for example, that Jesus taught his disciples "to despise the life led by the multitude," precisely as we would expect of a Greek philosopher (2.45). And Origen argues, against Celsus's sneers about the "poverty" of Christianity, that Jesus did not intend to praise poverty or condemn wealth without qualification. Rather, according to Origen, Jesus taught that *character,* not station in life, was what truly mattered (6.16). Origen's theme of divine condescension was a means of explaining what appeared to be "low class" aspects of Christian scripture, Christian doctrines, and Christian people without disrupting too greatly the divine hierarchy of the universe assumed as reality by Celsus *and* Origen. In this sense Origen was in basic agreement with Celsus about the fundamentals of nature and the divine.

Daimons

Where Origen significantly differs from Celsus is in the different roles they assign to daimons in their universes.[16] As we have seen,

Celsus is willing only momentarily to entertain the idea that a few daimons may misbehave. For the most part, he holds onto the classical philosophical position that daimons, as divine or quasi-divine beings, must be good and therefore do not harm except as punishment for injustice. Origen completely rejects that position. For Origen, daimons are completely evil, all of them (5.5). Daimons are the cause of diseases, plagues, famines, even stormy seas and other disasters (1.31; see similar lists at 8.31 and 54). They do so partly out of desire for human attention, especially sacrifices. In fact, daimons are gluttonous (3.29, 37). They crave the blood of sacrificial victims, and they feed on burnt-offerings, blood sacrifices, and even the odors of sacrifices (4.32, 7.35). People have correctly learned over the years that daimons can even be bribed by sacrifices (7.6).

The gods that most people worship, therefore, are actually daimons in disguise (3.2, passim). Asclepius is a daimon (3.25, 7.65), as is even the highest member of the pantheon, Zeus (5.46). The daimons of traditional religions *can* work amazing wonders and even beneficial miracles at times (3.31–32). They are the authors of divinations and oracles, for instance (4.92, 7.69, 8.25–26). But they wield only *local* power: they may be in charge of particular areas, especially particular sanctuaries, but only because there exists in those places something like a "vacuum" of the knowledge of God (3.36, 8.33).

Besides sacrifices, humans may also use magic to influence the actions and dispositions of daimons. Magicians are "in communion" with daimons and accomplish their deeds by daimonic power, when there is no stronger power in the vicinity. Origen explains that the "Magi" from the East followed the star that announced Jesus' birth because the advent of the divine Jesus had caused their daimonic power to fail, and the Magi wanted to find out the reason. The angelic visitors at Jesus' birth had overthrown the power of daimons on which the magic of the Magi depended

(1.60). Magic, in any case, is quintessentially daimonic (2.51, passim).

The nature of daimons is explained by their origin. Reflecting the beginnings of a long history of Christian demonology, Origen teaches that daimons were angels who "turned aside to evil," freely rebelling against God and thus becoming "angels of the devil" (8.25). Just as human beings had the power to choose to follow God or to rebel and sin, so did angels. Those "fallen" angels, therefore, joined the forces of the devil and became "daimons" (see also 7.69). They fell from heaven "to roam about the grosser bodies on earth which are unclean." This is how they impact the art of divination: they get into the bodies of wild beasts and with their limited knowledge of the future provide indications of it through the bodies of sacrificial victims and divinatory animals (4.92). In any case, they are purely evil, hoping to drag humans down with them through deceit and suffering.

Since Christianity is completely philanthropic, and daimons are completely misanthropic, daimons are absolutely opposed to Christianity. In the first place, Jesus put himself forward as the conqueror of daimons and the liberator of human beings, manifested clearly in his many exorcisms (3.36, 4.33–44). Christians are famous for continuing this exorcising ministry (1.25, 46, 67), even being known for casting daimons out of possessed animals (7.67). Moreover, Christian teaching against blood sacrifices has become so successful, Origen notes, that daimons were growing weaker, having been increasingly deprived of their gory meals, which explains why daimons have in their turn inspired the severe persecutions of Christians (4.32). Daimons provoke persecution of Christians out of sheer rage and vengeance against them (8.43–44). Daimons also try to destroy Christianity by attacking it from within; thus the presence of "heresies" among the churches is due, in Origen's opinion, to daimonic activity (6.11). All of this should prove to people that they should forsake daimons, as pure evil intent on destroying humanity, and join the Christians, the true benefactors of humanity.

Origen is willing to agree with Celsus that many of the blessings of life do come from beings intermediate between God and humans, but he insists that they are the angels, who are good. Angels may take credit for the fruits of the earth, the birth of animals, and such earthly blessings. But they do not desire worship in return. In fact, as proper subordinates to God, they are pleased when humans in thanksgiving worship God rather than themselves. They neither want nor can use the stuff of sacrifices: "They do not need the fumes of the earth" (8.57; see also 8.64). The good things, therefore, that Celsus and most people attribute to benign daimons, Origen attributes to good angels. Daimons are without exception evil, hateful, and malevolent.

The Optimal Universe Meets the Patronal Universe

The very different roles assigned to daimons by Celsus and Origen may initially seem to constitute a relatively minor difference between them. After all, we have seen that they share many assumptions about the universe, including the notion that there is an ontological hierarchy and an ethical hierarchy. They share the assumption that God may indeed inflict pain—though only for remedial purposes. And Celsus is even willing to entertain the notion, though faintly and reluctantly, that there *may* be a daimon here or there who might misbehave. But their overall demonologies are quite different from one another, and that difference provides a key by which we may understand more fundamental differences between the universes of Celsus and Origen. Celsus represents for the most part the traditional philosophical position that had once been the "new sensibility" of an optimal universe: the assumption that the ontological hierarchy of the universe is matched by an ethical hierarchy; that beings of higher nature will also be more ethical; that superior beings *cannot* commit evil because they *ought not* be evil. Thus daimons, as beings superior to even the best humans, must be benign, ethical entities, and thus to fear them would be both irrational and impious—that is, superstition. By teaching that daimons, though superior in power than humans in the chain of nature, are harmful, malevolent beings intent on destroying humanity, Origen introduces an element of belief that will destroy the optimal universe of classical philosophy, even though he may not himself have realized it.

This can be seen in the way Origen struggles with notions concerning the hierarchy of daimons in relation to humans. On the one hand, Origen claims that Christians need not fear daimons because Christians are "superior to them" (8.36). But the context in which he makes this claim says more than the mere statement. A long quotation is therefore necessary:

> It is *not* true, as Celsus supposes, that the *true* satraps, subordinate rulers, commanders, and stewards of God—that is, the angels—harm those who affront them. If some daimons harm people, about which Celsus himself has some inkling, they harm as evil beings, and in no way have they been entrusted with a satrapy or command or stewardship of God. And they harm those who are under their power and have submitted themselves to the daimons as their masters. And it may also be because of this that people are harmed when they break laws by eating in certain places foods that by law or custom are forbidden. But if such people are not among those subject to the daimon of the region and have not submitted themselves to it, they are free from any suffering caused by the daimon. They are able to laugh at such daimons, though if they otherwise, due to ignorance about the things, submitted themselves to the daimons, they would be

exposed to suffering. But not the Christian, the true Christian who has submitted himself to God alone and his Logos; he would suffer nothing from the hands of daimons, because he is superior to them. He would not suffer since "the angel of the Lord will encircle those who fear him and will save them" [Psalm 34:7]. . . . God does nothing less than appoint his own angels [for the care of] those who worship him so that the opposing angels—or even their ruler, the so-called "ruler of this world" [see John 14:30; 1 Cor. 2:6, 8]—will be unable to work anything against those who are consecrated to God. (8.36)

It is clear that in Origen's universe daimons are superior to humans in strength and materiality. Christians are "superior" to daimons *only because they have divine forces as their protectors.* Christians have God and his angelic hosts to "camp around" them and protect them from daimonic harm. Non-Christians have no such protection; they therefore have every reason to fear the malevolence of daimons, who may hurt them at will due to superior daimonic power.

Origen's universe is a patron-client system in which all human beings must choose their patron. Christians have God and his "logos," Christ, as their patrons; Christians therefore may take full advantage of the protection afforded by God's henchmen, angels (see also 8.60). Origen explains that God's spirit keeps daimons from invading the bodies of Christians (4.95). If one pays proper attention to God, then all those under him—angels, souls, spirits—will be kindly disposed also (8.64). Non-Christians, on the other hand, find themselves precariously outside "the family." They therefore, by default, fall under the power of daimons and all the forces of evil. Origen's universe is a world of two different patronal organizations in conflict with one another. The only real choice available to human beings is which "family" or "don" they will choose to serve.

The disruption of the classical philosophical hierarchy implied in Origen's position is made evident also in the way the term *divine* becomes almost imperceptibly altered. In the classical philosophical system, "divinity" referred to many possible positions along a graded scale. Thus even some human beings could be called "divine," as could, certainly, different gods and daimons and heroes. "Divinity" in the Greek world was basically a state of "more or less," referring to a relative position on a hierarchical scale from inferior to superior. We may have thought that Origen, as an adherent of "monotheistic" Christianity, would have reserved the term "divine" for the supreme God alone, perhaps along with his "logos," Christ. But Origen also is willing to call other superhuman beings "divine," as he explicitly designates angels (5.4). They are divine *because they minister for God and bring blessings.* Origen insists, on the other hand and against Celsus, that daimons are *not* divine in any sense *because they are evil* (5.46).

In Origen's hands, the term *divine* has become a purely *ethical* term, not referring necessarily to ontological superiority, but to ethical superiority. The ontological-ethical hierarchy of classical philosophy is ruptured and replaced with a simple *ethical* hierarchy in which "divine" is an ethical category: angels may be called divine, but daimons may not. This is an important development that allows for a complete redeployment of the roles of "superior" beings and the admission of evil daimons while retaining the idea that divinity equals goodness. And the existence of beings of superior power but evil inclination necessitates a patron-client system of protection.

Origen's patron-client universe should be placed alongside Celsus's optimal universe. Note how Celsus describes it:

Whatever exists in the world, the work of God or of angels or of other daimons or of heroes, do they not all have a law from the greatest God, and an apportioned power has been assigned over each thing as considered worthy? Shouldn't the worshipper of God, therefore, also quite justly also serve the being who has been allotted that authority by God? (7.70)

There is a universal law of the universe, completely in submission to the "greatest God." The universe is ruled by divinity, which is necessarily good. Superior powers are both good *and in control.* Evil is, for Celsus, mainly evil only in appearance. Or it is relatively inconsequential. Or it is merely the detritus of the act of creation. Or it is the resistance of necessary matter. But the universe is basically good and governed by a universal and benign law. All superior powers—angels, heroes, daimons—are inherently good and follow the "law from the greatest God." This is clearly an optimistic, even utopian, view of nature.

Actually, Origen's universe is closer in many ways to the pre-philosophical assumptions of traditional, popular Mediterranean religion. More precisely, though, we should say that with the Christian system, here represented for convenience by Origen, we encounter a third logic of the universe, in opposition to the "new sensibility" of philosophy but not a simple reaffirmation of traditional Greek and Roman piety either. The *traditional view,* to review briefly, was that the gods act like human beings do: they *generally* are predictable, but not always. They may be good or bad or both. They may help if they are friends, or they may hurt if they are enemies. People should stay out of their way when they are likely to be in a bad mood; people may learn which ones are likely to be for or against them; and people may win them over with gifts and appropriate behavior. Evil may indeed come from the gods, just as it may come from one's neighbors. That is a simple fact of social life: life with humans *and gods.*

The *philosophical view* labeled the traditional beliefs "superstition" and taught, on the contrary, that divine beings, as superior to humans, also *act* in a superior manner. They are necessarily good and benevolent. They do not harm—except on occasion to benefit, like a father or a physician. Worship of them is not done to change their inclinations, but to show appropriate gratitude and to join in their essence as much as possible. Evil is simply what we experience as the limits of necessity, the constraints of the possible, the necessary hard edges of reality.

The *Christian view,* at least as represented by Origen, teaches that the supreme God and all those angels and powers subservient to him are good and benevolent. Any harm from them is for our betterment. There are also some experiences we have that *seem* evil but are attributable to the constraints of reality. But there is also evil directly attributable to an entire force of the universe in temporary opposition to God—daimons and those under their influence. Daimons, which include the gods of the nations, are completely evil; they are fallen angels exercising their wills against God. Christians must choose either the protection of the latter or the destruction of the former.

It is not difficult to imagine how different people in different social locations would have found these different views of the universe more or less compelling. Think, for example, of the different social locations of intellectuals such as Celsus, upper-class gentlemen writing in the "Golden Age" of Roman imperial prosperity, compared with most Christians of the second or third century. A minority group, facing unpredictable, sporadic opposition and even persecution from forces more powerful than they, Christians could hardly see the world as a uniformly benign place. Most of the time their rulers ignored them; occasionally, they were hostile to them. The image of a benign, kindly deity ruling placidly and unchallenged over a bureaucratic hierarchy of similarly virtuous administrators could scarcely have grabbed their imaginations. The idea that the universe was a site of ongoing struggles between good and evil, on the other hand, would have struck them as commonsensical. The notion that governmental officials may be corrupt, amenable to bribes, hostile, even bloodthirsty would not have shocked Christians in the least. They knew that trusting a benign universe would get them nowhere. Trusting a powerful protector—a cosmic "protection racket" even—made much more sense. This is what Christianity, as interpreted even by the philosophical and sophisticated Origen, offered them. Since the optimal universe *was,* in the view of Christians, an *illusion,* what was needed was the protection afforded by a Universal Patron.

12

The Philosophers Turn

Philosophical Daimons in Late Antiquity

The previous chapter argued that the differences between Celsus and Origen about the nature of daimons were significant. Though both Celsus and Origen assumed a hierarchical universe, and both assumed that the divine must necessarily be also supremely ethical, Origen's insistence that there was an entire class of beings superior to humans in power and materiality but inferior to them ethically constituted an important challenge to the paired ontological and ethical hierarchies that had provided the logic for the philosophical condemnation of "superstition." Even though Celsus and a few philosophers before him had occasionally entertained the idea that there *might* be a daimon here or there of questionable moral character, their rejection of popular fears of daimons depended on their belief that daimons in general were divine or quasi-divine beings and that as such they were also moral. Origen's insistence, on the contrary, that *all* daimons, though perhaps higher than humans on the cosmic ladder of power and matter, were completely evil constituted a rejection of the logic underlying the classical philosophical position.

I do not intend to give the impression, however, that Origen knew what he was doing when he challenged the logic of a philosophical common sense. I believe he thought he was simply using philosophy appropriately. Precisely because the philosophical belief in an optimal universe was never an *explicitly expressed* theory of ancient philosophy—I have argued that it was an *assumption*—I suspect Origen did not realize that his theory of evil daimons undermined the very foundations of the ancient critique of superstition. I also do not wish to give the impression that I take Origen to be particularly innovative in his notions about daimons. In fact, it is clear that he is drawing on Jewish and Christian rhetoric before him, which had already identified the gods of "the nations" with daimons and which had already tended to treat those daimons as malevolent and dangerous, thus explaining Jews' and Christians' avoidance of idol worship or of even coming into contact with the paraphernalia of idolatry, such as food offered to idols. I have cited Origen not as the inventor of his demonology but as one representative of broader Jewish and Christian beliefs.

But even more than that caveat, I want to make it clear that I also do not attribute to Origen the invention of even the *philosophical* notion of evil daimons. I do not believe, that is, that the change of opinion in late antiquity—even among those with philosophical education—about the moral status of daimons was due entirely to Christian or Jewish influence. This chapter will attempt to sketch how other philosophers of the time around Origen also came to alter the classical philosophical position and to introduce, in significant ways, evil daimons into their *philosophical* universes.[1] The shift in demonology that occurred in late antiquity, I argue, reflected broader shifts in intellectual culture of the period and cannot simplistically be written off as due to Christian influence.

Plotinus and "Neoplatonism"

Whereas Greek and Roman philosophers had always, for the most part, admitted or assumed the reality of daimonic beings, those same philosophers had seldom if ever attempted to construct any elaborate demonology. That is, they seemed to feel no need to fit their beliefs about daimons into a philosophical system. But in late antiquity, in the philosophical movement that modern scholars call "Neoplatonism," daimons come to occupy more prominent positions and to play more important roles. And what is more important for my purposes, these late ancient Platonists come to ignore, for the most part, the classical philosophical assumption that daimons, precisely because they are superior beings to humans, must be morally superior. The late ancient philosophers, much more than their predecessors, become willing to admit the existence of evil daimons and to allow them a role in causing at least some of the sufferings of human beings.

According to most modern reckoning, the "founder" of Neoplatonism—that is, the philosopher who was especially influential in interpreting Plato's writings in new and different ways— was Plotinus (205–ca. 270), who lived from perhaps the age of forty until his death at age sixty-six in Rome.[2] Although giving daimons, along with other superhuman beings, a greater role as intermediaries between the highest divinities, on the one side, and humans and the material world, on the other, for the most part Plotinus adheres to the traditional belief that daimons do not harm humans and that they are necessarily moral. In an argument against the Gnostics' practice of exorcism, for instance, he counters with a traditional scientific account of disease.[3]

> If they [that is, Gnostics] claimed to cleanse people of dis-
> eases by self-control and suitable regimen, they would be
> speaking rightly, as also philosophers maintain. But as it is,
> they insinuate that the diseases are daimons, and they claim
> to be able to drive them out by means of a word. And they
> announce such things hoping to procure an honorable repu-
> tation among the masses, who admittedly admire the pow-
> ers manifested by magicians. Yet they [the Gnostics] would
> not be able to convince right thinking people that the dis-
> eases do not have [their own specific] causes—that is, in ex-
> haustion or surfeit or lack of nourishment or corruption,
> and in general from experiencing changes, whether from
> some external or some internal factor. These facts are made
> clear by the ways diseases are treated. For the bowel may be
> moved, or a drug given so that the disease is led out of the
> body from below, or blood is drawn, or it is healed by diet.
> For [in the case of fever] the cause [*aition*] is sufficient to
> bring about the fever [so recourse to a daimon is unneces-
> sary]. For it is laughable to suppose that together with the
> cause there occurs also a daimon, ready and willing to serve
> as an assistant in the case! (*Ennead* 2.9.14)

Plotinus, therefore, rejects the more "popular" idea (he explicitly
mentions "the masses") that daimons either are disease or cause
disease, himself invoking classical medical theories about disease
etiology.

Though it may not be obvious in this particular quotation,
part of what bothers Plotinus about attributing disease to daimons is the ethical issue: if daimons are taken as divine or divine-
like, that would mean accusing them of actions that would be
considered immoral if done by a human being. In another context Plotinus does advance this argument when insisting that

people should not take astrology to imply that the "sublunary deities" (the divine beings who occupy the space between the earth and the moon) actually cause people to be immoral:

> For it is not right to suggest that they [that is, divine beings] manipulate [all] human affairs, with the result that some people become thieves, others slave traders, burglars, temple robbers, and still others become cowardly or effeminate in their actions or passions, or they act shamefully. For not even a moderate man—or perhaps any human being at all—would do such things or arrange things in that way, much less a god. (*Ennead* 4.4.31)

Plotinus is able to mount the same ontological-ethical argument that we have seen philosophers turn against "superstition" from the fifth century BCE onward.

Given his expression of these sentiments, it is notable that Plotinus believes that magic is yet capable of compelling superhuman beings to do someone's bidding, apparently including causing sickness. He explains that though a wise man's "rational part," meaning his mind or will, cannot be affected by magic, his "irrational part," including the body but also some part of the soul, can indeed suffer harm due to magical operations. "As the irrational part is affected by spells, so also he, by using counter-spells and counter-charms, will destroy the power of the other. He may indeed, though, suffer death or disease or some such bodily condition from that sort of thing." And apparently magic operates through its power to compel daimons, mainly through the mechanism of "sympathy."[4] "Daimons themselves are not immune to suffering in their irrational part. It is not out of place to attribute to them memory and sensation and [to suppose that] they are naturally influenced by charms" (*Ennead* 4.4.43). Thus at least some daimons can be manipulated through magic, and magic can be used to cause sickness and other perturbations to the human body and lower aspects of the soul.[5]

So although Plotinus tends to hold onto the classical philosophical teaching that daimons as superior beings are moral and therefore do not harm humans or cause disease, he does allow *some* role for daimons in causing human suffering, due to the fact that their natures are susceptible to influence from other natural elements and forces. Plotinus has opened the door a crack for the invasion of evil daimons. His students Porphyry and Iamblichus will open that door even wider.

Porphyry

With Plotinus's student Porphyry (234–ca. 305), Neoplatonic demonology reaches a height both in complexity and in the harm and mischief attributed to daimons.[6] Though Porphyry speaks of daimons in several different contexts, the subject is especially central to his treatise *On Abstinence from Animal Food*, since his goal in this text, to urge vegetarianism, forces him to address also the issue of sacrifice and the difference between blood and bloodless sacrifices. One of Porphyry's main points is that people, or at least philosophers and those pursuing virtue and the contemplative life, should avoid eating animal flesh *even though* sacrificing is a traditional and generally appropriate religious activity. He argues, in the first place, that the gods really desire the "sacrifice" of a pure and virtuous mind and life, not of material things. Second, he maintains that nonanimal sacrifices (of grains, flowers, and the like) are pleasing to the gods, but that the gods do not desire sacrifices of flesh and blood. Third, he argues that animal sacrifices are really demanded only by daimons, not gods, though both "good" and "bad" daimons enjoy the materials produced by sacrifices (see 2.36). Fourth, Porphyry insists that it is only the evil daimons who attempt to pass themselves off as true gods, who demand immoral, disgusting things from people, and who harm people when offended.

The mistake made by "common people," Porphyry thinks, is that they wrongly treat all daimons alike and take them to be gods themselves. The "masses" mistakenly believe that "*all* of those commonly addressed by the name of daimons may in fact cause harm if irritated at being neglected and if the conventional services happen not to be rendered, but that again the same beings may become beneficent once propitiated by means of prayers and litanies, sacrifices and accompanying rituals" (*On Abstinence from Animal Food* 2.37). Unlike most of his philosophical predecessors, though, Porphyry argues against popular opinion not by denying the existence of evil daimons or arguing that since they are ontologically superior to humans they must also be ethically superior, but by insisting that people must distinguish between good and bad daimons.

The daimonic in Porphyry's system is to some extent a physiological issue. Daimons are the way they are (hungry for food, for instance) because of their physiology, and good daimons can be differentiated from evil ones by physique. Daimons are invisible and possess no *solid* body, but they are composed of a "pneumatic substance" that, insofar as it is corporeal, "is passive and corruptible." The physiques of daimons are more long-lived than those of humans, but they are not immortal. The issue is a fascinating one in Porphyry's thought and merits a long quotation:

> The bodies of the good [daimons] are symmetrical like those of the phenomena [that is, the visible gods], but those of daimons that commit evil are asymmetrical. And as the latter [that is, the evil daimons] are filled with the ability to suffer change [that is, they are most "pathetic"], they are assigned to the earthly region because there is no evil they will

not attempt. For in general, having a violent and deceitful character and being deprived of the guardianship of the better daimons, they commit vicious and sudden attacks, quite generally as ambushes, sometimes attempting to do so in secret, but at other times acting brazenly. So the sufferings that come from these daimons are swift. But the healings and corrections that come from the better daimons seem to be slower. For every good thing, being both docile and equable [*homalon*], proceeds in an orderly manner and does not transgress what is proper. Thus as long as you hold this opinion you will never inadvertently fall into the most inappropriate concept that evil may be related to good beings, and good to bad beings. For that reasoning is inappropriate not only with regard to this subject [that is, the nature of daimons]; rather, the masses accept the most foul assumptions even about the gods, and they pass such stuff along to the rest of humanity. (2.39)

The combination of the belief that evil cannot be the product of a good being with the belief that gods are good by definition, along with the admission that daimons exist and are the powers lying behind religious rituals, including those Porphyry finds distasteful or unethical, means that there must be some place for depraved daimons in Porphyry's system.

Maleficent daimons accomplish all sorts of damage. As we have seen to be the case in Origen, Porphyry also believes daimons are the cause of evils such as "pestilence, sterility, earthquakes, drought." But even worse, they have succeeded in convincing the great majority of humankind that they are also the beings who bring the good opposites of such things, that they also bring fertility in place of sterility, for example—as long, that is, as their demands are met. And even worse than that, they have convinced most people that they are gods themselves. They impersonate the gods, "making the majority of people their allies by igniting in them human desires, love, and longings for wealth, power, and pleasure, and indeed a lust for fame, from which spring rebellions and wars and other related disasters." Thus the worst of their actions is that they have convinced most people that the gods themselves do harm and cause suffering. "And not only the masses are so affected, but also not a few of those people familiar with philosophy" (2.40).

Porphyry uses the Platonic notion of "opposites" to argue that good cannot produce evil, nor can evil produce good. So bad things must not be caused by gods or good daimons. Porphyry willingly outlines the beneficent activities of good daimons (see 2.38, for instance). One of their most important benefactions is that they protect human beings from evil daimons. For example, they sometimes warn people in dreams of threats from evil daimons. Evil daimons, on the other hand, provide the power behind vicious magical practices. But people may protect themselves from evil daimons by living lives of purity. Indeed, a vegetarian diet may promote a purer life; animal bodies are, after all, attended by an "efflux of material daimons" (2.46). Evil daimons like to be mistaken for gods, but their physical nature, wrapped up in the gross materiality of flesh-and-blood sacrifice, ties them much too closely to the material world for them to be, in Porphyry's "transcendent" system, divine. "These are the beings that take joy 'in drink offerings and the smell of sacrifices' [*Iliad* 9.500], through which their pneumatic body grows fat. For it lives in vapors and exhalations, living an unstable existence through unstable materials, and gaining power by the fumes from blood and flesh" (2.42). In Porphyry's system the immorality of evil daimons is due to and an expression of their physiology.

Even our internal bodily processes are affected by their presence within our bodies, especially if we eat meat. According to Porphyry, daimons live in people's stomachs, feeding on the flesh rotting there in the process of digestion. In fact, according to Porphyry, that is the cause of flatulence: the gorging of daimons on rotten meat in people's bodies causes them to fart.[7] Here in late antiquity we have one of the most respected philosophers of his day admitting that even though daimons are higher than humans on an ontological scale, they are not necessarily superior to humans on a ethical one.[8] The presence of evil daimons is now a central part of respectable philosophical discourse. Consequently, "superstition" will have to be differently defined.

Iamblichus

With Porphyry's younger contemporary, Iamblichus (ca. 245–325), we encounter another Neoplatonic system with interesting differences from Porphyry's.[9] Some of the differences between Porphyry's theories about daimons and Iamblichus's are no doubt due to the fact that they had different goals in addressing the issue.

Porphyry wrote *On Abstinence from Animal Food* to advocate, mainly for a philosophical audience, vegetarianism. Since the slaughter and consumption of meat was implicated in sacrifice in the ancient world, Porphyry had to address the issue of animal sacrifice and, at least to some extent, distance it from the true, sublime worship of the gods. He therefore gave credit for the invention and continuation of sacrifice to daimons, beings who were superior to humans but inferior to true gods. Porphyry was thus led to a critique of just about all traditional forms of sacrifice.

Iamblichus was much more concerned than Porphyry to retain traditional religious practices, even some that had been criticized by earlier generations of philosophers. That meant, though, that Iamblichus had to reinterpret the rites and beliefs of traditional religion in order to make them fit notions of what was philosophically respectable, as many philosophers before him also had done with regard to other issues. And of course since one of the most central features of almost all ancient Mediterranean religions was sacrifice, Iamblichus provided philosophical defenses for it, countering Porphyry's criticisms and questions with elaborate explanations of what, on the surface, may seem like unphilosophical beliefs and deeds. Indeed, the differences between the accounts of daimons put forward by Porphyry and Iamblichus were due to a great extent to their different evaluations of traditional, and therefore animal, sacrifice.

Iamblichus has his own, sometimes elaborate, hierarchies of superhuman beings. First, there are the three main classes comprising (1) invisible gods, (2) visible gods, and then, much below both those categories, (3) daimons (*On the Mysteries* 1.20).[10] Iamblichus, when it is to his purpose, may subdivide these lower superhuman beings into other classes. On one occasion, he explains that there exist daimons, heroes, angels, and souls (2.2). Later he mentions archangels, angels, archons ("rulers"), and "material archons" (2.3). And the category of "daimons" is divided into "good daimons, avenging daimons, and depraved daimons" (2.7).

Iamblichus, in accord with classical philosophy, insists that gods are incapable of evil. Gods are the very essence of good, and therefore cannot commit evil deeds (4.6; see also 1.18 for Iamblichus's own philosophical explanation for the existence of evil). Traditional, mythological stories about the wrath of the gods, and thus the harm they may cause humans, are admitted to have some kernel of truth in them. But Iamblichus "demythologizes" such accounts, arguing that what people experience as divine anger is actually a reflection of our "distance" from their beneficent care. We ourselves withdraw or turn away from the gods and thus deprive ourselves of their light and purity. What is experienced as divine anger, therefore, is simply the deprivation, which we bring on ourselves, of their normal benevolence. The gods would not, cannot, experience the "passion" of actual anger, and they would never intentionally harm humans.

Daimons are another story. Daimons are said by Iamblichus (in direct disagreement with Porphyry) to be impassive and *not* subject to change (1.10). Daimons may have "a certain kind of body," but it is not, as the masses and even Porphyry think, the kind of body that is nourished by the stuff of sacrifices. A daimonic body, rather, is "unchanging and impassive, in the form of bright light and without need, so that neither does anything flow from it, not does it attach anything externally produced to itself" (5.10). It is ridiculous, Iamblichus claims, to think that daimonic bodies must be nourished by the stuff of sacrifices. That would make humans superior to daimons, since in that case daimons would be depending on human beneficence for their own existence (5.10). Human beings would then be "patrons" and daimons their "clients"! No, daimons are ontologically superior to human beings, and thus we must not imagine that their substance is affected in any way by the stuff of sacrifices.

But different kinds of daimons exist at different levels of morality or immorality. Good daimons work to benefit humans, and it is to them that much traditional religious cult is actually directed, in appreciation for their philanthropy toward us. But there are also "avenging daimons," that is, those daimons assigned the task of punishing humans for misdeeds. And below them, "accompanied by foul, blood-drinking, ferocious wild animals," are evil daimons (2.7).

Thus, as we have seen, against Porphyry's opinion that daimons may be affected by "exhalations" (such as smoke from sacrifices or different vapors from the earth), Iamblichus mounts a form of the "ontological-ethical hierarchy" argument we have already encountered so often: "You foolishly entertain such suspicions," he writes to Porphyry, "when you introduce problems inappropriate and unworthy of the gods, which would not be rightly said to apply to even a good man. For no sensible man, and one free from passions, would ever admit to allowing himself to be seduced by vapors rising from sacrifices—much less, then, would any of the more excellent beings" (5.4). Thus, for Iamblichus, daimons, or at least "excellent" daimons, are not compelled by "exhalations" to act in certain ways.

The "depraved" or "evil" daimons, however, seem to be more implicated in earthy materiality. They are deeply involved, for instance, in "sexual reproduction, human affairs, and earthly existences" (4.13). Some forms of divination, in which Iamblichus definitely believes, may be "disturbed" by interference from evil daimons. But according to Iamblichus, the virtuous person need fear no such interference. The true inspiration of the gods is quite capable of driving away any interference, which Iamblichus describes rather mechanistically, something like light "driving away" darkness (3.13). Certainly, immoral people may attract evil daimons to themselves due to their possession of natures similar in depravity to those of evil daimons. Iamblichus treats the relationship between the mass of less virtuous people and evil daimons by the logic of "like-to-like": the two bad forces attract each other. So it is entirely possible that morally inferior people will indeed experience trouble with evil daimons, even being led by them into deeper vice (3.21). But the virtuous man, keeping himself pure, need not fear them.

Finally, we should note that Iamblichus, though not here explicit about whether he is speaking of daimons in general or only those of the "depraved" class, admits that daimons are somehow involved in diseases. But in this context it seems to be a purely physiological fact. The presence of gods or angels brings lightness and health to the body. "That of daimons may indeed burden the body and confine it with illnesses. It also pulls the soul down to nature [*physis*]; it does not withdraw from bodies and the senses that are related to bodies. It imprisons about this [lower] region

those who aspire to the fire [above], and does not allow release
from the chains of destiny" (2.6). There is no talk here of daimonic evil *intention,* just the claim that their influence on the
body, due to the heavier materiality of their own substances,
drags it down. In sum, though daimons play a much less central
role in Iamblichus's theories of sacrifice and disease than in Porphyry's theories, Iamblichus nonetheless is willing to grant the existence of evil daimons, something earlier intellectuals were loath
to do. And he admits that daimons have some role in disease causation, something that the medical writers of previous generations adamantly rejected.

Is God in Nature?

There are, of course, many other ways in which the philosophy
of Iamblichus, and Neoplatonism more generally, differed from
classical Greek and Roman philosophy, but I will highlight only
one that is especially important for analyzing the shift from earlier to late antique notions of what counted as "superstition."[11] As
I have insisted throughout this study, ancient people—educated
and uneducated alike, philosophers and nonphilosophers—assumed that the gods and other superhuman forces and beings
were part of "nature." Nature included divinities. As we have
seen, Galen and Celsus explicitly criticized Jews and Christians
for failing to recognize this fact. The latter erroneously, and irrationally in Galen's and Celsus's view, thought that God could do
impossible and unnatural things. According to their argument,
everything that truly exists, including deities, is constrained by
necessity. So it is irrational to imagine that a god could go against
the very laws of nature or necessity and do the impossible. As we
saw was the case even for Origen, that would be like saying that
the divine could act in a manner contrary to its very nature. That
is not a theological truth, but only a self-contradictory statement.
Irrational.

Reflecting an important shift in late ancient philosophy, Iamblichus seems to disagree. He insists, for example, that sacrifices function by means of the sympathy of all things in the universe. A sacrifice may bring about changes because of a sympathetic reaction of the thing sacrificed with other powers of the world. (For other uses by Iamblichus of the principle of "sympathy" to explain everything from the efficacy of sacrifices, to divination, to medical pulse technique, to nourishment, see 5.12, 15–16, 20; 6.4; 10.3.) But Iamblichus does not believe that the gods themselves are involved in this "action and reaction" process, precisely because their existence transcends that system. "For the existence of the gods lies not in nature or natural necessity, which would render them capable of being affected by natural passions or powers dispersed throughout nature. Rather, their existence is separated by itself outside such things, having nothing in common with them, neither by way of existence, nor power, nor any other such thing" (5.7).

Whereas previous philosophers argued that even the gods were constrained by necessity and, if the philosopher believed in it, "fate," Iamblichus teaches the opposite:

> But the gods release that which has been fated. . . . So we appropriately accord to them every form of worship, in order that they, who alone are the rulers of necessity through the persuasion of minds, may set us free from all the evils set in store for us by Fate. But all things are not held in the nature of Fate; rather, there exists another principle [*archē*] of the soul superior to all nature and knowledge,[12] according to which we are able even to be made one with the gods and to rise above the cosmic order, and of sharing in the eternal life and energy of the gods who are above the heavens. According to this principle [of the soul], we are the sort of beings capable of freeing ourselves. For when the better parts in us become active, and the soul rises up to those better than it-

self, then it is separated in every way from those things that
hold it down in generation [that is, "becoming"], it with-
draws from the inferior, and exchanges one life for another.
It hands itself over to an other order of reality, forsaking entirely the former. (8.7)

Given the ability of some beings to exist higher than and outside the normal system of the world, it is not surprising that
Iamblichus believes that certain men, due to their superior natures, are "superior to all laws" (5.22). There are some beings, certainly the gods and even rare men, who are not bound by the
laws of the universe in the way the rest of us are. The ontological
transcendence of such beings seems to be matched by an ethical
transcendence. In regard to both the laws of nature and the laws
of behavior, there are just some beings who, due to their superiority, need not play by the same rules as the rest of the world.

We see, then, important shifts in philosophy represented by
Iamblichus's system. In the first place, the ontological-ethical hierarchy that I have been at such pains to describe—the notion
that beings who are superior in their natures must also be superior in their ethics—has been replaced by a simple *ethical* hierarchy, one of virtue, "excellence." True, there are beings who are
higher than humans on the scale of being, in particular, daimons.
But they are not necessarily moral beings. Just as there are good
and bad people, there are good and bad daimons. We may depend on the fact that *good* daimons will not do evil—precisely
because they are ethically superior beings, "more excellent." But
we may not take it as a fact that *all* daimons will behave themselves. In Iamblichus's system, so different in this respect from
classical philosophical systems, there is an ontological hierarchy
and there is an ethical hierarchy, *but there is no match between the
two scales.* A man may be morally superior to an evil daimon even
though he is lower than the daimon on the scale of power or sub-

stance. And thus the notion that there are, in fact, evil, depraved daimons is entirely reasonable.

In the second place, Iamblichus's system contains a great difference from classical philosophy in its placement of gods above nature, necessity, and constraint. Just as it is apparent that certain rare men are not bound by the same rules as the rest of us, so it is theologically rational that the gods are not bound by the same "laws of nature" that rule the cosmos. Again, this shift represents a collapse of the rigid ontological-ethical hierarchy of earlier classical philosophy and science.

We must recognize that Iamblichus is involved in a couple of interesting ironies. He uses the traditional ontological-ethical argument to insist that neither gods nor good daimons are allured or affected by sacrifices. Indeed, he gives almost no integral function to evil daimons, unlike Porphyry. But he nonetheless believes that evil daimons exist and may have detrimental effects on human activities and health—though only on those humans who are themselves immoral and depraved.[13] Thus Iamblichus employs the ontological-ethical argument while nonetheless retaining a nominal place in his system for evil daimons.

Furthermore, although Iamblichus can use the ontological-ethical argument to argue that gods cannot do evil, he has already surrendered the classical dogma that the gods are part of nature, bound by necessity like everyone else, and therefore cannot do the impossible or act contrary to nature. Iamblichus places the gods above nature and necessity, as Christians had. He thus forsakes the main assumption that had ruled so much of Greek and Roman science and caused the classical philosophers to bind the gods by the same rules as govern the rest of the cosmos. Even though evil daimons play a minor role in his system (unlike that of Porphyry, for instance), Iamblichus is even closer than Porphyry to the Christian assumption (and what I argue was the assumption of just about everyone else in the ancient world with the exception of those influenced by philosophy) that the divine stands outside any moral constraint of necessity and nature. The divine, after all, need not play by the same rules as the rest of the cosmos.[14]

The Late Antique Shift in Demonology

I have argued that two major assumptions in early Christianity struck Greek and Roman intellectuals as irrational: the Christian notion that God stood outside the normal constraints of "nature" and could therefore even accomplish "the impossible" (note Galen's and Celsus's criticisms of Jews and Christians on this point);[15] and the Christian belief that evil daimons existed, caused all sorts of harm, and in particular were the cause for many diseases. The second of these two assumptions made Christianity, in the minds of the educated Greeks and Romans, not only irrational but also superstitious. The classical definition of *deisidaimonia* as "fear of daimons" seemed to fit the Christians quite well. When Christians wanted to defend themselves against that charge, they could do so by explaining that *they* did not fear daimons because they had the protection of Christ. Nonetheless, they did believe, in contrast to the classical philosophical view, that daimons were in fact fearful realities.

The third- and fourth-century Neoplatonism of the likes of Porphyry and Iamblichus rejected much about Christianity, but it could no longer differentiate its own "science" from the "superstition" of Christianity on the basis of demonology.[16] One of the chief ways ancient science had differentiated itself from superstition, one of the most basic doctrines of classical philosophy and medicine, for example—that superhuman, divine, or semi-divine beings cannot commit evil and do not cause diseases—fell by the wayside in late antique philosophy. How do we explain this significant shift?

I think we may quickly dismiss one possible explanation. Someone might suggest that the late antique philosophers were themselves influenced in their notion of daimons by Christianity, say by coming into contact with the learned writings of someone like Origen. This seems to me not likely. For one thing, as I attempted to show in previous chapters, the seeds of a philosophical teaching about maleficent daimons existed in some forms of Platonism even as early as Xenocrates, and we can discern them also in Plutarch and Celsus. We do not need Christianity in order to have a "source" for the notion. In the second place, even if Christianity provided some encouragement to Porphyry and Iamblichus to accept the belief, we would then need to explain why they, and not earlier intellectuals, tended to be open to such persuasion. They could have argued against this Christian belief as easily as they did others. In other words, we need a more complex historical explanation than simply pointing to Christian influence.

I should remind the reader that, according to my account, the philosophical rejection of daimonic causation of disease or other misfortunes was never *the* Greek or Roman view. It is abundantly clear that Greeks generally, before the advent of Greek "scientific" medicine or philosophy, assumed that diseases and other calamities were brought on by gods, daimons, or other superhuman beings. It also seems clear that the vast majority of Greeks and Romans—along with probably most other peoples of the ancient Mediterranean—continued to believe generally the same things throughout the long period of history addressed by this book. The views found in ancient philosophical and "scientific" writings were those of a tiny fraction of the ancient population. The question that demands an answer is not "Why did so many people in the ancient world believe in evil daimons?" but rather "Why, for a few hundred years, did a few men reject that common belief?" The question should not be "Why did Christians and other people in late antiquity believe that daimons caused disease?" but rather "Why did Greco-Roman intellectuals finally —in late antiquity, mainly in the third century—give in to popular opinion and make daimonic causation of disease part of philosophy rather than condemning it as superstition?"

Though I will make no pretense of settling that problem completely, I will offer thoughts on it in the final chapter below, where I argue that broader changes in society and especially political structures in late antiquity led to an undermining of the ontological-ethical paired hierarchies that supported the philosophical sensibility about nature and superhuman beings. But before that, I now turn back to another major Christian apologist in late antiquity, Eusebius, in order to demonstrate still other significant shifts in the meaning of "superstition" that occurred in the heat of battle between Christians and their opponents.

13

Turning the Tables

Eusebius, the "Triumph" of Christianity, and the Superstition of the Greeks

The first chapter of this book focused on non-Christian authors who labeled Christianity a "superstition." Perhaps it is fitting that now, toward the end of the book, we come around to the writings of a Christian who turned the tables, who not only defended Christianity as the "only true philosophy" but also condemned Greek and Roman culture, including religion and philosophy, as superstition. Eusebius of Caesarea lived from about 260 to about 340. Educated by Pamphilus, who had himself been a disciple of Origen, Eusebius served much of his life as bishop of Caesarea, in Palestine.[1] He is most famous for his *Ecclesiastical History*, a history of the Christian church from its inception to his own day. His many other works include long defenses of Christianity and attacks on its opponents. Significantly for my purposes, Eusebius wrote at a time when Christianity was becoming an important political and social force, before and after Constantine's accession to the imperial throne and his conversion to Christianity. Eusebius witnessed the significant shift in the late ancient world when

Christianity went from being the religion of a persecuted minority to being the preferred and sponsored religion of the imperial family. He skillfully used that change to shift also the meaning of "superstition."

The Superstition of the Greeks and Romans

As we have seen, Origen and other predecessors to Eusebius had already begun the process of turning the tables on Greek and Roman religion and even philosophy. Eusebius appropriates and expands many of the themes we have already seen in Origen's defense against Celsus. I noted, for example, that ancient authors often appeal to the common opinion that "success proves truth." Rather than challenging the assumptions that underwrite such rhetoric, Eusebius simply turns them against the enemies of Christianity.

Eusebius gleefully recounts any available story by which he can illustrate the impotence of traditional gods. He points out that many gods have been unable to protect their own temples from natural disasters, such as lightning; gods who cannot even protect themselves, he insists, certainly do not deserve worship (*Preparation for the Gospel* 6.2–3). Just as non-Christians had persecuted Christians before the "triumph" of Constantine, so Christians persecuted their enemies later, which Eusebius uses to demonstrate the impotence or unreality of the Greek gods, obviously unable to protect their worshippers, sanctuaries, or images (*Life of Constantine* 3.57). The destruction of Jerusalem and its temple proves that Christianity has also superseded Judaism, due to divine providence (*Proof of the Gospel* 8).

Another proof of the decline of traditional Greek religion was the historical demise of oracles. Long before Eusebius's time, some, including philosophers and other intellectuals, had questioned why oracles had seemed more active in the past but had become weaker and rarer.[2] According to Eusebius, Christianity had brought about the decline of the power of daimons, the force behind the oracles. The daimons, deprived of worship and sacrifices, became progressively weaker, and thus oracles severely declined (see *Proof* 3.7, 8.5; *Preparation* 1.4).[3] Eusebius's ability to point to the successes of Christianity to prove its truth demonstrates a certain degree of cultural confidence on the part of Christians in their ability to turn the tables on their onetime persecutors.

Eusebius, moreover, is able to expand significantly the attempted appropriations by earlier Christian apologists of philosophical notions to brand Greek religion as superstition. Like Origen, for instance, Eusebius scathingly criticizes traditional myths. He points out the "ridiculous" stories about the origins of gods and their exploits.[4] At the base of these arguments is the philosophical doctrine that divine beings, if they are indeed divine, *cannot* be immoral, shameful, or passionate. As Eusebius elsewhere calls upon Plato to witness, "no good being can ever feel jealousy of anything."[5]

Eusebius also borrows philosophical criticisms of popular religious beliefs and practices, especially any that appeared to be motivated by fear. But whereas the philosophers had advocated philosophy itself as the liberator from the fear of *deisidaimonia,* Eusebius holds up Jesus as the bringer of *true* philosophy to the world, assigning to him all the benefits traditionally promised by classical philosophy:

> [Jesus] treated and cured the entire human race by means of the mild and gentle drugs administered through his words and with soothing and encouraging teachings. He delivered them from every kind of disease and suffering, no less of body than of soul. Everyone who came to him he set free from ancient superstition and fears of polytheistic deceit

and from a shameful and uncontrolled way of living. Those
who attached themselves to him he altered and transformed
from intemperance to a self-controlled life, from impiety to
piety, and from injustice to justice—indeed, from the power
of bitter daimons to the inspired acceptance of true piety.
(*Proof* 4.10, 163d–164a)

Except for the blanket condemnation of polytheism and the last
statement about daimons, everything said here about Jesus had
already been said by the Greeks about the influence of philosophy. Jesus was now the purveyor of the philosophy that cured by
means of its words and led people from the errors and immorality
encouraged by the Greek myths.[6]

Eusebius also makes a great deal out of the philosophical critique of sacrificial cult. He quotes long and numerous passages
from Porphyry and other Greek writers on sacrifice, but whereas
their purpose had been to reform popular opinion and sacrificial
practices (to make them less "superstitious"), Eusebius's purpose
is to turn their comments against all sacrificial cult entirely (to
make *all* of it appear "superstitious"). Thus he is able to present
Christianity as the *only* cult that meets divine approval. After all,
just about all religions of the ancient Mediterranean were based
on some sort of sacrificial rite. Even Jews, who had ceased to sacrifice with the destruction of the temple in Jerusalem in the first
century, still assumed the reality and validity of sacrifice in their
system, honoring it even in its absence by attentions to it in numerous rabbinic discussions. Christianity, though, practiced no
sacrificial cult, unless one took the rite of the eucharist to be
such, and Eusebius did not. Thus Eusebius capitalizes on a previous philosophical approbation of a nonsacrificial piety.

Porphyry was right, Eusebius says, to teach that only evil daimons would demand blood sacrifices, even to the extent of per-
suading people to sacrifice their fellow human beings. But Eu-

sebius turns Porphyry's ethical argument about the nature of daimons against him (Porphyry, it will be remembered, believed that only *some* daimons were evil). If the other Greek superhuman beings, those who did not desire animal sacrifice, were good daimons or gods, why did they not intervene and prohibit the evil daimons from misleading humanity? No, says Eusebius, *all* the Greek gods, and those of all peoples, have demanded and received sacrifices, and none attempted to stop the practice, even though surely the so-called good daimons and gods would have been powerful enough to call a halt to the evil practice. That they did not do so proves that even Porphyry's "good daimons" are actually evil daimons like the rest. And his "gods" are no gods at all, but other evil daimons. It is these evil daimons who are the instigators and advocates of sacrificial cults. Christianity, in contrast, is the only religion not tainted by the evil.[7]

Heretofore I've noted ways Eusebius borrows philosophical attacks on popular religious beliefs and "superstition" and turns them against Greek and Roman religion entirely. But Eusebius is also able to take over the rhetorical tactics of *internal* philosophical debates about religion and turn them against his philosophical opponents. There had long been a debate among philosophers, for instance, about the reality of oracles, with some philosophers defending them and others attacking them. Among the most famous of the ancient debates on the topic are Cicero's long work *On Divination,* in which Cicero gives himself the more skeptical position and his brother Quintus the position of defending the reality of oracles, and Plutarch's dialogue *On the Obsolescence of Oracles,* in which several different philosophical theories are presented. Eusebius selects various arguments from such debates and turns them against non-Christian religion and philosophy in general.

The first thing wrong with oracles is that they often demand unethical and even horrible actions from humans, such as human

sacrifice or futile warfare. More exasperating, though, is the ambiguity of oracles: answers to people's questions are framed in language that is so "poetic" and opaque that no matter what the out-
come the priests may claim that the oracles spoke the truth.
Whatever the explanation for oracles, the phenomenon should
not be honored. If oracles are truly divine, that just proves that
the god is either ignorant and so cannot provide a dependable
prediction, or that the god is immoral and wicked, intentionally
misleading humans to their own destruction.[8] According to Eusebius, the oracles are too real to be the product of mere human
trickery, and are more likely the product of some superhuman
force—specifically, misanthropic and maleficent daimons, who
grab every opportunity to harm humans. But Eusebius is able to
arrive at this conclusion, to a great extent, by depending on earlier philosophical debates about oracles.

Likewise on the topic of "fate," Eusebius appropriates moral
arguments previously found in philosophical debates.[9] In the first
place, Eusebius argues, the doctrine of fate, if true, would make
individual morality impossible. If great men are fated to accomplish great things, then evil men must be fated to do evil.[10] In the
second place, why should men strive to excel or do good if their
actions are already foreordained? We should stop praising virtuous men if they are virtuous only because they cannot help being
so. If fate is real, free will is destroyed and so all moral responsibility or blame is nonsense. Moreover, we should certainly recognize that prayers are senseless if the futures of both ourselves and
those to whom we pray are predetermined.[11]

Thus Eusebius expands many of Origen's themes, appropriating, as had Origen, philosophical attacks on "superstition" to attack Greek religion and even philosophy itself. The beliefs in
myths, sacrifice, oracles, and fate all reveal traditional religion to
be superstition. And even philosophers, in spite of their criticisms
of *some* of the aspects of popular religion, still implicate them-

selves in superstition by continuing to worship the same gods and participate in many of the same religious activities. Christianity, according to Eusebius, emerges as the only true philosophical religion.

Christianity as an Ancient Religion, Christians as a New Nation

As we have seen, Celsus and other critics attacked Christianity because it was recent and disconnected to the traditional religion of a particular ethnicity. Origen, building on Jewish and Christian apologists before him, countered by showing how even Greek writers admitted that Moses predated Greek religion and Homer himself. By claiming Moses' scripture as their own, Christians asserted a pedigree more ancient than that of their Greek opponents.[12] Moreover, Origen had countered the accusation that Christians encouraged people to forsake their ancestral ("ethnic") religions by pointing out that philosophers did the same: when philosophers tried to wean people from "superstitious" practices and beliefs, they were actually encouraging people to adopt novel, though admittedly superior, religious notions. Eusebius learns from Origen but pushes such arguments in his own directions. In the first place, Eusebius goes even further to demonstrate the greater antiquity of Christianity *as a religion.* In the second place, and here more creatively, Eusebius readily admits that Christianity constitutes something new: Christians are members of a new *ethnos,* a new nation—in fact, Eusebius presents Christianity as the first and only *universal ethnos.*[13]

Eusebius concedes that Jesus first appeared rather recently, but there was nothing "novel or foreign" about his teaching (*Ecclesiastical History* 1.4). Jesus taught many things related to a philosophical, moral life. But for Eusebius the most salient of Jesus' accomplishments was his destruction of idolatry, his teachings against

"polytheistic error," the "ancient superstition" of the worship of
daimons. According to Eusebius, humanity had originally known
only the worship of God, but over many years human societies
had devolved from natural monotheism into the worship first of
heavenly bodies, then of great men, then of beasts, and daimons,
and all sorts of disgusting things—into a degraded polytheism.[14]
Thus, although Eusebius is fond of calling polytheism "the ancient error" (*Life of Constantine* 3.54) or "the ancient disease" (*Ecclesiastical History* 2.3.2), he insists that Christianity, which for all
practical purposes in these contexts means monotheism, is more
ancient still.[15]

Furthermore, Christianity is older even than Judaism.[16] Eusebius here borrows a Christian rhetorical tradition that one could
argue goes back even to the Apostle Paul, who had pointed to the
"faith of Abraham" to insist that Gentiles could become members
of the people of God without following the Mosaic law, since
Abraham, after all, lived centuries before Moses and was declared
"righteous by faith apart from works of the law" (Gal. 3:15–18;
Rom. 4:9–12). According to Eusebius, though originally monotheists, human beings by the time of Abraham had declined into
the worship of many gods. Abraham's rejection of the worship of
idols constituted the rejection of the "*deisidaimonia* and per-
verted previous life of his fathers" (*Ecclesiastical History* 1.4.13).
Abraham turned his back on the "ancestral superstition" of polytheism (*Proof* 1.2).

Much of the first book of Eusebius's *Proof of the Gospel* is an argument from Jewish scripture that the religion of Abraham, Isaac,
and Jacob, the Jewish patriarchs, was basically Christianity before
the appearance of Jesus. The religion of the patriarchs, after all,
was certainly not Judaism, since they existed before the giving of
the law of Moses. They thus did not follow all the religious practices for which the Jews of Eusebius's time were famous. But neither were the patriarchs like the Greeks or other nations, since

they were no longer "held captive by the polytheistic superstition" (*Proof* 1.2). They were Christians before their time. Christianity for Eusebius is the great third way, neither Judaism nor Hellenism, but the philosophical, monotheistic religion that preceded both.

In fact, Christians do not follow Jewish (that is, "Mosaic") laws and customs because, in Eusebius's reckoning, the law of Moses was only a temporary imposition upon the Jews because they had proven themselves unable to avoid idolatry without the special safeguards put in place by Moses. Because the "solution" of Moses was only temporary, Christians must not be expected by their Greek detractors to follow Jewish customs and law. Christians possess, instead, the true and ancient philosophy of monotheism, known intuitively at the foundation of humanity, recovered presciently by Abraham and the patriarchs, and now revealed to the world in the philosophy of Christ. Eusebius has turned the accusation of novelty around. Building on the Greek intellectual admission of the antiquity of Jewish literature, and on the Jewish admission that the faith of Abraham predated Moses' law, Eusebius insists that Christianity is more ancient than either polytheism or Judaism.

On the other hand, however, Eusebius is perfectly willing to admit that Christianity represents something entirely new, in this case, a new, universal *ethnos*. A common assumption of the ancient world, as we have seen, was that each people, each *ethnos*, had its own religious practices. Christianity was offensive because it was a religion without an *ethnos*, and at least to some people that seemed ridiculous, or even dangerous. Eusebius's answer to this problem is interesting because instead of simply dismissing the notion that religions must be attached to ethnic groups, he defines Christians as constituting an ethnic group of their own.[17]

Though Eusebius mentions many different ethnic categories (Egyptians, Persians, Romans, or sometimes simply "barbarians," as well as others), when addressing the issue of the ethnicity of Christianity he generally speaks only of the two *ethnē* that really matter to him: Greeks and Jews. And in that scheme Christianity is "neither Hellenism nor Judaism, but a new and true kind of divine philosophy" (*Preparation* 1.5.16d). Christians constitute a "third *ethnos*" alongside Greeks and Jews. Thus, even though he claims that Christianity professes the most ancient religion, Eusebius admits that Christians constitute a "new *ethnos*" (see *Ecclesiastical History* 1.4.2, 4).

Furthermore, Eusebius capitalizes on the cosmopolitan and universal tendencies of his age to present Christianity as *the universal ethnos,* the *ethnos* that is not limited to traditional ethnic boundaries. The *universality* of Christianity is one of the things that make it superior to all ethnically based cult or religion, including Judaism (*Proof* 1.5, 1.6.19a).[18] Eusebius is here doing something that would initially have struck ancient people as strange: proclaiming, oxymoronically, the existence of a *universal ethnos.*[19] The very category of ethnicity was one that divided the world's peoples into discernible groups with their own customs, characteristics, and religions. To speak of a universal people was entirely possible, of course, especially given the tradition of philosophical cosmopolitanism. But in that case, one usually did away with the category of ethnicity entirely. Eusebius wants to have it both ways: to portray Christianity as an *ethnos,* but also as universal. Rather than simply rejecting the notion that any religion must be linked to an *ethnos,* Eusebius radically redefines *"ethnos"* to be a universal (rather than "ethnic") category, and then argues that only Christianity can fill the bill.

Though the notion would have seemed counterintuitive to many, we can also imagine its allure. It capitalized on a wider felt need for a universal vision that seems to have been increasing in the late antique world. A certain drive for universalism in late ancient politics, philosophy, and culture enabled Eusebius to hit upon a timely strategy in portraying Christianity as a universal *ethnos,* indeed, as the only truly universal *ethnos* and religion. Eusebius turned a weakness of Christianity—that it was a religion without an *ethnos*—into a strength. Christianity was now the vehicle for a universal human race.

Monotheism and Monarchy

The theme of *universalism* introduces a key for understanding some of the fundamentals of Eusebius's universe—his political theology and its meaning for his understanding of superstition and the reality of daimons. For Eusebius, human history may be plotted as a great Divine Comedy: it began in universal monotheism; it later descended into polytheism and idolatry; and it has recently begun to be restored to monotheism.[20] To usher in the last act of the drama, two providentially arranged events occurred at the same time: the establishment of the Roman empire by Augustus and the advent of Christ on earth. Jesus was born, Eusebius explains, just after Augustus had established his control as sole ruler over the Roman empire, turning what had been a republic into (in Eusebius's view) a monarchy. Jesus began his ministry of liberation from error and superstition during the reign of Augustus's (adopted) son, Tiberius. The conjunction of these events for Eusebius is not at all coincidental, but is the work of divine timing.

By coordinating the advent of Christ with that of Augustus, God began the final act of human history: the establishment of divine peace where before had been strife and suffering.

Before him [Jesus] much polyarchy existed, and all the nations were ruled either by tyrannies or democracies, since humans enjoyed no intercourse with one another, but each carried on privately. Egyptians were ruled by their own king, as were the Arabs, Idumeans, Phoenicians, Syrians, and all other peoples. And there were uprisings of peoples against peoples, cities against cities, countless sieges and taking of prisoners in every locale and region, until the Savior and Lord arrived. And at the same time as his appearance to humanity, the first Roman conqueror of all nations, Augustus, destroyed most polyarchy and spread peace to the entire earth, in accordance with the prophecy at hand, which prophesied clearly about Christ's disciples: "Therefore they shall be magnified to the ends of the earth, and this shall be peace." (*Proof* 7.2.344d; the same claim, almost word for word, is made in *In Praise of Constantine* 16.5–7)

The reason Augustus signifies universal unity is because he established monarchy for the world. And monarchy, for Eusebius, is always equated with monotheism, whereas "polyarchy" represents polytheism.[21]

Incidentally, modern English readers are at something of a disadvantage in recognizing the heavily monarchical slant of Eusebius's language because many modern translations render *basileus*, his normal term for Augustus *and* Constantine, into "emperor," though "king" would be its more normal translation. Although the earliest Roman emperors were wary of monarchical language, preferring the title *princeps* ("first" among senatorial "equals"), Eusebius never hesitates to call the emperors "kings."

Eusebius is never squeamish about "kingship" language because for him monarchy is clearly the superior polity. As Eusebius proclaims in his speech praising Constantine, who is for Eusebius the "new Augustus," "For this [monarchic rule] is the law of royal authority, the law which decrees one rule over everybody" (*Praise* 3.5; trans. H. A. Drake). One of the signs of the superiority of monarchy is that only humans, and not animals, are capable of maintaining this constitution. Eusebius implies that beasts are so bestial because they are incapable of monarchy! The main alternatives to monarchy envisioned by Eusebius are the rule of several rulers and democracy. In the former case, true unity and peace are not possible because the rulers fight one another. Having several rulers or multiple constitutions is condemned, with the same rhetoric turned against polytheism; "polyarchy" is the political expression of "polytheism," which is, as we have by now learned, the rule of daimons, enslavement to *deisidaimonia*, superstition, "fear of daimons."[22] "For which reason [that is, the superiority of monarchy] there is one God, not two or three or even more. For strictly speaking, belief in many gods is godless" (*Praise* 3.6; trans. Drake). But according to Eusebius, democracy is no better than oligarchy. Democracy is "a polyarchy based on equality" and always results in anarchy and civil war (*Praise* 3.6). Monarchy is much preferable to rule by the "ungodly multitude" (*Life* 3.1).[23]

Eusebius's monotheistic theology is thus reflected in his monarchical ideology, and they are both reflected in his general deprecation of plurality or multiplicity and preference for unity. The cross, for instance, is the *one* standard for Constantine's army, in opposition to the *several* images of different deities used by the army of Licinius, Constantine's rival for the imperial throne. Not surprisingly, the orderliness and efficiency of Constantine's troops are contrasted to the plurality and confusion of Licinius's, a reflection of the unity and control of monotheism *versus* the multiplicity and chaos of polytheism (*Life* 2.16). Whereas the empire before Constantine was divided into East and West, each with its own emperor and caesar, Constantine's rule is vastly superior because now the entire empire is united under one king. Universalism—the uniting of the entire world under one rule—is possible only under monarchy, the proper expression of monotheism. Empire is thus also the proper political conclusion of theological universalism.

Perhaps ironically, it is important for Eusebius's "monotheistic" vision that Constantine become identified with God and Christ, as is especially apparent in his *Life of Constantine* and in his speech *In Praise of Constantine*.[24] Constantine and God are mingled in the narrative as basically one single liberator of humanity, and Constantine's political opponents, such as Maxentius and Maximin, are the representatives of daimons. The "bad" rulers are portrayed with the traditional invective used against tyrants: both the evil rulers and daimons are misanthropic and enslave the people they should be governing with benevolence. Sometimes Eusebius so conflates the characters that it is difficult to discern when he means to refer to God or Christ or Constantine, on one side, and the "tyrants" or daimons on the other (see, for example, *Life* 1.5). Constantine and his children (that is, his dynasty) are "the slayers of the dragon," the apocalyptic representation of Satan (*Life* 3.3). Just as God is the "universal King" (*Life* 3.12), so Constantine is "the sole monarch of the world" (3.46).[25] The Roman peace, inaugurated with God's blessings on Augustus but culminating in the reign of Constantine, is depicted as "the demise of daimons" (*Proof* 3.7.140b; *Preparation* 1.4.12). But Constantine, in defeating his opponent and the enemy of Christianity, Maxentius, may also be portrayed as Moses.[26] Maxentius is defeated in battle and comes to his ignoble end by drowning, just as Pharaoh and his armies had drowned in the Red Sea (*Life* 1.38; *Ecclesiastical History* 9.9; see also ibid., 8.13).

Admittedly, Eusebius reports Constantine's demurral at being equated with Christ; Constantine humbly insists that only the rule of Christ is eternal (*Life* 4.48). But Eusebius himself is not so reticent. As H. A. Drake notes, "Although Eusebius theoretically establishes a hierarchy of God-Logos-Emperor, in practice he treats Constantine and the Logos as relatively equal coordinates."[27] Note how Eusebius pairs Christ's subjugation of daimonic forces with Constantine's subjugation of those more visible: "Our common Universal Savior, by invisible and divine power, keeps the rebellious powers—all those who used to fly though the earth's air and infect men's souls—at a distance, just as a good shepherd keeps wild beasts from his flock. And His friend [Constantine], armed against his enemies with standards from Him above, subdues and chastizes the visible opponents of truth by the law of combat" (*Praise* 2.3; trans. Drake).

The basic theological opposition in Eusebius's writings, therefore, is between monotheism on the one side and polytheism, which is always "superstition" *(deisidaimonia)*, on the other. But as we have seen, lined up along the two opposing sides of that dichotomy are many other oppositions, interlocking with others on each side to form a remarkably stable and pervasive theological, political, and ideological system in Eusebius's writings, as may be illustrated by a table:

Monotheism	Polytheism
monarchy	chaos, democracy, multiple rulers
rule of law	bestial chaos
liberty	slavery
peace	warfare and strife
God-Christ	Satan-daimons
Constantine	the tyrant persecutors
Moses	Pharaoh
Romans (Christians)	barbarians (idolators)
Christianity	Hellenism
philosophy	superstition
unity	plurality

The list could, of course, be expanded, but this basic dualistic opposition rules Eusebius's entire corpus.

For Eusebius, anything but monarchy means division, pluralism, and chaos. And just as monarchy is the necessary political

constitution of monotheism, "polyarchy" results from "polytheism" (see also *Praise* 12.9). And just as monarchy is for Eusebius
"liberty" (ironically from the perspective of the ancient Athenians
and Romans), so polyarchy and polytheism constitute slavery to
despotic rulers, those whose souls in turn are enslaved to daimons. "For how could one bear the likeness of monarchical authority who has formed in his soul the myriad falsely depicted
images of demons? How can he be ruler and lord of all who has
bound himself to countless malignant masters, who is a slave of
shameful pleasures, a slave of unbridled lust, a slave of ill-gotten
gain, a slave of ill-temper and wrath, a slave of fear and frights, a
slave of blood-thirsty demons, a slave of soul-destroying spirits?"
(*Praise* 5.3; trans. Drake). Monarchy is the only good constitution. And monarchy *must* be monotheistic.[28]

Imperial Patron or Optimal Universe?

It should now be clear how Eusebius's theology and political ideology are key for understanding how he meets the problems of
evil daimons. First, we must note that Eusebius's demonology
is much like that of Origen and other Christians before him.
Daimons are thoroughly evil, the very creators of polytheism and
idolatry, all of which is subsumed for Eusebius under the term
"superstition," *deisidaimonia* (see *Preparation* 7.16.330a; the notion, though, pervades Eusebius's works). They deceive people
through the inspiration of oracles and divination. They manipulate people through magic. They have inspired the persecution of
Christians and the invention of heresies. Yet, fortunately, they
have grown weaker as more people have rejected polytheism and
been converted to Christianity. Christianity has enervated the
daimons.[29]

Thus Christians need not fear daimons—not indeed for the
reasons given by classical philosophy, that daimons are, as supe-

rior beings, virtuous and harmless, but because Christians have a more powerful patron, Jesus Christ. In place of the belief in a balanced, self-regulating universe that ruled classical philosophy, Eusebius, like Origen, depends on faith in a patron-client system of protection. Christians do not fear daimons, Eusebius claims, because they can depend absolutely on the protection of "our common Universal Savior," who rids the world of daimons (*Praise* 2.3; quoted above). The failures of the traditional "gods" to protect their followers prove for Eusebius not that they do not exist but just that they are poor, weak, and even evil patrons who cannot protect their clients or even themselves (see, for example, *Preparation* 4.16). Christian miracle workers, on the other hand, destroy the evil machinations of daimons by appealing to their own more powerful patrons, God and Christ (see the story in *Ecclesiastical History* 7.17, for instance). It is not coincidental that many of the sentiments here quoted occur in a sermon Eusebius delivered at the dedication of a church in Tyre, in which Eusebius portrays God as the ultimate patron and Christians as God's "friends," that is, clients.[30] Moreover, God is portrayed as especially the patron of the emperor Constantine (see *Ecclesiastical History* 10.8). Eusebius's theological answer to the problem of evil daimons is implicated in his ideology of monarchy and empire.

The Divine Comedy of world history has reached its culmination in the triumph of Constantine—indeed, in what Garth Fowden calls "Constantine's marriage of imperial Rome to Christian monotheism."[31] As I mentioned above, Eusebius praises Constantine as the slayer of the eschatological, satanic "dragon" (*Life* 3.3). Eusebius feels no need to await a restored holy city, as promised by the book of Revelation, because the Jerusalem rebuilt by Constantine is already "the New Jerusalem" (*Life* 3.33). All of one chapter in his speech *In Praise of Constantine* is a celebration of the triumph of Constantine as a signal that the eschatologically promised triumph over daimons has already been to a great extent accomplished (*Praise* 7). Eusebius has indeed turned the diachronic apocalypticism of earlier Christianity, which awaited the coming of the kingdom of God *in the immediate future,* into a synchronic "realized eschatology" that sees Constantine's empire as a model of the heavenly kingdom: "God has formed the earthly kingdom in resemblance to the heavenly, the goal he sets for all humankind, holding before them this beautiful aspiration" (*Praise* 4.2).

I will bring my treatment of this topic to a close with a rather long quotation, but one that I think merits quoting because it contains, in several lines, so many different aspects of Eusebius's political theology, ideology, and view of history here examined. Toward the end of his life, Eusebius composed a speech to be given at festivities surrounding the dedication of the Church of the Holy Sepulchre, built at Constantine's command, in Jerusalem in 335. At one of the climaxes of the speech, Eusebius waxes eloquent in his panegyric of both the empire and Christianity:

> But two great powers—the Roman Empire, which became a monarchy at that time, and the teaching of Christ—proceeding as if from a single starting point, at once tamed and reconciled all to friendship. Thus each blossomed at the same time and place as the other. For while the power of Our Savior destroyed the polyarchy and polytheism of the demons and heralded the one kingdom of God to Greeks and barbarians and all men to the farthest extent of the earth, the Roman Empire, now that the causes of the manifold governments had been abolished, subdued the visible governments, in order to merge the entire race into one unity and concord. Already it has united most of the various peoples, and it is further destined to obtain all those not yet united, right up to the very limits of the inhabited world. For with divine power the salutary instruction prepares the

way for it and causes everything to be smooth. This, if nothing else, must be a great miracle to those who direct their attention to the truth and do not wish to belittle these blessings. For at one and the same time that the error of the demons was refuted, the eternal enmity and warfare of the nations was resolved. Moreover, as One God and one knowledge of this God was heralded to all, one empire waxed strong among men, and the entire race of mankind was redirected into peace and friendship as all acknowledged each other brothers and discovered their related nature. All at once, as if sons of one father, the One God, and children of one mother, true religion, they greeted and received each other peaceably, so that from that time the whole inhabited world differed in no way from a single well-ordered and related household. (*Praise* 16.5–7; trans. Drake)

Only in the nuclear family of monotheism, with God the father, Christianity the mother, and all humanity as children, and only under the divine constitution of monarchy, is there eternal peace.

Certainly Garth Fowden is right to insist that monotheism does not necessarily carry universalism and empire in its wake.[32] There have been monotheisms that did not necessarily bring universalistic imperialisms along with them. But in the political theology of late antiquity, it is easy to see the cooperation of universalism, and therefore empire, with monotheism (and vice versa). And monotheism with its attendants universalism and monarchy provides the structure that delivers Eusebius from "the fear of daimons." The patronage of the one God with his agents Christ and even Constantine protects Christians from the maleficence of daimons. Christians need not believe in the counterintuitive notion that daimons are not evil because they ought not be evil. They need not accept the answer offered by classical philosophy. The divine patron protects them instead.

Conclusion

The Rise and Fall of a Grand Optimal Illusion

$\int$uperstition" was a category invented by ancient intellectuals, especially those we call philosophers. They came to believe that traditional notions about nature and divine beings could not be true, and they criticized all sorts of beliefs and practices that their contemporaries simply assumed were legitimate. The philosophers, by and large, never rejected basic religion, but they did criticize religious behavior they considered excessive or embarrassing. They argued that popular notions that the gods were capricious and immoral were false. They taught that traditional myths about divine misdeeds must not be true. They pointed out that the gods surely weren't the type of beings that could be "bought off" by sacrifices, much less by shameful or disgusting offerings. The Greek and Roman writers also mocked the hasty importation of "foreign" religious practices into their own culture, though they clearly never halted the flow of imports and were never "pure" from foreign taint themselves. The most central characteristic of "superstition" attacked by ancient intellectuals was the idea that gods, daimons, or any other superhuman being caused disease or other unnecessary harm to human beings. Gods and daimons may heal and help, but they do not harm.

I have shown through analysis of the writings of several ancient intellectuals that the philosophical notion of the workings of nature and superhuman beings assumed a match between what had previously been seen as two distinct hierarchies: the ontological hierarchy in which different beings in the universe were seen as occupying different positions of superiority or inferiority, and an ethical hierarchy in which different beings were assumed to be better or worse. This new notion may be termed the "Grand Optimal Illusion" of ancient philosophy and science. It was "Grand" in that it presumed to redescribe the entire universe. It was "Optimal" because it assumed that since the world *ought* to be so, then it necessarily *was* so. And it was an "Illusion" because, quite simply, the ancient thinkers who advocated these ideas had no new "data," "facts," or "evidence" from nature that could have demonstrated its truth. The Hippocratics, Plato, Aristotle, Theophrastus, and all the other thinkers had not "discovered" new facts about the gods, nature, or daimons that disproved popular notions; they took these new notions to be true because they felt that they ought to be true.

This was certainly an intellectual revolution in the ancient world, though we must be careful not to make the mistake of previous generations of historians and depict it as the same sort of revolution as that precipitated in the modern world by the "Enlightenment" and *its* redefinition of nature and "supernature." As we have seen, the ancients never rejected "supernatural" intervention in "natural cause and effect"—precisely because they never invented the category of "the supernatural" in the first place. Another significant difference between the ancient shift of nature and the modern one is that the Enlightenment truly revolutionized the modern world. It changed religion, eventually, even on the popular level. It led to modern science, which influences the lives of us all. In contrast, the ancient shift of opinion actually had little effect—there is simply no evidence that the majority of people in the ancient Mediterranean ever gave up most of the ideas and behaviors labeled "superstitious" by the philosophers.

The evidence that most among the ancient population either never heard the philosophers' critique of "superstition" or ignored it is overwhelming. In the first place, we simply find no indication in the historical sources that most people gave up common understandings and practices of sacrifice. They apparently continued to assume that divine beings gave them blessings in return for sacrificial offerings and that divine beings would withhold blessings and even harm them if they ceased sacrificing. Second, we do have evidence from throughout the ancient world that people still assumed that superhuman beings—gods, daimons, heroes, ghosts—were frightful and harmful. Most still attributed at least some diseases (though certainly not *all* diseases) to gods or daimons. In the course of this book I have indirectly indicated some of that evidence in the condemnations of the philosophers themselves. The writings of Theophrastus show that people of his day used all sorts of "superstitious" prophylactics to guard themselves from pollutions or from attacks by Hecate or other gods, even though Theophrastus was writing at the end of the fourth and the beginning of the third century BCE, long after these beliefs had come under attack from the Hippocratics, Plato, and Aristotle. The same beliefs are still fully visible in the first century BCE, as shown by the writings of Diodorus Siculus, in the first and second centuries CE as evident in the writings of Seneca and Plutarch, not to mention the New Testament, and later in the second century as shown by Celsus and Galen. The continuing assault on "superstition" mounted by intellectuals throughout antiquity is in itself one piece of evidence that the beliefs they attacked continued to be held.

Much evidence not cited thus far in this book confirms the picture. The satires of Lucian of Samosata in the second century

CE, to name only one such source, provide evidence that people of his day continued to assume that daimons might need to be exorcised from a house by Egyptian spells or that the god or daimon of a household statue might send fevers.[1] Lucian may be exaggerating when he depicts such beliefs as being advocated even by philosophers (though we should not be too sure), but he certainly is not making up the beliefs entirely: we may assume that he is reflecting actual convictions current in his society and recognizable to his readers. Though we must rely mostly on the writings of the educated classes from the ancient world, even those sources suggest that *most* people never gave up those traditional beliefs labeled "superstitious" by the philosophers. The Grand Optimal Illusion never convinced the majority.

We may now sit back and ponder what caused ancient thinkers to develop this new concept of nature and the divine. How did it come about? What convinced that small minority of men to change their minds about nature and the divine, to come to believe that superhuman beings do not harm? We cannot have a firm answer to this problem, I believe, because no writing from the ancient world actually *narrates or explains* the shift. As we have seen, the earliest writings attacking superstition simply *assume* that the gods *as divine* are happy, blessed, *and good.* Neither the Hippocratic writers, nor Plato, nor Aristotle, nor even Theophrastus (our earliest source for the use of *deisidaimonia* in the negative sense) tells us *how* they knew "for a fact" that superhuman beings are also morally superior. So we must guess about the sources of the belief. What caused the rise of the Grand Optimal Illusion?

The Rise

Let me first reiterate one thing we can say for certain: older historians were simply wrong when they implied that the rejection of superstitious beliefs was due to the rise of "rationalism" or "empiricism" in the ancient world. As we have seen, ancient intellectuals never *demonstrated* that the gods were good; they *assumed* it. They did not discover new "evidence" about the nature of the divine. Moreover, they offered alternative explanations of disease (in humoral theory, for instance) that were based on no more "fact" (from the modern point of view) than was belief in divine causation. No, the rejection of divine and daimonic causation of disease did not come about simply because certain Greek men were suddenly "rational" thinkers whereas all their countrymen were "irrational," nor because they suddenly became "empiricists" whereas their countrymen couldn't see nature in front of their faces. The modernist depiction of ancient "science" as caused by a development of "empiricism" or "rationality" is misleading and ultimately not supported by the evidence. Rather, we must look to ancient *social* and *cultural* sources for the invention of "superstition."

Probably there were many such factors that influenced the shift in ancient thought that some modern scholars have called "the Greek Enlightenment" and I call "the Grand Optimal Illusion." But certainly one must be the significant and widespread changes in politics and political theory in sixth- and fifth-century BCE Greece. And one of the most important political notions advanced in that period was the idea of universal law and "equality before the law": *isonomia*. Many years ago Gregory Vlastos suggested that the ancient political notion of *isonomia* was one of the prime influences in ancient medicine and science; a political idea became a central tenet in ancient science.[2] And it is not difficult to imagine how this happened, though imagine we must since no ancient writer, to my knowledge, explicitly admits that it was politics that influenced theology. If we analyze the theme of *isonomia* and universal law from political debates, however, we will make some sense of the shift in philosophical theology.

Fragments of the sixth-century BCE Athenian politician and lawgiver, Solon, provide a starting point for our search. In one such fragment, Solon explains the rationale for the polity he established in Athens:

> To the *demos* [common people] I gave as much privilege as is sufficient,
> Neither taking away honor nor offering more.
> Those possessing power and who were admired because of their wealth [that is, the upper class],
> Also them I protected from experiencing anything dishonorable.
> I took a stand, covering both sides with a great shield
> So that neither would defeat the other unjustly.[3]

Several aspects of this quotation are notable. In the first place, all of politics is set up as a dualistic opposition, that between the majority of the people and the aristocratic party, who were fewer in number but more powerful. In the whole course of Greek political rhetoric and theory, from the earliest times into the Roman empire, politics will be portrayed in this obviously oversimplified opposition. So we see here the famous Greek assumption of conflict, the "agonistic" presupposition of Greek culture, as well as the tendency to place that conflict in a dualistic relation of two opposed forces. We also see an early expression of the sense that balance or equilibrium between these two forces is what constitutes a successful constitution. Moderation is necessary. Excessive power on the part of either the demos or the wealthy is assumed to be the source of political problems.

This emphasis on moderation and the avoidance of excess emerges also in other Solonian fragments. In Fragment 4, Solon insists that an excess of greed leads to civic strife, and that the law exists to curb such excess. He is referring, as will also become commonplace in Greek rhetoric, both to the possibility of too much wealth on the part of the rich and too much envy on the part of the poor. He thus urges the wealthy to be moderate (Fragments 4 and 4c). Furthermore, in dealing with the people, in "treating" the body politic as it were, moderation is also necessary:

> The *demos* follows its leaders best
> When it is not trusted too much nor treated violently.
> Surfeit gives birth to hubris. Whenever wealth attends
> Human beings, they manifest no good sense. (Fragment 6)

In such a situation of dualistic opposing forces, Solon claims that his laws were intended to be followed by all the people, no matter what their station. "I wrote laws for all, for high and low alike" (Fragment 36; trans. M. L. West).[4]

The medical and philosophical appropriations of these political notions are obvious. Greek intellectuals assumed that material forces in the cosmos also existed, when in their proper state, in balanced antagonism, often portrayed as dualisms. Here too, disruption of balance, in either excess or deficiency of matter or power, could lead to disaster. Furthermore, these same intellectuals, arguing against popular opinion (that is, "superstition"), insisted that all beings and forces of the cosmos, including even the gods, had to obey the *same universal laws of behavior.* The dynamics of the cosmos were governed by the same principles as ruled the polis.

Solon's reforms in the sixth century, though not themselves constituting a democracy, are usually seen by modern scholars as having paved the way for the Athenian democracy that began with the reforms of Cleisthenes in 508–507 BCE. As several scholars have pointed out, the actual term *democracy (dēmokratia)* does not occur in the earliest references to the new form of government. In fact, the term used early on to refer to the democratic system was *isonomia,* precisely the word used by Alcmaeon, one of our earliest medical writers, to describe the balanced state of a healthy body.

Alcmaeon was probably active in the first half of the fifth century BCE (around 475 BCE).[5] The following quotation survives in the writings of Aetius, an author of the first century CE, but most scholars believe it does reflect the teachings of Alcmaeon:

> Alcmaeon holds that what preserves health is the equality [*isonomia*] of the powers—moist and dry, cold and hot, bitter and sweet and the rest—and the supremacy [*monarchia*] of any one of them causes disease; for the supremacy of either is destructive. The cause of disease is an excess of heat or cold; the occasion of it surfeit or deficiency of nourishment; the location of it blood, marrow or the brain. Disease may come about from external causes, from the quality of water, local environment or toil or torture. Health, on the other hand, is a harmonious blending of the qualities.[6]

It should be obvious that Alcmaeon is appropriating what was initially political rhetoric and applying it to the human body. As Jacques Jouanna points out, "It is generally agreed . . . that the picturesque terms 'isonomy' and 'monarchy,' borrowed from political vocabulary, may be traced back to Alcmaeon of Croton himself."[7]

Indeed, in his treatment of the subject, Gregory Vlastos argued persuasively that one of the earliest occurrences we possess of the use of *isonomia* is from a "drinking song" that celebrated, most probably, events leading up to the establishment of the democracy by Cleisthenes. The word occurs in what is called the "Song of Harmodius":

> In a myrtle bough I'll carry my sword,
> Like Harmodius and Aristogeiton,

When they slew the tyrant,
And made Athens *isonomous*.[8]

The assumption here is that the rule of a tyrant, "one-man" rule, is not government of "equality with regard to the law," for the tyrant is "above" the law. Quite likely, *isonomia* was invented by the apologists for the democracy to refer to the "lawful equality" of all the citizens conferred first by democracy. In any case, *isonomia* quickly became, if it was not originally, the "watchword of democracy," as can be seen by its occurrence in a political speech provided by Herodotus.[9]

In what was to become a classic typology in ancient Greek political theory, Herodotus sets up three short speeches on the best constitution, comparing democracy, oligarchy, and monarchy.[10] The advocate of democracy—oddly enough, a Persian recommending it for Persians—argues, "How could a monarchy ever be suitably arranged—with someone who is unaccountable to anyone else being able to do whatever he likes? For even the best of men, placed in such a situation, would not be able to maintain his normal character. He would become arrogant due to his current good fortune. And jealousy is a natural product of human nature" (Herodotus 3.80). The lone ruler is impossible to please, completely unpredictable about how he will react to his subjects. "Respect him appropriately, and he is irritated because he is not being fawned over sufficiently. Fawn over him, and he is irritated because you are a flatterer. But the greatest perils I will mention are that he disrupts the laws of the land, violates women, and murders men without trial." The only way to avoid this seemingly unavoidable political predicament is by instituting a democratic government (though, it should be noted, Herodotus does not here use the actual term *dēmokratia*):

But when the many rule, in the first place they possess the most excellent of all names: *isonomia* [equality before the law], and secondly, they commit none of these evils of monarchy. Offices are assigned by casting lots, accountability for each office is maintained, and all decisions are referred to the united citizenry. I move, therefore, that we set aside monarchy and allow the majority to rule. For everything belongs to the many. (3.80)[11]

The speaker explicitly connects *isonomia* only with democracy. In fact, he maintains that only a democratic constitution is truly lawful at all. The problem with monarchy, in his view, is that the king (or tyrant; any sole ruler is what the speaker means), being politically superior, may act capriciously, harming his subjects. He is above the law. Note also the themes of excess and extravagance. Democracy, *isonomia,* is presented as the system of moderation, balance, and law.

Of course, the other two speakers will paint entirely different pictures of oligarchy, on the one hand, and monarchy, on the other. They both insist that democracy is precisely the most *unlawful* system, since the crowd is fickle, easily swayed, and most inclined to excess. The oligarch also believes he is advocating a "balance of powers." He opposes the greater numbers of "the people" *(dēmos)* with greater power put into the hands of the few "best" men, the men of higher station and greater wealth. In his view, only by giving greater power to "the few" can the greater numbers of "the many" be balanced. The advocate of monarchy, who eventually wins the debate, counters the democrat's accusations by insisting that the true monarch will be benevolent and morally outstanding. He will not incline to the excesses feared by the democrat because he possesses a superior nature, which is the proof that he ought to rule in the first place (3.81). Importantly, the advocates of both democracy and oligarchy appeal to a sense of "balance" and "equilibrium" between the opposed parties of the many and the few. The term *isonomia,* though, is reserved for use by the democrat, leading most modern scholars to agree that it was a slogan that originated in prodemocratic rhetoric and was later sometimes appropriated by advocates for other constitutions.[12] For my purposes it is important to note that here, in one of the earliest uses of the word *isonomia,* it refers to a balance of powers and to universal law and shows its origins in political, and specifically democratic, rhetoric.[13]

More such political evidence could be marshaled, but this is sufficient to support my suggestion that the later philosophical notions underwriting the rejection of "superstition" owe much to early Greek political theory and rhetoric. The political use of these notions can be discerned in sources dating back to the late sixth century BCE (in Solon's poems quoted above), whereas the earliest occurrence of them in ancient "science" does not occur until later in the fifth century, first perhaps in Alcmaeon's formulation, and later in Hippocratic texts. The constitutional Greek polis—especially the democracy—nurtured ideas of universal law: *isonomia* meant that all citizens (*theoretically,* of course) were equally protected by and responsible to the same law. No one was above the law, even those of the highest class, even rulers. The claim that a king or emperor might be above the law was explicitly condemned. It is certainly not a coincidence that this is the same sensibility extended by philosophers even to the heavens. Philosophical theology—in opposition to popular religious opinion—taught that the gods and other superhuman beings basically had to play by the same moral rules as human beings. Therefore, if it was wrong for human beings to commit injustice and harm, it was wrong also for gods and daimons. The philosophers extended political notions of universal law and *isonomia* to the gods.

When universal law was combined with the Socratic-Platonic doctrine that the wise, good man will harm no one, not even his enemies, the result was a change in opinion about the nature of nature and the nature of the divine. The good man is the only one who is truly happy, "blessed"; and the truly good man will not harm. Since the gods are by definition the most happy and blessed, it must follow that they are also good; and if good, they will not commit injustice or unnecessarily harm. The combination of universal law with the Socratic rejection of "help friends, harm enemies" led to the philosophical doctrine, accepted eventually by all schools after Socrates, that the gods as superior beings are necessarily also superior morally. The Grand Optimal Illusion was born.

The Fall

By late antiquity the illusion had eroded away. Even well-educated intellectuals and the most respected philosophers of the day were willing to accept the notion, which had doubtless never lost its sway over the vast majority of the population, that superhuman beings were just as morally ambivalent as human beings. Though these intellectuals did not admit the possibility that *gods* might do evil, they did admit that other beings superior to humans, especially daimons, might indeed harm people, cause diseases, or be the authors of all sorts of disasters and suffering. In late ancient philosophy there is still an ontological hierarchy (some beings are superior to others) and there is still an ethical hierarchy (some beings, such as gods and certain wise men, are morally more "excellent" than others), but the two hierarchies are no longer expected to match one another. Thus disease, in the systems of Porphyry, Iamblichus, and Eusebius (and I remind the reader that I am taking these thinkers to be representative, not idiosyncratic, in this regard), may indeed be caused by those conditions taught by traditional medical theory, such as imbalance, separation, *miasma,* and so forth. But diseases may *also* be the result of daimonic influence, even malicious and evil daimonic powers. The earlier dependence of ancient medicine and science on the central notion of *isonomia,* meaning a "balance of powers" and even, in some situations, "equality," is disrupted.

I insist that this does not mean that people in the late antique world were personally more frightened of daimons than were people in previous generations. As we have seen from Origen and Eusebius, themselves pictures of confidence and self-assurance, there existed different mechanisms in their own world for protection against daimonic harm. In place of the belief in a balanced, self-regulating universe that ruled so much earlier medicine, Origen and Eusebius depend on faith in a patron-client system of protection. Christians do not fear daimons because they can depend absolutely on the protection of their patrons, God and Christ. The mechanism that offers liberation from fear of daimons, therefore, is the patronage of God, Christ, and Constantine, often mingled together indiscriminately (see, for example, Eusebius, *Life of Constantine* 1.5). A previous cosmos characterized by a balance of powers and the stability of an onto-ethical hierarchy has been replaced by a cosmos ruled by the dynamics of a patron-client system. There is no more need for fear in the latter than in the former—as long as one has the right patron.

The expectations about disease causation are also obviously expressions of political ideologies. Just as the classical medical systems were expressions of principles derived partly from democratic and republican ideologies, which emphasized *isonomia,* balance of powers, and the notion that all beings must be subject to precisely the same rules, so the late ancient assumptions about disease and healing are expressions of late ancient ideologies supporting empire and monarchy. Beings higher up in the power structure of the cosmos do not necessarily live by the same rules as those lower down. A "balance of powers" is no longer so necessary because there is, in the end, only one power that truly matters, and it must be assumed to be a benevolent one. Of course, any belief that the basic structures of the universe reflect a society of "equals" seems, in late antiquity, incredible. In classical Greek medicine *isonomia* is health and *monarchia* is disease. In the late ancient ideological commitment to *monarchia,* the solidity of that classical assumption must certainly be severely shaken, if not altogether destroyed. The hierarchy of having *one* ruler *on top (monarchia)* replaced the balance of powers *(isonomia)* in politics as well as health.

Social Science

I do not think it is surprising that the classical scientific assumptions no longer held such a powerful hold on late ancient intellectuals. The social situation had simply changed too much. Certainly the world of the early Greek democracies was profoundly different from the world of Constantine's empire. But the world of Constantine's empire was also profoundly different from that of Augustus and the empire's beginnings.[14] The reality and significance of these differences are recognized as truisms in scholarship (to the extent, perhaps, that some scholars would urge reexamination). But the shifts from early to late empire have not yet been sufficiently taken into account when analyzing precisely *how* late ancient intellectual culture differed from classical Greco-Roman medicine, science, and philosophy. A growing emphasis on the ideology of monarchy and empire replaced previous rhetoric derived from the ideology (if not the actual structures) of democracy and republic, and this shift in political ideology and rhetoric is indispensible for interpreting "what changed" in the science and philosophy of late antiquity.

Note, for example, the contrast between the figures of Augustus and Constantine sketched by H. A. Drake: "the one [Augustus], heir to one of the oldest of Rome's houses, champion of the Italic blood, dressed with studied simplicity in a coarse gown of home-woven cloth; the other [Constantine], rumored the bastard son of a stablemaid, born in a region known to Augustus, if at all, only by its barbaric rebelliousness, arrayed in the bejewelled and tinted robes of absolute majesty."[15] The republican, antimonarchical sentiments of upper-class Romans in Augustan Rome meant that the shape, appearance, and supporting rhetoric of the first emperor had *to appear* more egalitarian. I say "appear" because it must be admitted that Augustus was not the head of anything like a democracy or even a republic. He firmly held the reins of the army. And as Drake notes, on that score Augustus and Constantine were alike: "The army held the balance of power. On it depended Augustus' Republican affectations as much as Constantine's monarchical pretensions. By it were both men autocrats, differing only in the techniques by which they disguised their power."[16]

But the techniques of power, the different rhetorics of empire, *were* quite different. And these shifts in rhetoric, in the different ideologies that supported the later versus the earlier emperors, were coupled with shifts in social and economic realities. As Drake proceeds to explain,

> As the *princeps,* first among equals and first in the State, Augustus established a theoretical right to rule that served his successors for a good two centuries. But such a system could no longer serve Constantine. Incursions on Senatorial prestige by less cautious autocrats, combined with new and severe crises on the borders of the Empire, had taken their toll on the Roman Senate. In the mid-third century, the Emperor Gallienus, opting for a professional general staff to deal with the deteriorating military situation, denied control of the legions to Senators, and thereby severed another of that body's slender threads to political reality.[17]

The decrease in the power of the Senate, though, was exceeded by an even more pronounced decrease in the power of republican rhetoric and ideology. When the troops of the emperor Aurelian (who reigned from 270 to 275) rebelled against his authority, he claimed that they could not do so, and he appealed not to the support or legitimacy given his office by voice of the Senate, but to divine appointment. When Diocletian wanted to legitimate his rule in 284, as Drake explains, "he did so by aligning his house not with the Senate, but with the chief of the Roman gods, Jupiter."[18] Constantinian propaganda changed the gods, from Jupiter to Jesus, but not the principle of legitimation. Any myth of a "first among equals" or "balance of powers" *(isonomia)* was no longer supportable.[19]

The philosophers' view of nature based on notions of balance, moderation, and universal rule of a unitary law was an application to nature of principles formed in politics. It should come as no surprise that those principles no longer seemed so self-evident when the political and social situation had so radically changed. The principles supporting the Grand Optimal Illusion lost their hegemony over even the educated classes (they had never exercised much influence over the rest of the people) in the late ancient world because the world itself had changed so much. What is surprising is not that late ancient intellectuals abandoned principles that had originally been forged in the furnace of democratic or republican rhetoric, but rather that those principles survived centuries after democracies and republics had long been things of the past. After all, writers such as Plutarch, Galen, and Celsus lived in a monarchical empire, not a democracy or republic. But the ideology and rhetoric of republicanism still hung in the atmosphere surrounding them. What changed in late antiquity was that those scents had finally, and not surprisingly, dissipated, replaced by the ideology and rhetoric of absolute monarchy. Changes in views of nature and the world finally caught up with already long-established changes in actual political structures.

*   *   *

By the time of Eusebius, the Grand Optimal Illusion—or at least its near-universal hold on philosophically educated people—had collapsed under the weight of its own implausibility. The classical medical writers and philosophers, after all, had rejected the divine and daimonic causation of disease *not* simply because they saw that gods and daimons did not in fact cause disease. That is, they did not believe that the hierarchy of nature was also an ethical hierarchy simply because they "saw that it was so." Rather, their views of nature and its workings reproduce the rest of their world, including political and social structures and the ideologies supporting them. Once those structures had been long ago replaced by others, it should be expected that accompanying ideologies would also be replaced by others, and that nature would therefore look different as well. And that is what happened over a long period of time in late antiquity. The most significant aspect of the philosophical critique of "superstition" was the classical notion that daimons do not cause disease or harm humans. In late antiquity, even the philosophers believed that daimons probably did.

I have argued that Christianity did not itself bring about this change. In fact, Christianity had always been closer to the assumptions of "the masses," which is not surprising since it started out as a movement among the uneducated and continued to draw its greatest numbers from the nonelite.[20] Most people in the ancient world had always assumed that gods and daimons were unpredictable and might attempt some mischief from time to time. They assumed that superhuman beings acted pretty much the way people acted, sometimes nobly, sometimes badly. Only the intellectuals had rejected this common sense, replacing it with the claim, which must have seemed implausible to most people throughout antiquity, that superhuman beings act not the way people act, but the way people, or at least upper-class gentlemen, *ought* to act. That philosophical assumption fell apart because it became less and less compelling due to social and political changes in late antiquity, not because Christianity taught otherwise.

Of course, Christianity may indeed have been as successful as it was because, among other factors, it offered answers to a problem that most people considered a real one: the threat of harm from possibly malicious daimons. Christianity, unlike classical philosophy, did not answer the problem by insisting that evil daimons did not exist. Instead, it offered an antidote more powerful than the poison, a drug stronger than the disease: healing and exorcism in the name of Jesus. More and more in the last several years, scholars have recognized the importance of healing and exorcism for the success of Christian propaganda.[21] In its demonology, Christianity tapped into an assumed reality and met a need in a way classical philosophy had failed to do. So it was more successful eventually in winning over the masses than philosophy had ever been.

Eusebius and other Christian intellectuals also eventually succeeded in defending Christianity as the only true philosophy and in turning the tables by tarring all of hellenic religion and philosophical theology as *deisidaimonia*. Just as Greek intellectuals had been right, from their point of view, in labeling Christianity as a superstition, so Christian intellectuals were right, from their point of view, in branding hellenic religion and philosophy with the same term. In the end, "Christianity the superstition" was replaced by "Christianity the only true philosophy." From that point onward, the meaning of "superstition" changed in important ways. It was thereafter "superstitious" (in the increasingly dominant discourse of Christianity) to worship the "pagan" gods. The reality of harmful, evil daimons reentered nature, and the "philosophy of Christ" was offered as the only protection from vicious daimons and the only alternative to "superstition."

Notes

1. Superstitious Christians

1. See Rudolf Freudenberger, *Das Verhalten der römischen Behörden gegen die Christen im 2. Jahrhundert* (Munich: Beck, 1967); Robert Wilken, *The Christians as the Romans Saw Them* (New Haven: Yale University Press, 1984), 15–30.

2. The term *malefica* itself often carried connotations of evil magic, and Christians were often accused of such. See Morton Smith, *Clement of Alexandria and a Secret Gospel of Mark* (Cambridge: Harvard University Press, 1973), 234; Wilken, *Christians as the Romans Saw Them*, 98.

3. The literature on the question is extensive, partly because there has been debate and ongoing discussion about several questions related to Roman persecution of Christians, such as: On what precise charge were Christians arrested? Was Christianity ever truly "illegal"? What laws were Christians accused of breaking, if any? How much actual persecution was there and when? My central point, in any case (that persecution was occasional and local rather than centralized, official, and empirewide), is widely acknowledged. For good surveys of the "state of the question," see Bart D. Ehrman, *The New Testament: A Historical Introduction to the Early Christian*

Writings, 2d ed. (New York: Oxford University Press, 2000), 392–397; Elizabeth A. Castelli, *Martyrdom and Memory: Early Christian Culture Making* (New York: Columbia University Press, 2004), chapter 2.

4. H. Armin Moellering, "Deisidaimonia, a Footnote to Acts 17:22," *Concordia Theological Monthly* 34 (1963): 466–471.

5. The older English versions (King James and Douey) have "superstition," as they both have "too superstitious" at Acts 17:22. But almost all of the more modern translations have "religion."

6. The text does not specify that the audience on the Areopagus comprised philosophers, but since the scene began with an argument between Paul and Stoics and Epicureans, it could have been *assumed* that the Areopagus audience was likewise mainly philosophers.

7. So, for example, Moellering, "Deisidaimonia."

8. Mark D. Given, "Not Either/or but Both/and in Paul's Areopagus Speech," *Biblical Interpretation* 3 (1995):356–372. Some of the article recurs in Given's book, *Paul's True Rhetoric: Ambiguity, Cunning, and Deception in Greece and Rome* (Harrisburg, Pa.: Trinity Press International, 2001). The book provides much more elaborate demonstration of the several ambiguities of the text of Acts and the portrait of Paul in Acts as well as in his own letters.

9. Given, "Not Either/or," 365–366.

10. *Another* possible complication, one not discussed by Given, occurs when we realize that it was precisely the *philosophers* who had invented and promoted the "insulting" meaning of *deisidaimonia,* as I will demonstrate in several chapters that follow. Most people of the first century may well have taken the term to mean "pious," but by the first century CE, I will argue, philosophers were united in using the term only in its pejorative sense. This raises a complication for Given's thesis with regard to the intentions of the author of Acts—or at least with regard to his sophistication. According to Given, the author presents Paul as, so to speak, pulling the wool over the eyes of his philosophical audience: he means the term as a criticism but realizes that they will probably take it as a compliment because it occurs where one would expect the *captatio benevolentiae* of a speech. But would this trick have fooled any real philosophers? Is the narrator, that is, sophisticated enough to know that the hearers, precisely because they were philosophers,

would have been insulted, though nonphilosophers would not have? By setting up *philosophers* (the inventors of the *negative* meaning of *deisidamonia*) as the butt of his joke on the double meaning of *deisidaimonia,* the author may be revealing that he knows less about philosophers than he pretends. Perhaps the joke would have been on the narrator in the end. Or perhaps this should be taken as evidence that the author could not have "intended" to depict the philosophers as deceived after all. Or perhaps the entire exercise just demonstrates the problems that necessarily arise when we focus on authorial intention but really admit all the different possibilities of intention or lack thereof.

2. Problems of Definition

1. See the use of this way of speaking of "superstition," though of a different period, in Ramsay MacMullen, *Christianity and Paganism in the Fourth to Eighth Centuries* (New Haven: Yale University Press, 1997), 74–75.

2. Iona Opie and Moira Tatem, eds., *A Dictionary of Superstition* (Oxford: Oxford University Press, 1989), v.

3. For an even more confused attempt to define *superstition* (here in a way that will hold true universally), see Sophie Lasne and André Pascal Gaultier, *A Dictionary of Superstitions* (Englewood Cliffs, N.J.: Prentice-Hall, 1984). A much better account is provided by B. Gladigow ("Aberglaube," in Hubert Cancik et al., eds., *Handbuch religionswissenschaftlicher Grundbegriffe* [Stuttgart: Verlag W. Kohlhammer, 1988], s.v.), who points out that accusations of superstition relate not to some kind of universal phenomenon but to "interreligious polemic."

4. To cite a few examples picked practically at random: Fielding H. Garrison, *An Introduction to the History of Medicine,* 3d ed., revised and enlarged (Philadelphia: W. B. Saunders, 1924), 103–106; Georg Luck, *Arcana Mundi: Magic and the Occult in the Greek and Roman Worlds* (Baltimore: Johns Hopkins University Press, 1985), 16; James Longrigg, *Greek Rational Medicine: Philosophy and Medicine from Alcmaeon to the Alexandrians* (London: Routledge, 1993), 1, 2, 8, 26, passim; Plinio Prioreschi, *A History of Medicine,* vol. 3: *Roman Medicine* (Omaha: Horatius Press, 1998), 482, 494–495.

5. *The Corinthian Body* (New Haven: Yale University Press, 1995), 4–6.

6. The point is gradually gaining recognition among historians and classicists: see Derek Collins, "Nature, Cause, and Agency in Greek Magic," *Transactions of the American Philological Association* 133 (2003):17–49, esp. 28–29.

7. See, for example, Seneca's discussion of lightning in Book 2 of *Natural Questions.* Though Seneca is interested in disputing popular ideas that gods *personally* and *directly* cause specific lightning strikes, he nonetheless still believes that lightning is in effect a "divine power" (*divina potentia,* 2.31.1), and divine working does operate within the events that unfold in fulfillment of omens derived from certain kinds of lightning (2.32.3–4).

8. Petronius, *Satyricon* 30; Pliny, *Natural History* 28.5.28, 28.4.19.

9. Hellebore: see Dioscorides, *Materia Medica* 4.151. The practice of spitting on one's chest is well attested: see, for example, *Satyricon* 74; Theophrastus, *Characters* 16; see also Theocritus, *Idyll* 6.39, 20.11, for similar cases.

10. It is not always easy to discern Pliny's own opinions about many of the beliefs he relates. But his attitudes toward the "science" of his day are often equally ambiguous. For Pliny's views of physicians, for example, see Vivian Nutton, "The Perils of Patriotism: Pliny and Roman Medicine," in *Science in the Early Roman Empire: Pliny the Elder, His Sources and Influence,* ed. Roger French and Frank Greenaway (London: Croom Helm, 1986), 30–58.

11. Cicero, *On Divination* 1.99, 1.77.

12. See Pliny, *Natural History* 11.90.222; Plutarch, *On Superstition* 8 (*Moralia* 168F); Nicander, *Alexipharmaca* 312. The "scientific" explanation is that bull's blood coagulates quickly in the body, thus killing the person who drank it.

13. Columella, *On Agriculture* 12.18.4; 2.21.3–4; 11.2.98; 6.2.3.

14. Among the many possibilities, the following may be taken as representative. Astrology: Marcus Manilius, *Astronomica;* Firmicus Maternus, *Matheseos Libri viii;* for English translations of ancient astrologers, see *Ancient Astrology: Theory and Practice,* trans. Jean Rhys Bram (Park Ridge, N.J.: Noyes, 1975); for introduction into the rather difficult terrain of ancient astrology, see Tamsyn Barton, *Ancient Astrology* (London: Routledge, 1994). Pharmacology: Dioscorides, *Materia Medica;* Nicander, *Alexi-*

pharmaka. Agriculture: *Geoponica* (*Geoponika sive Cassiani Bassi scholastici De re rustica eclogae* [Leipzig: Teubner, 1895]). The Greek novels published together in B. P. Reardon, ed., *Collected Ancient Greek Novels* (Berkeley: University of California Press, 1989), are rich in the details of popular religious beliefs and practices. And on the Latin side, Petronius's *Satyricon* and Apuleius's *The Golden Ass* are especially entertaining.

15. For the variety of things the words *daimōn* and *daimonion* could refer to, and to get an idea of the difficulties in defining them, see Walter Burkert, *Greek Religion* (Cambridge: Harvard University Press, 1985), 179–181. Burkert's is also one of the fullest and most authoritative treatments of Greek religion in general.

16. Peter John Koets notes and criticizes this historical account; see his *Deisidaimonia: A Contribution to the Knowledge of the Religious Terminology in Greek* (Purmerend, the Netherlands: J. Muusses, 1929).

17. *Inscriptiones Graecae* 14.1683; see the discussion in Koets, 29–30.

3. Inventing *Deisidaimonia*

1. See the "Introduction" by Jeffrey Rustin to Theophrastus, *Characters* in the Loeb edition (Cambridge: Harvard University Press, 1993), 4–6; *Theophrastus of Eresus: Sources for His Life, Writings, Thought, and Influence,* ed. and trans. William W. Fortenbaugh et al., part 1 (Leiden: Brill, 1992), 1.

2. For the debate on the importance of Theophrastus, see Richard Sorabji, "Is Theophrastus a Significant Philosopher?" in *Theophrastus: Reappraising the Sources,* ed. Johannes M. van Ophuijsen and Marlein van Raalte, Rutgers University Studies in Classical Humanities, vol. 8 (New Brunswick: Transaction Publishers, 1998), 203–221, and other essays in the same volume.

3. For another attempt to use the *Character Sketches,* in the absence of other extant, more serious philosophical texts by Theophrastus on the subject (in this case anger rather than superstition and religion), see William W. Fortenbaugh, "Theophrastus on Emotion," in *Theophrastus of Eresus: On His Life and Work,* ed. William W. Fortenbaugh et al., Rutgers University Studies in Classical Humanities, vol. 2 (New Brunswick: Transaction Books, 1985), 209–229, esp. 222.

4. For one portrayal of basic piety and impiety in Greek popular

thought of the time, see Jon D. Mikalson, *Athenian Popular Religion* (Chapel Hill: University of North Carolina Press, 1983), 91–105.

5. Theophrastus Fragment 584A, quoted in Porphyry, *On Abstinence from Eating Animals* 2.5.1–2; numbers given in the text are those from Porphyry's text. See *Theophrastus of Eresus,* ed. and trans. Fortenbaugh et al., part 2, pp. 405–433. For commentary on the fragment, see Fortenbaugh, *Quellen zur Ethik Theophrasts* (Amsterdam: B. R. Grüner, 1984), 262–274; and see discussion by Dirk Obbink, "The Origin of Greek Sacrifice: Theophrastus on Religion and Cultural History," in *Theophrastean Studies: On Natural Science, Physics and Metaphysics, Ethics, Religion, and Rhetoric,* ed. William W. Fortenbaugh and Robert W. Sharples, Rutgers University Studies in Classical Humanities, vol. 3 (New Brunswick: Transaction Books, 1988), 272–295.

6. "Atheism," when used by ancient authors, refers more accurately to "despising" or "ignoring" the gods rather than to the more modern notion that beings superior to humans simply do not exist at all. Though ancient authors sometimes speak of "atheists," even apparently meaning people who deny the existence of the gods, it is strikingly difficult to find an actual atheist in the ancient world. All sorts of people were called "atheists" (including Christians and Epicureans) who did not actually deny the existence of *any* god.

7. Theophrastus's rejection of animal sacrifice, and his particular stance on vegetarianism, would have been controversial in his day; see Sorabji, "Is Theophrastus a Significant Philosopher?" 16; Obbink, "Origin of Greek Sacrifice," 283, 285. For a good overview of ancient philosophies and their relation to religion, see Harold Attridge, "The Philosophical Critique of Religion in the Early Empire," *Aufstief und Niedergang der römischen Welt* 2.26.1 (Berlin: Walter de Gruyter, 1978), 45–78. For background in the early "natural" philosophers, see Werner Jaeger, *The Theology of the Early Greek Philosophers* (Oxford: Clarendon, 1947); Lloyd Gerson, *God and Greek Philosophy: Studies in the Early History of Natural Theology* (London: Routledge, 1990).

8. For evidence, including use of the term *deisidaimonia* (though we cannot be certain whether the word is Porphyry's or Theophrastus's in the context), see also Fragment 584D in Fortenbaugh et al., quoted from Porphyry, *On Abstinence* 2.59.1–61.2.

9. Though scholars now believe this definition to be a later interpolation and not authored by Theophrastus himself, it nonetheless represents a sentiment assumed in the section.

10. *Inquiry into Plants* 9.8.6; Pliny the Elder also mentions such beliefs. See his *Natural History* 27.60.85, 25.10.29.

11. Many of these recommendations are paralleled in other ancient texts. Pliny the Elder also passes them along; see *Natural History* 25.50.

4. Dealing with Disease

1. According to Owsei Temkin, *On the Sacred Disease* is "the most enlightened work of the Hippocratic collection" ("An Essay on the Usefulness of Medical History for Medicine," *Bulletin for the History of Medicine* 19 [1946]:9–47, at 13). For John Chadwick and W. N. Mann, who present Hippocratic medicine as an almost spookily prescient version of modern empirical and experimental medicine, the Hippocratic argument about the "natural" causes of the sacred disease is a flagship example of the "modern" in Hippocratic medicine (*The Medical Works of Hippocrates* [Oxford: Blackwell, 1950], 4). W. H. S. Jones actually preferred *Airs, Waters, Places* and *On Ancient Medicine* over *Sacred Disease* as examples of excellent Greek scientific thinking, mainly because he felt that the former were less tainted by philosophy or rhetoric and were more "empirical" (see Loeb edition, vol. 2, pp. 131–132; and *Philosophy and Medicine in Ancient Greece; with an edition of peri archaiēs iētrikēs* [Baltimore: Johns Hopkins Press, 1946], 4). Jacques Jouanna identifies *Sacred Disease* as "the earliest known text in which a rational medicine is opposed to a religious and magical medicine" ("The Birth of Western Medical Art," in *Western Medical Thought from Antiquity to the Middle Ages,* ed. Mirko D. Grmek [Cambridge: Harvard University Press, 1998], 22–71, at 39). See also Harold W. Miller, "The Concept of the Divine in *De Morbo Sacro,*" *Transactions of the American Philological Association* 84 (1953):1.

2. See the discussion of the document, including recognition that the author is portraying popular Greek practices and beliefs, in G. E. R. Lloyd, *Magic, Reason and Experience: Studies in the Origin and Development of Greek Science* (Cambridge: Cambridge University Press, 1979), esp. 15, 38.

3. We must remember that the Greek word for the speech act used in

Sacred Disease 1—*epaoidē* (or *epōidē*)—can be translated into any of these English terms. The Greek terminology is ambiguous, and we English speakers must often decide on our own whether what is being referred to is something we would call a prayer, a religious song, a magical spell, or a less formal spoken incantation.

4. See Wesley D. Smith, "So-called Possession in Pre-Christian Greece," *Transactions of the American Philological Association* 96 (1965):403–426, who argues that the idea of daimonic *possession* (as opposed to the view that the god or daimon simply acts *upon* the person's body) is found only in late antiquity (the earliest reference, in his view, is from Lucian, who lived in the second century CE) and due to "eastern influence." (See also Roy Kotansky, "Greek Exorcistic Amulets," in *Ancient Magic and Ritual Power,* ed. Marvin Meyer and Paul Mirecki [Leiden: Brill, 1995], 243–277.) Though I demure from attributing such a development to "eastern influence" (a favorite historical explanation of earlier generations of scholars that is, gradually but thankfully, falling out of favor), it does seem that the earlier texts prefer to depict the daimon or god more as "attacking" or "falling on" the person than actually entering the body.

5. Jones offers an alternative reading, *katharmatōn,* which would refer to the "refuse" or "offscourings" left over after the "cleansing." The logic of pollution is similar whichever reading is chosen: the "cleansing agent" takes the pollution onto itself and thus becomes a pollutant, or the residue of pollution retains the power to pollute after being removed from the patient. The idea that things (such as a divine being, holy area, or magical material) that can purify someone from pollution may also pollute someone is not unusual, either in the ancient world or in other cultures, in spite of the Hippocratic author's sense, expressed in this same section, that the notion is ridiculous.

6. D. R. Jordan, "The Inscribed Lead Tablet from Phalasarna," *Zeitschrift für Papyrologie und Epigraphik* 94 (1992):191–194 (an inscribed lead tablet from Crete, dated to the fourth-third centuries BCE); see also William D. Furley, "Zur Form und Funktion von EPOIDAI in der griechischen Zaubermedizin," in *Philanthropia kai Eusebeia: Festschrift für Albrecht Dihle zum 70. Geburtstag,* ed. Glenn W. Most et al. (Göttingen: Vandenhoeck, 1994), 80–104, esp. 96–99; and discussion in Kotansky, "Greek Exorcistic

Amulets," 254. On the near ubiquity and variety of magic in the Greek and Roman worlds, see Fritz Graf, *Magic in the Ancient World* (Cambridge: Harvard University Press, 1997); Pedro Lain Entralgo, *The Therapy of the Word in Classical Antiquity* (New Haven: Yale University Press, 1970), 22–31. For discussion of healers contemporary with or predating the Hippocratic writers, see Walter Burkert, *The Orientalizing Revolution: Near Eastern Influence on Greek Culture in the Early Archaic Age* (Cambridge: Harvard University Press, 1992), 41–87.

7. The most abundant evidence comes from the Asclepian inscriptions. See Emma J. Edelstein and Ludwig Edelstein, *Asclepius: Collection and Interpretation of the Testamonies* (Baltimore: Johns Hopkins University Press, 1998).

8. R. J. Hankinson is right to point out that a central issue in the Hippocratic (and more generally ancient scientific) argument against *personal* divine causation of disease is that of *fear.* Though here speaking of the divine role assigned to heat in the treatise *On Fleshes,* Hankinson insists, "even if it [heat] is conceived literally as a pantheistic cognitive force, [it] is not something to be feared or propitiated: rather it is to be *understood*" ("Magic, Religion and Science: Divine and Human in the Hippocratic Corpus," *Apeiron* 31 [1998], 23). What Hankinson does *not* explain is why divine forces should *not* be feared. My thesis in this book constitutes an attempt to explain *why* the ancient scientists believed that it was irrational (superstitious) to take divine forces to be fearsome—and why there was little empirical reason for the rest of the population to accept their view on this issue.

9. The point that ancient medicine did not attribute disease causation to contagion is now a commonplace; see, for example, Jacques Jouanna, *Hippocrates* (Baltimore: Johns Hopkins University Press, 1999), 152. See also J. C. F. Poole and A. J. Holladay, "Thucydides and the Plague of Athens," *Classical Quarterly* n.s. 29 (1979):282–300; Volker Langholf, *Medical Theories in Hippocrates: Early Texts and the "Epidemics"* (Berlin: Walter de Gruyter, 1990), 220–221. The historian Thucydides famously used a notion of contagion to explain the spread of the Athenian plague (see *Peloponnesian War* 2.50), but he was virtually alone among *educated* authors in doing so. There are other occasional hints at notions of disease contagion in educated authors. (I would argue that the notion was quite common in the general

populace, reflected, for instance, in all sorts of beliefs about pollution.) Plato, *Phaedrus* 255E, speaks of getting a disease from another person's gaze. Isocrates mentions people's fears that nursing those suffering from a certain disease may make themselves sick as well (*Aegineticus* [*Discourse* 19] 29). The pseudo-Aristotelian *Problems* 1.7 (859b) notes that people may get the plague from being near sick persons; but it proceeds to explain that this is due to the feverish patient's body heating up the body of the person standing nearby. For another brief discussion of some contagious diseases, see *Problems* 7.8. As Dainelle Gourevitch points out, however, the Hippocratic authors ignore notions of contagion even though those notions occur in contemporary popular conceptions, as she demonstrates in a study of veterinary accounts of disease contagion in flocks and herds: "La medicina ippocratica e l'opera *Delle arie, acque, luoghi:* Breve storia della nascità e del potere di un *inganna* scientifico," *Medicina nei Secoli* 7 (1995):425–433.

10. In his discussion of the oath, Heinrich von Staden puts into nice context the concern expressed for purity and holiness with regard to entering a god's precinct in a suitable state. See "'In A Pure and Holy Way': Personal and Professional Conduct in the Hippocratic Oath?" *Journal of the History of Medicine and Allied Sciences* 51 (1996):404–437.

11. I should draw attention to one "case history" based on a funerary inscription that illustrates the mixture of what we would call "medical" and "religious" therapies practiced by a Greek physician, though not, as far as we can tell, a "Hippocratic" physician in particular (whatever that *would* mean). The inscription, composed according to Bruno Meinecke by the treating physician himself, describes the sicknesses and death of a four-year-old boy. The different roles played by divine beings (good and bad) and the easy mixture of scientific-medical actions and assumptions with religious (popular) beliefs are significant. The inscription is from Smyrna, probably third-second centuries BCE. See "A Quasi-autobiographical Case History of an Ancient Greek Child," *Bulletin of the History of Medicine* 8 (1940):1022–1031.

12. *On Breaths* 3; this translation by Volker Langholf brings out, correctly I think, the more "personal" sound of the Greek. See his discussion of the document in *Medical Theories in Hippocrates,* 244, on which my treatment here depends.

13. There was a wide variety of belief about how the penetration in intercourse affected menstruation, and not every writer seems to believe that a virgin must be penetrated in order to begin menstruation (see, for example, a different point of view in the Hippocratic *Nature of the Child* 20). But the idea that penetration at least aided menstruation was common. See, for example, *Diseases of Women* 1.1 (Ann Ellis Hanson, "Hippocrates: Diseases of Women I," *Signs* 1 [1975]:567–584, esp. 572); *On Semen* 4. Other medical writings do provide evidence, though, that some people believed menstruation could not even begin apart from penetration. The later medical writer Soranus (first to second centuries CE) provides evidence for such beliefs, though he rejects them himself (see his *Gynecology* 1.7.31, 1.8.33). And a near contemporary of Soranus, Rufus, provides similar evidence: see his "Regimen for Virgins" 18.1–2, 25. Rufus's text is contained in a collection of medical writings compiled in late antiquity by Oribasius, *Collectionum medicorum reliquiae,* ed. Ioannes Raeder (Amsterdam: Adolf M. Hakkert, 1964), vol. 4, pp. 106–109.

14. The confusion that has resulted by reading the modern Enlightenment's "secularizing" project back into the concerns of the ancients pervades much modern scholarship. Plinio Prioreschi, for example, puzzles over the presence of "theological" statements coupled with "naturalistic" explanations in the presocratics ("Supernatural Elements in Hippocratic Medicine," *Journal of the History of Medicine and Allied Sciences* 47 [1992]:389–404). Prioreschi is correct to note the presence of religious beliefs in ancient science. What is misleading is to consider such things "supernatural" and, implicitly, as mere vestiges of something basically foreign to the science. Ann Ellis Hanson finds it a problem that "scientific" gynecological texts sometimes advocate or allow the wearing of an "amulet" for pregnant women. She explains the presence of the "amulet" in medical writings as a leftover piece of "magico-religious" practice that for some reason went undetected by the medical writers: "some Hippocratic contributors missed the fact that this medicament was appealing to the magico-religious principle that like cures like." Soranus later committed the same oversight; he "failed to notice that [the object worn] was an amulet" ("Talking Recipes in the Gynaecological Texts of the *Hippocratic Corpus,*" in *Parchments of Gender: Deciphering the Bodies of Antiquity,* ed. Maria Wyke [Oxford: Clarendon,

1998], 71–94, at 83). This explanation fails to recognize that *if* a practice, whether derived originally from "folk" or "magical" or "religious" contexts is "rationalized" by being interpreted along the lines of the scientific rationality of the system, *then* the prescription is *by definition* "scientific" rather than "magical." (The Hippocratics did indeed assume a principle of "like-to-like," admittedly not usually in curative mechanisms, but certainly in their theories of nutrition and drug therapy.) Langholf makes a similar mistake when he simply designates a belief in prayer and dream divination found in some Hippocratic texts as "inconsistency" (Langholf, *Medical Theories in Hippocrates*, 237–238). It strikes Langholf as an "obvious inconsistency" that someone could believe both in "natural laws" and at the same time the efficacy of prayer. This shows a remarkable ignorance of the many and diverse forms of religious belief and practice that have been noted by scholars of religion and cultural anthropologists. In Christianity, for instance, whole religious movements have had no trouble reconciling a belief in intercessory prayer (understood, admittedly, in various ways) with "natural laws" or even divine necessity and predestination. Traditional Calvinists, to cite one example, never allowed a firm belief in predestination to preclude intercessory prayer. Though the combination of such beliefs may seem "obviously contradictory" to an outsider, that probably indicates that the outsider does not sufficiently understand the system being observed. The presence in Hippocratic texts of both assumptions should prompt modernist historians to interrogate their own presuppositions rather than dismiss such elements as "irrational" or "inconsistent" "vestiges" retained a bit out of place in scientific writings.

15. See Langholf, *Medical Theories in Hippocrates*, 235–236, and references there cited.

5. Solidifying a New Sensibility

1. *Iliad* 6.205, 6.428; 9.533; 19.59; and especially 24.606.

2. See this idea suggested in James Longrigg, *Greek Rational Medicine: Philosophy and Medicine from Alcmaeon to the Alexandrians* (London: Routledge, 1993), 14.

3. See the discussion in ibid., 12–13.

4. For a good sense of the complexity and variety of religion in Greece

in the time of Plato, see Michael L. Morgan, *Platonic Piety: Philosophy and Ritual in Fourth-Century Athens* (New Haven: Yale University Press, 1990), 17–21.

5. For the variety of ideas about daimons in Greek thought of the time, see Jon D. Mikalson, *Athenian Popular Religion* (Chapel Hill: University of North Carolina Press, 1983), 65–66.

6. On the setting and aims of the *Republic,* see Morgan, *Platonic Piety,* 104–105.

7. Ibid., 115.

8. See similar hierarchies in *Republic* 388A, 391D–395D, and 431B.

9. See the portrayal of common assumptions about the gods in K. J. Dover, *Greek Popular Morality in the Time of Plato and Aristotle* (Indianapolis: Hackett, 1994), 75–81; Mikalson, *Athenian Popular Religion,* 63–64.

10. Dover, *Greek Popular Morality,* 180–184.

11. *Iliad* 5.344; 20.443; 16.698–709; 21.596–611; 11.437; 22.214–366.

12. Mary Whitlock Blundell, *Helping Friends and Harming Enemies: A Study in Sophocles and Greek Ethics* (Cambridge: Cambridge University Press, 1989), 1.

13. Ibid., 56; but see 56 n.146 for what Blundell calls possible "antecedents" before Socrates. See also D. A. Hester, "To Help One's Friends and Harm One's Enemies: A Study in the *Oedipus at Colonus,*" *Antichthon* 11 (1977):22–41.

14. See Plato, *Crito* 49B–C; Xenophon, *Memorabilia* 4.8.11. See also Cicero, *De officiis* 1.25.88, 1.14.43; Plutarch, *Moralia (How to Profit from One's Enemies)* 90F; Diogenes Laertius, *Lives of Philosophers* 8.23.

15. In this discussion, as most of the time in discussing the ancient philosophical notions of person, I avoid gender-inclusive language and use the term "man," even when the ancients would admit that their statements *could* be applied also to women. Ancient philosophy and science were absolutely male-centric; women were included only as "imperfect" or "incomplete" versions of the male body. Thus to use gender-inclusive language and avoid the universalizing term "man" when referring to human beings would be to give the ancient conceptions a gender-egalitarian appearance that would be entirely misleading.

16. It should be noted that Aristotle does not want to use the term "virtue" to describe the gods. For Aristotle, virtue is a means to the end of bless-

edness. The gods do not need the "means" because they already enjoy the "end." Thus although Aristotle would not say precisely that the gods are "virtuous," he certainly would not accept the counterproposal that they commit "vice." The gods are above "virtue," not below it.

17. For an accessible account of "the mean" in Aristotle's ethics, see D. K. Hutchinson, "Ethics," in *The Cambridge Companion to Aristotle,* ed. Jonathan Barnes (Cambridge: Cambridge University Press, 1995), 195–232, esp. 217–228. See also J. O. Urmson, "Aristotle's Doctrine of the Mean," *American Philosophical Quarterly* 10 (1973):223–230, also published in *Essays on Aristotle's Ethics,* ed. Amélie Oksenberg Rorty (Berkeley: University of California Press, 1980); David Pears, "Courage as a Mean," in ibid., 171–187.

18. For an in-depth discussion of *why* (and *how*) habituation is necessary for virtue in Aristotle's ethics, see Troels Engberg-Pedersen, *Aristotle's Theory of Moral Insight* (Oxford: Oxford University Press, 1983); and Rosalind Hursthouse, "Moral Habituation: A Review of Troels Engberg-Pedersen, *Aristotle's Theory of Moral Insight,*" *Oxford Studies in Ancient Philosophy* 6 (1988):201–219.

19. Aristotle always recognized the centrality of education and habit (socialization) for virtue. See M. F. Burnyeat, "Aristotle on Learning to Be Good," in *Essays on Aristotle's Ethics,* ed. Rorty, 69–92.

20. For a study that sets Aristotelian teleology within the broader context of his philosophy—as well as noting *problems* with the doctrine—see Joseph Owens, "The Teleology of Nature in Aristotle," *Monist* 52 (1968):159–173; also published in Joseph Owens, *Aristotle: The Collected Papers of Joseph Owen* (Albany: State University of New York Press, 1981), 136–147. On the complexities of Aristotle's teleology as well as its relation to Platonic thought and earlier Greek sensibilities, see John M. Rist, "Some Aspects of Aristotelian Teleology," *Transactions of the American Philological Association* 96 (1965):337–349. On how influential Aristotelian teleology was—and some differences between Aristotle's teleology and that of much subsequent European thought—see W. Wieland, "The Problem of Teleology," in *Articles on Aristotle,* vol. 1: *Science,* ed. Jonathan Barnes, Malcolm Schofield, and Richard Sorabji (London: Duckworth, 1975), 141–160.

21. See W. D. Ross, *Aristotle's Physics: A Revised Text with Introduction and Commentary* (Oxford: Clarendon, 1955), esp. 35–37.

22. See also Aristotle, *Physics* 2.8 (198b10–199a19); *Politics* 1.2 (1253a7–10), but the theme recurs throughout Aristotle's writings.

23. On the "perception of limited good" in the ancient Mediterranean, see Bruce J. Malina, *The New Testament World: Insights from Cultural Anthropology*, rev. ed. (Louisville: Westminster/John Knox, 1993), 94–96, 103–112. For other modern scholarly treatments on the theme, see also Alvin W. Gouldner, *Enter Plato: Classical Greece and the Origins of Social Theory* (New York: Basic Books, 1965), 49–60; John Winkler, *The Constraints of Desire: The Anthropology of Sex and Gender in Ancient Greece* (New York: Routledge, 1990), 47, passim; David Cohen, *Law, Sexuality, and Society: The Enforcement of Morals in Classical Athens* (Cambridge: Cambridge University Press, 1992), 35–69; Cohen, *Law, Violence, and Community in Classical Athens* (Cambridge: Cambridge University Press, 1995), 26, 63; Josiah Ober, *The Athenian Revolution: Essays on Ancient Greek Democracy and Political Theory* (Princeton: Princeton University Press, 1996), 101. For the function of the theme in ancient asceticism and medical theory, see my "Contradictions of Masculinity: Ascetic Inseminators and Menstruating Men in Greco-Roman Culture," in *Generation and Degeneration: Tropes of Reproduction in Literature and History from Antiquity to Early Modern Europe*, ed. Valeria Finucci and Kevin Brownlee (Durham: Duke University Press, 2001), 81–108, at 93–95.

24. For another example in which teleology, necessity, zero-sum, and hierarchy all come together, see Aristotle's explanation for why only humans among all animals have eyelashes on both upper and lower eyelids: *Parts of Animals* 2.14 (658a31–658b2).

25. For the special influence of the *Timaeus*, for example, on later philosophy *and* Christian thought, see John Whittaker, "Plutarch, Platonism and Christianity," in *Neoplatonism and Early Christian Thought: Essays in Honour of A. H. Armstrong*, ed. H. J. Blumenthal and R. A. Markus (London: Variorum, 1981), 50–63, at 57–59.

6. Diodorus Siculus and the Failure of Philosophy

1. Unfortunately, Koets, who is careful to address the different meanings of *deisidaimonia* in Diodorus, does not give sufficient attention to these

texts in which the element of fear is absent. See Peter John Koets, *Deisidai-monia: A Contribution to the Knowledge of the Religious Terminology in Greek* (Purmerend: J. Muusses, 1929).

2. I leave out of consideration here texts that discuss the possible salu-tary social function of *deisidaimonia*. According to these statements, many people are unlikely to be virtuous for the right reasons, so must be kept in line by laws, threats, and fear of divine retribution (34/35.2.47). These state-ments have a distinctly philosophical ring, implying that Diodorus himself would not accept most popular religious beliefs about divine punishments, but that he, along with philosophers and educated rulers, believes such be-liefs are useful for controlling the "masses" and encouraging virtue in non-philosophical persons. Such statements, though, tend to occur in the frag-ments of Diodorus found in other authors; this, for instance, comes from Eusebius. I have not made use of the fragmentary materials because I fear the wording may not preserve that of Diodorus. These statements on *deisi-daimonia*, for example, sound distinctly "un-Diodoran" in their more nega-tive portrayal of *deisidaimonia*. Robert Drews notes Diodorus's usually pietistic editing of his sources; he sometimes *changes* his sources (such as Polybius) to emphasize traditional pious beliefs about divine retribution for sacrilege ("Diodorus and His Sources," *American Journal of Philology* 83 [1962]:383–392). The exact wording in these less "pious" fragments, there-fore, may reflect the sentiments and terminology of other, later writers who are here excerpting Diodorus.

3. See especially Martha Nussbaum, *The Therapy of Desire: Theory and Practice in Hellenistic Ethics* (Princeton: Princeton University Press, 1994).

4. *Deisidaimonia* is elsewhere explicitly connected with *manteis:* for ex-ample, 13.12.6, 13.86.1–3.

5. See Kenneth S. Sacks, *Diodorus Siculus and the First Century* (Prince-ton: Princeton University Press, 1990), 189.

6. For Diodorus's social and class location, see ibid., 184.

7. Cracks in the Philosophical System

1. See Martin P. Nilsson, *Greek Popular Religion* (New York: Columbia University Press, 1940), 10–13.

2. See Everett Ferguson, *Demonology of the Early Christian World* (New York: Edwin Mellon, 1984), 37; "Agathon daimon," *Oxford Classical Dictionary*, s.v.

3. Hesiod, *Alcestis* 1003; *Theogony* 991; Aeschylus, *Persians* 620.

4. For a full treatment of the many problems of the demonology in this treatise—and the many different interpretations of it—see Frederick E. Brenk, *In Mist Apparelled: Religious Themes in Plutarch's* Moralia *and* Lives (Lugduni Batavorum: Brill, 1977), esp. 85–112. For a discussion of Plutarch's demonology in the context of Platonism more generally, see John M. Dillon, *The Middle Platonists, 80 B.C. to A.D. 220* (Ithaca, N.Y.: Cornell University Press, 1977), 216–221.

5. See Brenk, *In Mist Apparelled*, 114–131.

6. H. Armin Moellering, *Plutarch on Superstition: Plutarch's* De Superstitione, *Its Place in the Changing Meaning of Deisidaimonia and in the Context of His Theological Writings* (Boston: Christopher, 1963). Theories of development are notoriously difficult to establish. Moellering's thesis has not convinced everyone by any means.

7. Morton Smith, "*De superstitione* (*Moralia* 164E–171F)," in *Plutarch's Theological Writings and Early Christian Literature*, ed. H. D. Betz (Leiden: Brill, 1975), 1–35. The most telling problem with Smith's suggestion is that in *On Isis and Osiris* Plutarch *three times* makes the same exact statement that furnishes the thesis for *On Superstition:* that atheism and superstition are two opposite extremes the "mean" for which is true religion: 355D; 378A; 379E. Such quotations from *On Superstition* in another work seem unlikely if Plutarch did not write it. For references to other studies of Plutarch's seemingly contradictory stances on "superstition," see Brenk, *In Mist Apparelled*, 9–15.

8. Frederick E. Brenk, "'A Most Strange Doctrine'": *Daimon* in Plutarch," *Classical Journal* 69 (1973):1–11. And more fully, Brenk, *In Mist Apparelled.* See also "An Imperial Heritage: The Religious Spirit of Plutarch of Chaironeia," *Aufstieg und Niedergang der römischen Welt* 2.36.1 (Berlin: Walter de Gruyter, 1987), 248–349, esp. 275–294 on Plutarch's demonology.

9. For other references to daimons leading people astray or harming them, see *Crassus* 22; *Alexander* 50; *Sulla* 24.

10. Brenk, "A Most Strange Doctrine," 11; see also *In Mist Apparelled,* 145–164.

11. Brenk's later, fuller treatment seems to allow for more inconsistency in Plutarch's views of daimons than this 1973 article suggests. See *In Mist Apparelled.*

8. Galen on the Necessity of Nature and the Theology of Teleology

1. As Lesley Dean-Jones has put it, "We have more works from the hand of Galen than from any other single author of antiquity." See *Women's Bodies in Classical Greek Science* (Oxford: Clarendon, 1994), 24. For dates and chronology of Galen, I follow V. Nutton, "Chronology of Galen's Early Career," *Classical Quarterly* 23 (1973):158–171.

2. *In Hippocratis librum VI epidemiarum commentarii* 091.17b.256.2. See Ernst Wenkebach and Franz Pfaff, eds., *Galeni in Hippocratis sextum librum epidemiarum commentaria I–VI* (Leipzig: 1940) (CMG V.10.2.2).

3. *On the Doctrines of Hippocrates and Plato* 3.3.6.

4. Richard Walzer, *Galen on Jews and Christians* (London: Oxford University Press, 1949).

5. Ibid., 10–16. In the passage cited here, Galen compares Moses, Epicurus, and Plato. But "Plato" stands also for "other Greeks who properly discern the rationality of nature," that is, other philosophers who think like Galen. And doubtless "Moses" stands certainly for Jews and perhaps also Christians. In three other references, Galen explicitly criticizes "the followers of Moses and Christ" mainly for trusting in faith rather than demonstration. See esp. Walzer, 14–15.

6. *On the Usefulness of the Parts* 11.14 (Kühn 8.904; Helmreich 2.158). Subsequent use of "K" numbers in cites to Galen refers to the standard edition of Galen's works: C. G. Kühn, *Claudii Galeni Opera omnia* (Paris: De Boccard, 2003; reprint of the edition of 1821–1823).

7. Well-known, though brief, treatments of Galen's religious beliefs include Walzer, *Galen on Jews and Christians;* Fridolf Kudlein, "Galen's Religious Belief," in *Galen: Problems and Prospects,* ed. Vivian Nutton (London: Wellcome Institute for the History of Medicine, 1981), 117–127. For a typically modernist description of the function of religion in Galen's thought that I reject, see *The Western Medical Tradition 800 BC to AD 1800,* ed. Law-

rence I. Conrad et al. (Cambridge: Cambridge University Press, 1995), which depicts Galen's religion as "a private affair" and his medicine as "a system of healing independent of the divine" (72, 16). The author passes on the traditional modern belief that classical medicine was "secular," and that what changed in late antiquity was that "secularization" was reversed and religion reintroduced into medicine. "Secular" is an anachronistic and misleading way to characterize Galen's system. It is instead theological through and through.

8. We don't know where Galen delivered his own lectures, but it would be rash to insist that he *never* did so in an Asclepian sanctuary. See Heinrich von Staden, "Anatomy as Rhetoric: Galen on Dissection and Persuasion," *Journal of the History of Medicine and Allied Sciences* 50 (1995):47–66, esp. 61.

9. See other examples mentioned by Vivian Nutton in his commentary to *On Prognosis,* 169n2 (Berlin: Adademie-Verlag, 1979), 174.

10. These examples are from *An Exhortation to Study the Arts* 9 (K 1.22).

11. *On Examination by Which the Best Physicians Are Recognized,* ed. and trans. Albert Z. Iskander, 1.9 (pp. 44–45) (Berlin: Akademie, 1988). For other references by Galen to divination, see Iskander, p. 145.

12. For dreams used with other forms of divination, see *On Prognosis* 2.12 (K 14.608), and commentary at pp. 159–160, 225.

13. *The Order of My Books* 4 (K 19.59); *On the Therapeutic Method* 10.4 (K 10.609); *On Prognosis* 2.12 (K 14.608); see also commentary at Iskander, *On Examination,* pp. 143–144.

14. Galen, *On the Therapeutic Method, Books I and II,* trans. and comm. R. J. Hankinson (Oxford: Clarendon, 1991), xxi; *My Own Books* 2 (K 19.18–19); *On Prognosis* 9.5–8 (K 14.649–651; and see Nutton's commentary at pp. 211–212).

15. *On the Sects for Beginners* 2 (Helmreich 3); *On Treatment by Venesection* 23 (K 11.314–315); and see the commentary by Iskander to *On Examination,* p. 143.

16. See K 6.832–835. For English translation and helpful notes, see Lee T. Pearcy, *Galen on Diagnosis in Dreams* (Ancient Medicine/Medicina Antiqua, web site: http://www.ea.pvt.k12.pa.us/medant/). Galen mentions elsewhere (*Natural Faculties* 1.12 [K 2.29]) that he had written a work on dreams, but it is apparently not this text.

17. *Exhortation to Study the Arts* 5 (K 1.7), 9 (K 1.21); *To Thrasyboulos* 26 (K 5.853).

18. The best work for noting such language is *The Usefulness of the Parts*. See, for example, 5.6 (Helmreich 1.270–271) for Galen's characterization of Nature as "well educated."

19. The term occurs many times in Galen, but see *Construction of the Embryo* 2 (K 4.657), and comments by Peter Singer, *Selected Works* (Oxford: Oxford University Press, 1997), note to p. 191.

20. *The Best Constitution of Our Bodies* 2 (K 4.740–741). See also *On Anatomical Procedures* 6.1 (K 2.537), where Galen claims to have written that work in order to show people how they could conduct dissections to demonstrate for themselves that Nature does nothing in vain. His own dissections of even "lower" animals such as cats, mice, reptiles, birds, and fish, he says, were undertaken "to persuade myself firmly that one Mind put all these together and so that the body of the animal is suitable to its character [*ēthos*] in all aspects." See also 4.6 (K 2.448). For one study emphasizing the importance of teleology, in this case for Galen's theories of respiration, see chapter 4 of Armelle Debru, *Le corps respirant: La pensée physiologique chez Galien* (Leiden: Brill, 1996).

21. Although most intellectuals of Galen's day would have, I think, agreed with him that nature and the divine are constrained by "the possible," some philosophers, probably some Stoics and others under their influence, had put forth arguments to the contrary. See the discussion and references in Walzer, *Galen on Jews and Christians*, 28–31.

22. I say "would" because Galen never *explicitly* targets Christians with this criticism. In one case he actually praises Christians for their contempt of death, due to their belief in an afterlife, and their sexual asceticism (see Walzer, 15–16; the passage is preserved in an Arabic source, but Walzer provides text and translation). Galen finds this remarkable because Christians seem to be acting "philosophically" without philosophical training. Elsewhere, as noted above in note 5, Galen criticizes Jews and Christians ("the followers of Moses and Christ") for accepting doctrines on "faith" without philosophical demonstration (Walzer, 13–15). But since Galen does couple "the followers of Moses and Christ" in these passages, I take it that he also would have included the Christian view of nature, God, and the possible in his attack on "Moses."

9. Roman *Superstitio* and Roman Power

1. Michele R. Salzman, "'Superstitio' in the *Codex Theodosianus* and the Persecution of Pagans," *Vigiliae Christianae* 41 (1987):172–188, esp. 174.

2. For one study on the relation of *superstitio* to *deisidaimonia,* see S. Calderone, *"Superstitio,"* in *Aufstieg und Niedergang der römischen Welt* (Berlin: Walter de Gruyter, 1972), 1.2.377–396.

3. Seneca, *Moral Epistles* 123.16; see also Cicero, *Nature of the Gods* 1.42.117.

4. Seneca, *Moral Epistles* 121.4; Cicero, *Nature of the Gods* 1.17.45; *De finibus* 1.18.60; *Laws* 1.11.32.

5. For example, Tacitus, *Annals* 12.59.

6. See all of Book 30 of his *Natural History.*

7. See Mary Beagon, *Roman Nature: The Thought of Pliny the Elder* (Oxford: Clarendon, 1992), 46. Beagon is misleading when she implies that Pliny rejected magic because its claims to be able to manipulate nature were false (97) or because magicians assumed a "supernatural" causation that Pliny rejected (106–108). She is confused that Pliny rejects magical things but accepts other remedies or beliefs that seem to her (and to moderns in general) no less "magical" (see 107, 111). But Beagon introduces the confusion herself by introducing the modern notion of "supernatural" as opposed to "natural" causation. She is right about several points: Pliny rejects magic because of what he considers its bizarre choice of ingredients, the gibberish of incantations that disturb his "practicality" (I would say more likely his "etiquette"), magicians' use of ingredients that offend "dignity," and their vain and proud attempts to order nature around (they wrongly place themselves in a position superior to nature). But these are all issues of morality or etiquette, not epistemology about cause and effect in nature. Beagon sees Pliny as having a "dilemma": "in dismissing the inflated claims of the Magi and their believers, he risks underestimating *vis naturae* [the power of nature]" (111). But this is misleading because both Pliny and the magi share the same assumptions about the working of nature. Pliny's dilemma, if he has one, arises because he must reject the magi for *social* rather than *physiological* or *methodological* reasons. The practices of magicians are wrong because they are practiced by magicians, who are evil enemies of humankind (see, for example, 28.27.94–95).

8. Salzman, *"Superstitio,"* 173.

9. L. F. Janssen, "'Superstitio' and the Persecution of Christians," *Vigiliae Christianae* 33 (1979):131–159, at 141.

10. See Salzman, *"Superstitio,"* esp. 173.

11. See Livy 1.31.6, 29.14.2; Janssen, "'Superstitio' and Persecution."

12. Among the many references, see *The War Rule* (1QM) XV–XIX; *Commentary on Habakkuk* (1QpHab) III.

13. See Salzman, *"Superstitio,"* for the legal texts.

14. Janssen, "'Superstitio' and Persecution," 155.

15. The author of the Acts of the Apostles has Paul assert such a claim (Acts 16:37, 22:27). But Paul never mentions this in his own correspondence, so there is at least the possibility that this is one of those cases in which the author of Acts embellishes his portrait to Paul's benefit.

16. For a history of different interpretations, see Wesley Carr, "The Rulers of This Age—I Corinthians II.6–8," *New Testament Studies* 23 (1976–1977):20–25; *Angels and Principalities: The Background, Meaning and Development of the Pauline Phrase* hai archai kai hai exousiai (Cambridge: Cambridge University Press, 1981). I disagree with Carr's conclusion, though, that Paul must not be here referring to superhuman agents; see *The Corinthian Body* (New Haven: Yale University Press, 1995), 62 and 262 n.65.

10. Celsus and the Attack on Christianity

1. On Celsus himself, see Jean Daniélou, *Origen* (New York: Sheed and Ward, 1955), 99–101, 106; Michael Frede, "Origen's Treatise *Against Celsus*," in *Apologetics in the Roman Empire: Pagans, Jews, and Christians*, ed. Mark Edwards et al. (Oxford: Oxford University Press, 1999), 131–155.

2. To place Celsus's critique within the broader context of other ancient attacks on Christianity, see the Introduction by Henry Chadwick in *Contra Celsum*, trans. Chadwick (Cambridge: Cambridge University Press, 1953); T. R. Glover, *The Conflict of Religions in the Early Roman Empire* (London: Methuen, 1918); Carl Andresen, *Logos und Nomos: Die Polemik des Kelsos wider das Christentum* (Berlin: Walter de Gruyter, 1955); Stephen Benko, "Pagan Criticism of Christianity during the First Two Centuries," *Aufstieg und Niedergand der römischen Welt* 2.23.2.1055–1118 (Berlin: Walter de

Gruyter, 1980); Eugene V. Gallagher, *Divine Man or Magician? Celsus and Origen on Jesus* (Chico, Calif.: Scholars Press, 1982); Robert Wilken, *Christians as the Romans Saw Them* (New Haven: Yale University Press, 1984).

3. For one attempt actually to reconstruct the text, see Celsus, *On the True Doctrine: A Discourse against the Christians,* ed. and trans. R. Joseph Hoffmann (New York: Oxford University Press, 1987).

4. For Celsus as a representative of "a sort of Platonist consensus" in the second century, see John M. Dillon, *The Middle Platonists, 80 B.C. to A.D. 220* (Ithaca, N.Y.: Cornell University Press, 1977), 400–401.

5. *Contra Celsum* 6.49, 6.60. I cite the text according to the edition of Marcel Borrett, *Contre Celse* (Paris: Editions du Cerf, 1967–1976). As usual, most of the time I furnish my own translations from the Greek, but for an English translation of the whole, see Chadwick's *Contra Celsum.*

6. *Contra Celsum* 1.32. See Chadwick, p. 31, n.3, for other ancient and modern discussions of the tradition. My own opinion is that critics of Christianity early seized on the Christian claim that Jesus was born of a virgin *(parthenos)* and altered the letters so that Jesus's father was a *pantheros,* which was a common name and nickname for soldiers. See L. Patterson, "Origin of the Name Panthera," *Journal of Theological Studies* 19 (1917): 79–80.

7. Is Celsus showing some knowledge of Christians labeled by their enemies as Docetists?—those Christians who, aware of the philosophical problems in having God actually *become* flesh, insisted that Christ was only *apparently* flesh?

8. See Isaiah 52:14, 53:2–3; Clement of Alexandria, *Paedagogus* 3.1.

9. Apuleius, a contemporary of Celsus and also knowledgeable about the Platonic philosophy of his time, shares this sort of view of daimons: they possess "airy" bodies, share intelligence with both gods and humans, share immortality with gods, and embodiedness with humans. But they are good, benevolent beings, superior to humans both ontologically and ethically. See Apuleius, *On the God of Socrates.*

10. On the possible audience and impact of Celsus's book, see Frede, "Origen's Treatise *Against Celsus,*" 148, 152–155.

11. For placement of Celsus's, Galen's, and Porphyry's critiques in context with other intellectual attacks on Christianity, see John G. Cook,

"Some Hellenistic Responses to the Gospels and Gospel Traditions," *Zeitschrift für die Neutestamentliche Wissenschaft und die Kunde der Älteren Kirche* 84 (1993):233–254; see also R. Joseph Hoffman, *Porphyry's Against the Christians: The Literary Remains* (Amherst, N.Y.: Prometheus Books, 1994).

12. Galen, *On the Passions of the Soul*, ch. 3 (for an English translation, see *On the Passions and Errors of the Soul*, trans. Paul W. Harkins; introduction and interpretation by Walter Riese [Columbus: Ohio State University Press, 1963], 32); see also Dale B. Martin, *The Corinthian Body* (New Haven: Yale University Press, 1995), 36.

13. See *Meditations* 11.3. I am not convinced by C. R. Haines's suggestions that the reference to Christians here is an interpolation. See the Loeb edition, ed. and trans. Haines, pp. 295, 383–387. In any case, the sentiment expressed against excessive pursuit of martyrdom is one Marcus certainly would have shared with other men of his day and class.

14. See my further discussion of this difference between Paul and the more rigorous philosophers, especially the Stoics, in "Paul without Passion: On Paul's Rejection of Desire in Sex and Marriage," in *Constructing Early Christian Families: Family as Social Reality and Metaphor*, ed. Halvor Moxnes (London: Routledge, 1997), 201–215, at 210.

15. For a recent study of the New Testament evidence, see John J. Pilch, *Healing in the New Testament: Insights from Medical and Mediterranean Anthropology* (Minneapolis: Fortress, 2000). For a survey of the evidence after the New Testament, see R. J. S. Barrett-Lennard, *Christian Healing after the New Testament: Some Approaches to Illness in the Second, Third and Fourth Centuries* (Lanham, N.Y.: University Press of America, 1994).

11. Origen and the Defense of Christianity

1. For a good, concise introduction to Origen, see Joseph W. Trigg, *Origen* (London: Routledge, 1998). For older, more comprehensive treatments, see Jean Daniélou, *Origen* (New York: Sheed and Ward, 1955), and Pierre Nautin, *Origène: sa vie et son ouevre* (Paris: Beauchesne, 1977).

2. On the "failure" of Origen's apology, see Michael Frede, "Origen's Treatise *Against Celsus*," in *Apologetics in the Roman Empire: Pagans, Jews, and Christians*, ed. Mark Edwards et al. (Oxford: Oxford University Press, 1999), 145–152.

3. On the philosophical climate of Origen's work, see Daniélou, *Origen,* 73–98.

4. See Timothy D. Barnes, *Constantine and Eusebius* (Cambridge: Harvard University Press, 1981), 136, 186. Barnes is commenting on Eusebius, but this is one of the many instances in which Eusebius is following the lead of his hero and apologetic predecessor, Origen.

5. For other instances of the "success" theme, see 1.43, 47; 3.29, 33–34, 39; 7.17, passim.

6. For Origen's dependence on Philo, see Annewies van den Hoek, "Philo and Origen: A Descriptive Catalogue of Their Relationship," *Studia Philonica Annual* 12 (2000):44–121.

7. Origen's own attack on sacrificial practices depends on philosophical and Jewish critiques of sacrifice before him; see Frances M. Young, *The Use of Sacrificial Ideas in Greek Christian Writings from the New Testament to John Chrysostom,* Patristic Monograph Series 5 (Cambridge, Mass.: Philadelphia Patristic Foundation, 1979).

8. Origen was not the first to promote Christianity as a "philosophy." Justin Martyr and Clement of Alexandria had already done so in the second century. See Justin, *Dialogue with Trypho,* 8; Clement, *Strommateis,* passim; Trigg, *Origen,* 13.

9. See Arthur J. Droge and James D. Tabor, *A Noble Death: Suicide and Martyrdom among Christians and Jews in Antiquity* (San Francisco: HarperSanFrancisco, 1992).

10. For philosophical precursors to Origen's comments, see *Contra Celsum,* trans. Henry Chadwick (Cambridge: Cambridge University Press, 1953), 143, n.2.

11. See Justin Martyr, *Apology* 1.2; Peter John Koets, *Deisidaimonia* (Purmerend: J. Muusses, 1929), 87–91.

12. *Contra Celsum* 4.65; as Chadwick notes, Celsus is drawing here on Plato, *Republic* 379C and *Theaetetus* 176A.

13. Modern scholars would specify that Jesus probably spoke *Aramaic;* Origen and others of his period would not have carefully differentiated the two dialects.

14. For Origen, though, Jesus' *soul* suffered, but not the divine *logos;* see Peter J. Gorday, "Becoming Truly Human: Origen's Theology of the Cross," in *The Cross in Christian Tradition: From Paul to Bonaventure,*

ed. Elizabeth A. Dreyer (New York: Paulist, 2000), 93–125, esp. 99–100, 105–107.

15. A similar analysis could explain Origen's defense of the doctrine of the resurrection of the body. Origen follows a rather "Pauline" defense of the resurrection by agreeing that the resurrected body is *not* that of "flesh and blood" but of the higher elements of the human self: 2.16, 5.18–20, 6.29. For an analysis of Paul's views along these lines, see my *Corinthian Body* (New Haven: Yale University Press, 1995), 104–136.

16. I here deal with Origen's demonology as it appears in *Contra Celsus,* but for Origen's more "systematic" treatment of daimons, see his *Peri Archon (On First Principles)* 1.5, 3.2; for an English translation of this work, see *Origen: On First Principles,* ed. G. W. Butterworth (Gloucester, Mass.: Peter Smith, 1993).

12. The Philosophers Turn

1. For an important comparison of Origen's ideas to a major philosophical figure of his day, see Henri Crouzel, *Origèn et Plotin: Comparaisons doctrinales* (Paris: Pierre Téqui, 1991).

2. See R. T. Wallis, *Neoplatonism* (New York: Charles Scribner's Sons, 1972); John M. Rist, *Plotinus: The Road to Reality* (Cambridge: Cambridge University Press, 1967), esp. 2–20 for Plotinus's life. For an excellent introduction to and study of Plotinus, see Margaret R. Miles, *Plotinus on Body and Beauty: Society, Philosophy, and Religion in Third-Century Rome* (Oxford: Blackwell, 1999).

3. For Neoplatonism in relation to Gnostics and Christianity, see the various essays in Richard T. Wallis and Jay Bregman, eds., *Neoplatonism and Gnosticism* (Albany: State University of New York Press, 1992); for discussion of the possible identity of those we call Plotinus's "Gnostics" (Porphyry was actually the one to use this term for them), see Christos Evangeliou, "Plotinus's Anti-Gnostic Polemic and Porphyry's *Against the Christians,*" in *Neoplatonism and Gnosticism,* 111–128.

4. See Rist, *Plotinus,* 237–246, on sympathy and magic in Plotinus's thought.

5. See discussion in Wallis, *Neoplatonism,* 71–72; Miles, *Plotinus on Body and Beauty,* 81, 121.

6. For introduction and discussion of Porphyry and Iamblichus, see Wallis, *Neoplatonism*, 94–137.

7. The reference is from a lost work of Porphyry, *On the Philosophy to Be Derived from Oracles*, quoted by Eusebius, *Preparation for the Gospel* 4.23.174–175.

8. E. R. Dodds called Porphyry "the best scholar of his time" (*Pagan and Christian in an Age of Anxiety* [Cambridge: Cambridge University Press, 1965], 126); Michael Frede has called him "the most distinguished philosopher of his day" ("Eusebius' Apologetic Writings," in *Apologetics in the Roman Empire*, ed. Mark Edwards et al. [Oxford: Oxford University Press, 1999], 238).

9. Tradition held that Iamblichus was a student of Porphyry, but that has been questioned: see Henry J. Blumenthal and E. Gillian Clark, eds., *The Divine Iamblichus: Philosopher and Man of Gods* (London: Duckworth, 1993), 1–2.

10. All references given in the text are to Iamblichus, *On the Mysteries of the Egyptians, Chaldeans, and Assyrians,* cited by book and chapter number. For the original Greek text, see Jamblique, *Les Mystères D'Égypte,* ed. and French trans. Édouard des Places (Paris: Belles Lettres, 1966). Though the translations from the Greek are here my own, one may consult the English translation by Thomas Taylor (3d ed., London: Stuard and Watkins, 1968; originally published 1821).

11. For the developments of Platonism into the third century, see John M. Dillon, *The Middle Platonists, 80 B.C. to A.D. 220* (Ithaca, N.Y.: Cornell University Press, 1977). Other scholars, reacting to previous portrayals of Neoplatonism as a radical departure (and degeneracy) from Platonism, have stressed the similarities and connections; see, for example, Philip Merlan, *From Platonism to Neoplatonism,* 3d ed. rev. (The Hague: Martinus Nijhoff, 1975).

12. Reading *gnōsis* with des Places; an alternative reading here supplies *genesis*—that is, "superior to reproduction."

13. Andrew Smith, "Iamblichus' Views on the Relationship of Philosophy to Religion in De Mysteriis," in *The Divine Iamblichus,* 74–86, at 80.

14. I have concentrated in this section on the three "greats" of late ancient Platonism ("Neoplatonism"), but I insist that the doctrine in their systems of most concern for my purposes—their acceptance of maleficent

daimons and the daimonic causation of disease—was widely held by late ancient intellectuals. Though both the dates and the intellectual status of the *Hermetic Corpus* are hotly debated (the consensus assigns the documents to the two centuries between the late first and late third centuries CE), those texts show influence from both philosophy and broader intellectual currents, and they provide evidence of a belief in evil daimons. One of the treatises in the *Corpus* gives daimons credit for adultery, murder, violence to parents, impiety, strangling, and suicides (*Corpus Hermeticum* 9.3; see also 16.13). For recent translations with introduction and commentary, see Brian Copenhaver, *Hermetica: The Greek* Corpus Hermeticum *and the Latin* Asclepius *in a New English Translation with Notes and Introduction* (Cambridge: Cambridge University Press, 1992); *The Way of Hermes: The Corpus Hermeticum*, trans. Clement Salaman, Dorine van Oyen, and William D. Wharton (London: Duckworth, 1999). I do not make much of the hermetic literature for my own purposes here precisely because some scholars would insist that it is not truly "philosophical" or representative of high intellectual culture. Others would insist that there are chronological problems with placing this literature in the same context with Porphyry, Iamblichus, and Eusebius, arguing rather that it is either much earlier or later than them. For a good discussion of the various problems, see Garth Fowden, *The Egyptian Hermes: A Historical Approach to the Late Pagan Mind* (Cambridge: Cambridge University Press, 1986); for roles assigned to daimons by the *Corpus Hermeticum* as well as by other late ancient intellectuals such as Zosimus and Lactantius, see ibid., 78, 122, 206–207.

15. See Richard Walzer, *Galen on Jews and Christians* (London: Geoffrey Cumberlege/Oxford University Press, 1949), 11–12, 23–37.

16. Note, for example, the analysis of Anthony Meredith, "Porphyry and Julian against the Christians," *Aufsteig und Niedergang der römischen Welt* 2.23.2.1119–1149. Neoplatonists attacked Christianity by means of several different rhetorical strategies—by accusing it of contradiction, for instance —but they couldn't do so simply by reusing older Greek intellectual arguments against certain Christian doctrines, such as the centrality of revelation. As Meredith points out, "It may well have been the feeling that the Christians were so close to them that made the Neoplatonists protest so bitterly against them" (1141). This would also be the case, I maintain, with re-

gard to demonology, and also in this regard, it was philosophy that had changed, not Christianity.

13. Turning the Tables

1. On Eusebius's relationship to Origen, see Timothy D. Barnes, *Constantine and Eusebius* (Cambridge: Harvard University Press, 1981), 80–125.

2. The most famous ancient discussion of the issue is found in a dialogue written by Plutarch probably in the late first century, *On the Obsolescence of Oracles,* which I have already mentioned in the chapter on Plutarch above. For one survey of the evidence and discussion, see Saul Levin, "The Old Greek Oracles in Decline," *Aufstieg und Niedergang der römischen Welt* (Berlin: Walter de Gruyter, 1989), 2.18.2.1599–1649.

3. There are many other strategies in Eusebius's writings by which he attempts to prove the superiority of Christianity by focusing on its successes—for example, to explain why Christians themselves have suffered so much in past persecutions, Eusebius employs the Greco-Roman theme of the "noble death" of the philosopher or virtuous martyr we have already encountered in Origen. See *Ecclesiastical History* 5, introduction; 8.9, 14. On the "noble death" tradition, see Arthur J. Droge and James D. Tabor, *A Noble Death: Suicide and Martyrdom among Christians and Jews in Antiquity* (New York: HarperCollins, 1992), esp. 17–51. See Aryeh Kofsky, *Eusebius of Caesarea Against Paganism* (Leiden: Brill, 2000), 220–224, for a survey of the *different* explanations offered by Eusebius for the persecutions of the Christians.

4. See *Preparation for the Gospel* 2.1–5; 2.2.59a–61b; 2.5.69b–70d; 2.6.74b; 14.16; *Praise of Constantine* 7.4; 13.4.

5. *Against Hierocles* 6, published in the Loeb edition of Philostratus, *The Life of Apollonius.*

6. It should be noted that although the philosophers would not have gone out of their way to condemn polytheism, there had by Eusebius's time developed a strong tradition even among Greek and Roman philosophers that supported monotheism, at least if that term may be used to include the idea, popular among intellectuals throughout antiquity, that all the various "gods" were actually just different expressions or manifestations of the one,

high, true, and ineffable divine being. See Michael Frede, "Monotheism and Pagan Philosophy in Later Antiquity," in *Pagan Monotheism in Late Antiquity,* ed. Polymnia Athanassiadi and Michael Frede (Oxford: Clarendon, 1999), 41–67. The several essays in the latter book demonstrate that monotheism (at least to the extent that Christians could be called monotheists) was a growing tendency in late antiquity, at least among intellectuals of the Greek East. See also H. A. Drake, *Constantine and the Bishops: The Politics of Intolerance* (Baltimore: Johns Hopkins University Press, 2000), 136–139.

7. See *Preparation* 5.1–2; 4.10; passim.

8. On the ambiguity of oracles, see *Preparation,* 5.20.211–212. In all of this, Eusebius is borrowing mainly from Oenamaus, a Cynic philosopher who lived around 120 and criticized popular beliefs, writing a book called *The Detection of Impostors* (or *Against Oracles*), no longer extant. Eusebius quotes Oenomaus's satirical comment: "How odd the toys of the gods" (*Preparation* 5.21.213b).

9. Eusebius addresses the issue primarily in two places in his writings, predictably using arguments already set forth by his predecessors, in this case especially Origen. At the end of his book *Against Hierocles* (actually an attack on the Greek sage and holy man Apollonius of Tyana), Eusebius appends an entire chapter detailing just how ridiculous, impious, and immoral are both popular and philosophical notions about fate. In his book *Preparation for the Gospel* he devotes a long chapter to the subject.

10. Philosophical writers would reject the starting point of the criticism. Plotinus, for example, though accepting the reality of fate, insists that divinities do *not* cause people to pursue evil lives: *Ennead* 4.4.31.

11. Eusebius is careful to maintain a Christian doctrine of providence: God can see the future and may guide the lives of persons. But God does so without destroying free will and without *himself* being constrained by fate. See, for example, *Against Hierocles* 41.

12. Both Origen and Eusebius are building on previous apologists in the argument based on the antiquity of Judaism. See Justin, *First Apology* 44–45; Clement of Alexandria, *Stromateis* 5.89, 5.140, passim; Michael Frede, "Eusebius' Apologetic Writings," in *Apologetics in the Roman Empire,* ed. Mark Edwards et al. (Oxford: Oxford University Press, 1999), 223–250, esp. 248 and n.25.

13. The translation "nation" for the Greek *ethnos* (plural: *ethnē*) is not en-

tirely felicitous. *Ethnos* in the ancient world did not precisely mean what is meant by the modern term *nation*—and certainly not the even more problematic term *race*. But *ethnos* did refer to a "people" that was understood to have its own language, history, traditions, laws, and religion—that is, to what we would today include under the large category "culture." If we avoid the modern assumptions about political unity and self-determination often implied by the term *nation,* it is perhaps not a bad translation for *ethnos.* I will, however, most often use the Greek term itself.

14. See *Proof of the Gospel* 9.2; *Preparation* 2.2.51d, 10.1.460d.

15. See also *Preparation* 1.9: polytheism is the later invention.

16. For a full study of Eusebius's interpretation of the Jews and Judaism in his Christian historiography, see Jörg Ulrich, *Euseb von Caesarea und die Juden: Studien zur Rolle der Juden in der Theologie des Eusebius von Caesarea* (Berlin: Walter de Gruyter, 1999); "Euseb und die Juden: der origeneische Hintergrund," in *Origeniana Septima,* ed. W. A. Bienert and U. Kühneweg (Leuven, Belgium: Leuven University Press; Peters, 1999), 135–140.

17. Here again, as in so many cases, Eusebius is drawing on Christian apologetics before him. The earliest Christian writing we possess that moves in this direction of designating Christians a "third people" is the anonymous *Preaching of Peter,* from the first part of the second century and now found in quotations in Clement of Alexandria (*Stromateis* 6.5.41). There, Christians are not actually called a "third *ethnos*" but are distinguished from Jews and Greeks because of "worshipping in a third manner" *(tritōi genei sebomenoi).* The *Epistle to Diognetus* does not call Christians a "third *ethnos*" or "race," but does present Christians as treated by Jews and Greeks alike as "another tribe" *(allophyloi,* 5.17). See discussion in Adolf Harnack, *The Mission and Expansion of Christianity in the First Three Centuries* (New York: Harper and Brothers, 1972), 246–251; Abraham J. Malherbe, "The Apologetic Theology of the *Preaching of Peter,*" *Restoration Quarterly* 13 (1970):205–223, esp. 220–221. Eusebius may also be drawing on Clement, *Stromateis* 3.10, 5.14.98.

18. Moses was the lawgiver for only one nation, the Jews; Christ is superior to Moses because he is a universal lawgiver and leader for peoples of the entire world (*Proof* 9.11). Whereas Moses led only the Jews, Christ leads Greeks and barbarians (9.13; see also 10.7).

19. See Vincent Twomey, *Apostolikos Thronos* (Münster: Aschendorff,

1982), 190. Garth Fowden (though not in connection to Eusebius) mentions the impossibility of a universal *ethnic* religion. *Empire to Commonwealth: Consequences of Monotheism in Late Antiquity* (Princeton: Princeton University Press, 1993), 71.

20. For instances of the "decline into polytheism" theme, see, for example, *Proof* 1.2, 4.9.160c; *Praise* 13.4. For non-Christian precursors of Eusebius's tendency to depict history as an eventual progress rather then the usual decline, see Arthur J. Droge, "The Apologetic Dimensions of the *Ecclesiastical History,*" in *Eusebius, Christianity, and Judaism,* ed. Harold W. Attridge and Gohei Hata (Detroit: Wayne State University Press, 1992), 492–509, at 497.

21. Note the introduction and commentary to Eusebius, *Life of Constantine,* by Averil Cameron and Stuart G. Hill (Oxford: Clarendon, 1999), esp. p. 3. As in many other cases, Eusebius is here borrowing from and building on his predecessors. As Francis Dvornik has demonstrated, other Christian writers had produced similar arguments on the Pax Romana and the "monarchy" of the Roman emperor. In *Contra Celsum* 2.30, Origen spoke of the Roman peace and Augustus's rule as the beginning of a providentially established Roman empire. (Even before Origen, in the second century Melito of Sardis linked the birth of Jesus to the reign of Augustus as due to providence, as seen in Eusebius's own quotation of the Melito fragment: *Ecclesiastical History* 4.26.7–8.) Lactantius would similarly link monotheism to monarchy (*Divine Institutes* 1.3). As Dvornik notes, though, Eusebius is the first Christian writer to argue so *thoroughly* for the theory that linked monotheism to monarchy. See Francis Dvornik, *Early Christian and Byzantine Political Philosophy: Origins and Background* (Washington: Dumbarton Oaks, 1966), vol. 2, pp. 603–605, 613–622.

22. The themes occur regularly in Eusebius's many writings, but see *Preparation* 1.4, 5.1.178 (where polytheism is explicitly equated with rule by many rulers).

23. There are antidemocratic hints in several places in Eusebius's writings. In *Preparation* 3.14.123b, for example, he calls "superstition" *pandēmon,* "vulgar," "common," literally something that belongs to "all the people."

24. For a discussion of these works in the context of Eusebius's life and other works, see Averil Cameron, "Eusebius of Caesarea and the Re-

thinking of History," in *Tria Corda: Scritti in onore di Arnaldo Momigliano,* ed. Emilio Gabba (Como: New Press, 1983), 71–89; for the identification of Constantine with Christ, see esp. Barnes, *Constantine and Eusebius,* 249–254.

25. Of course, Christ is also represented as the emperor of the world. See, for example, *Ecclesiastical History* 10.4. For Eusebius's concerns to promote the Constantinian *dynasty* (rather than Constantine alone), see Barnes, *Constantine and Eusebius,* 267; Timothy C. G. Thornton, "Eusebius of Caesarea, Constantine II and the Imperfections of Constantine the Great (*Vita Constantini* 4.31 and 4.54)," *Studia Patristica* 29 (1997):158–163. For more Constantinian propaganda insisting that unity and universal rule must coexist, see Miriam Raub Vivian, "Eusebius and Constantine's Letter to Shapur: Its Place in the *Vita Constantini,*" *Studia Patristica* 29 (1997):164–169, esp. 168.

26. As Averil Cameron points out, the theme occurs in the *Ecclesiastical History* but is expanded in the *Life:* "Eusebius' *Vita Constantini* and the Construction of Constantine," in *Portraits: Biographical Representation in the Greek and Latin Literature of the Roman Empire,* ed. M. J. Edwards and Simon Swain (Oxford: Clarendon Press, 1997), 145–174.

27. H. A. Drake, *In Praise of Constantine: A Historical Study and New Translation of Eusebius' Tricennial Orations,* University of California Publications, Classical Studies, vol. 15 (Berkeley: University of California Press, 1976), 75. I should point out that I am here treating Eusebius's *mature* view. Other scholars have argued that we may discern stages in Eusebius's views on the relation of church and empire, and that in his earlier stages, church and state were seen as distinct. See, for example, Hans Eger, "Kaiser und Kirche in der geschichtlichen Theologie Eusebs von Caesarea," *ZNTW* 38 (1939):97–115. I am here unconcerned with the historical accuracy of Eger's thesis, only with the mature conclusions of Eusebius's views of history embodied in the texts here analyzed.

28. For studies of the monotheism = monarchy theme, see Raffaele Farina, *L'Impero e l'Imperatore cristiano in Eusebio di Cesarea: La prima teologia politica del Cristianesimo* (Zürich: Pas Verlag, 1966), esp. 119–123, 132–136; Drake, *Constantine and the Bishops,* 364. For Greek and Jewish precursors to the theme, see Erik Peterson, *Der Monotheismus als politisches Problem: Ein*

Beitrag zur Geschichte der politische Theologie im Imperium Romanum (Leipzig: Jakob Hegner, 1935). As Peterson points out, even "pagans" could use monarchical theology by pointing out that "one-rule" does not mean that only one god *exists,* just that only one *rules* (53–56). In this theme, as in so many others, Eusebius is borrowing on and expanding material adopted from his Christian intellectual forebears, especially Origen (see Peterson, pp. 34–35 for Justin Martyr, and 71–79 for Origen).

29. On daimons as the power behind oracles, see *Preparation* 3.17. On daimons and magic, see *Against Hierocles* 31; *Life* 1.36. On daimons as the inventors of "heresy," see *Life* 2.61–62, 73; *Ecclesiastical History* 5.16. Daimons pervade Eusebius's works, providing explanations for all sorts of evils and suffering; for a few other references, see *Preparation* 5.2.181a; also *Praise* 7.2, 13.4; *Proof* 10.8.503c–d; *Preparation* 5.2.181b. For the context, see Jonathan Z. Smith, "Towards Interpreting Daimonic Powers in Hellenistic and Roman Antiquity," in *Aufstieg und Niedergang der römischen Welt* 2.16.1 (Berlin: Walter de Gruyter, 1978), 425–439. For Christianity as enervating the daimons, see *Preparation* 4.17.164d, 5.17.208a.

30. *Ecclesiastical History* 10.4; see the opening of the speech for the use of the term "friends" in this way. For the use of "friendship" language to designate a patron-client relationship, see my *Slavery as Salvation* (New Haven: Yale University Press, 1990), 24, 191 n.116, and references there cited.

31. Fowden, *Empire to Commonwealth,* 4. As Fowden points out, though, Constantine was not the first emperor to link *one-man* rule to *one-god* rule; Caracalla had already done so (50).

32. Ibid., 5.

Conclusion

1. Lucian, *Lover of Lies,* passim. For the exorcisms, see 16 and 31; for the statue sending fevers, see 18.

2. Gregory Vlastos, *"Isonomia," American Journal of Philology* 74 (1953): 337–366; see also his "Equality and Justice in Early Greek Cosmologies," *Classical Philology* 42 (1947):156–178.

3. Solon Fragment 5. Greek text: M. L. West, ed., *Iambi et elegi Graeci ante Alexandrum Cantati* (Oxford: Oxford University Press, 1989–1992),

vol. 2, p. 124. I here, as usual, offer my own translation, but for alternative translations of Solon's fragments, see M. L. West, *Greek Lyric Poetry: The Poems and Fragments of the Greek Iambic, Elegiac, and Melic Poets (Excluding Pindar and Bacchylides) Down to 450 BC* (Oxford: Oxford University Press, 1994), 75–76. See also Fragment 37, in which the "crowd" is opposed to the wealthy. For discussion of the quotation in the context of the development of Athenian democracy, see John Thorley, *Athenian Democracy* (London: Routledge, 1996), 16.

4. It is quite unlikely that Solon himself invented all this: the assumption of an ongoing agonistic relationship between two opposing forces, the few who are powerful and the many who are weaker; the notion that a balance of the two powers is necessary for a stable polity; the belief that excess or deficiency will upset that balance; the argument that a single system of law that must be universally obeyed without regard to status is the mechanism that will assure stability. I believe Solon was reflecting political ideas that were more generally current in sixth-century BCE, and possibly earlier, political contexts in different Greek cities. On the way Greek historians by their composition of scenes show this same tendency to set up conflicts as (usually dualistic) sets of opposed speeches, see Harry C. Avery, "The Resolution of Rhetorical Conflict in Greek Historians," in *Conflict, Antithesis, and the Ancient Historian* ed. June W. Allison (Columbus: Ohio State University Press, 1990), 92–111.

5. James Longrigg, *Greek Rational Medicine: Philosophy and Medicine from Alcmaeon to the Alexandrians* (London: Routledge, 1993), places his work "around the second quarter of the fifth century BC" (p. 51). See pp. 47–64 for Alcmaeon's probable dates, theories, and influence.

6. For this translation, see Longrigg, *Greek Rational Medicine,* 52. For the Greek, see *Die Fragmente der Vorsokratiker,* 7th ed., ed. Hermann Diels and Walther Kranz (Berlin: Weidmannsche, 1951–1954), 24B4, vol. 1, pp. 215–216. The identification of health with *isonomia* and disease with *monarchia* apparently was known throughout the ancient world, even though the two terms do not occur often in this sense explicitly in the medical texts. Note, for example, the citation, using both *isonomia* and *monarchia,* in (the pseudo-Galenic?) *On the History of Philosophy* 58 (K 19.343), listed in Kühn as "spurious" (K 19.222–345).

7. Jacques Jouanna, *Hippocrates* (Baltimore: Johns Hopkins University Press, 1999), 327.

8. For the Greek, see Diels and Kranz, *Fragmente der Vorsokratiker*. See Gregory Vlastos, *"Isonomia,"* 340. Vlastos himself suggests, though he did not to my knowledge follow up the idea further, that the medical view that health is *krasis* of equal powers and *monarchia* disease "is certainly patterned on a democratic concept of the political order, though it is by no means necessary to assume that Alcmaeon so used it *because* he was himself a partisan of democracy" (363). See also Vlastos, "Equality and Justice."

9. For the phrase "watchword of democracy," see Victor Ehrenberg, "Origins of Democracy," *Historia* 1 (1950), at 531; followed by Vlastos, *"Isonomia,"* 339. S. Sara Monoson calls *isonomia* "the celebrated democratic principle." See "Frank Speech, Democracy, and Philosophy: Plato's Debt to a Democratic Strategy of Civic Discourse," in *Athenian Political Thought and the Reconstruction of American Democracy*, ed. J. Peter Euben et al. (Ithaca: Cornell University Press, 1994), 172–197, at 192. See also Arlene W. Saxonhouse, *Athenian Democracy: Modern Mythmakers and Ancient Theorists* (Notre Dame: University of Notre Dame Press, 1996), 57.

10. Some other contexts in which the comparison recurs: Aristotle, *Nichomachean Ethics* 8.10; Dio Chrysostom, *Oration* 3.45; Plutarch, *Moralia* 826a–827d.

11. J. M. Moore, trans., *Aristotle and Xenophon on Democracy and Oligarchy* (Berkeley: University of California Press, 1986), 155–156.

12. See Monoson, "Frank Speech, Democracy, and Philosophy," 192; Vlastos, *"Isonomia,"* 339, 347, passim; Vlastos, "Equality and Justice"; Saxonhouse, *Athenian Democracy*, 32–33, 57; Mogens Herman Hansen, *The Athenian Democracy in the Age of Demosthenes: Structure, Principles, and Ideology* (Oxford: Blackwell, 1991), 75–85.

13. Similar connections of *isonomia* (or sometimes just *nomos* and *ison* occurring together) are found in Thucydides, *History of the Peloponnesian War*. See, for example, 2.37.1–3, 3.82.8, 4.78.3, 6.38.5.

14. For one description, see T. G. Elliott, *The Christianity of Constantine the Great* (Scranton: University of Scranton Press, 1996), 6–8, 63–64, though readers should be wary of Elliott's almost hagiographic treatment of Constantine. For a thorough study of the "reforms" of both Constantine

and his predecessor Diocletian and the consequent changes of the empire in late antiquity, see Timothy D. Barnes, *The New Empire of Diocletian and Constantine* (Cambridge: Harvard University Press, 1982).

15. H. A. Drake, *In Praise of Constantine,* University of California Publications, Classical Studies, vol. 15 (Berkeley: University of California Press, 1976), 12. See also Drake, *Constantine and the Bishops* (Baltimore: Johns Hopkins University Press, 2000), 36–57. For background information on Constantine's rise, see Timothy D. Barnes, *Constantine and Eusebius* (Cambridge: Harvard University Press, 1981), 3–77.

16. Drake, *In Praise of Constantine,* 12.

17. Drake, *In Praise of Constantine,* 13. See also S. R. F. Price, *Rituals of Power: The Roman Imperial Cult in Asia Minor* (Cambridge: Cambridge University Press, 1984), 245–247.

18. Drake, *In Praise of Constantine,* 13.

19. See also Elliott, *Christianity of Constantine the Great,* 6–8. Ramsay MacMullen well illustrates the shifts from the early to the late empire in comparing depictions of the *humanity* of early emperors to the god-like remoteness of Constantine's public image (see *Constantine* [New York: Dial, 1969], 3–4, 11, 197). Of course, we should remember that what changed was not that the later images were "divine" whereas the earlier were "human." As can be easily seen by noting how often even Augustus or any other early emperor was depicted in sculpture in the guise or the nakedness of a god, the emperors had long been portrayed as divine. What changed was the conception of the divine itself, from being "nearer" (and therefore more "human") to being more "remote."

20. The older idea that Christianity was almost exclusively a lower-class movement, represented, for example, by a famous Marxist study by Karl Kautsky, *Foundations of Christianity: A Study in Christian Origins* (London: Allen & Unwin, 1925), was displaced (among scholars if not in popular opinion) by a later consensus that held that early Christian groups, especially Pauline churches, comprised a population represented by a wider diversity of class origins. The most important representatives of the consensus have been Edwin A. Judge, *The Social Pattern of Christian Groups in the First Century* (London: Tyndale, 1960); Gerd Theissen, *The Social Setting of Pauline Christianity: Essays on Corinth,* ed. and trans. John H. Schütz (Philadel-

phia: Fortress, 1982); Wayne A. Meeks, *The First Urban Christians: The Social World of the Apostle Paul* (New Haven: Yale University Press, 1983). Though the consensus still holds for the most part (see, for example, Harry Y. Gamble, *Books and Readers in the Early Church: A History of Early Christian Texts* [New Haven: Yale University Press, 1995], 5–6), it has been recently challenged, though not in my opinion overturned: see Justin J. Meggitt, *Paul, Poverty and Survival* (Edinburgh: T. and T. Clark, 1998); Dale B. Martin, "Review essay: Justin J. Meggitt, *Paul, Poverty and Survival*," *Journal for the Study of the New Testament* 84 (2001):51–64.

21. See, for example, Peter Brown, *The World of Late Antiquity 150–750* (London: Thames and Hudson, 1971), 54–55; Ramsay MacMullen, *Christianizing the Roman Empire (AD 100–400)* (New Haven: Yale University Press, 1984); Bernd Kollmann, *Jesus und die Christen als Wundertäter: Studien zu Magie, Medizin, und Schamanismus in Antike und Christentum* (Göttingen: Vandenhoeck and Ruprecht, 1996); Hector Avalos, *Health Care and the Rise of Christianity* (Peabody, Mass.: Hendrickson, 1999).

Works Cited

Note: For editions and translations of most Greek and Latin sources, readers may consult the Loeb Classical Library editions. Unless otherwise noted, all translations in this book are my own. Bibliographical references for ancient sources not found in the Loeb Classical Library are provided below.

Andresen, Carl. *Logos und Nomos: Die Polemik des Kelsos wider das Christentum.* Berlin: Walter de Gruyter, 1955.

Apuleius. *Apuleius: Rhetorical Works.* Trans. and annotated Stephen Harrison, John Hilton, and Vincent Hunink; ed. S. J. Harrison. Oxford: Oxford University Press, 2002.

Athanassiadi, Polymnia, and Michael Frede, eds. *Pagan Monotheism in Late Antiquity.* Oxford: Clarendon, 1999.

Attridge, Harold W. "The Philosophical Critique of Religion in the Early Empire." *Aufstief und Niedergang der römischen Welt* 2.26.1.45–78. Berlin: Walter de Gruyter, 1978.

Attridge, Harold W., and Gohei Hata, eds. *Eusebius, Christianity, and Judaism.* Detroit: Wayne State University Press, 1992.

Avalos, Hector. *Health Care and the Rise of Christianity.* Peabody, Mass.: Hendrickson, 1999.

Avery, Harry C. "The Resolution of Rhetorical Conflict in Greek Histo-
    rians." In *Conflict, Antithesis, and the Ancient Historian,* ed. June
    W. Allison, 92–111. Columbus: Ohio State University Press,
    1990.

Barnes, Timothy D. *Constantine and Eusebius.* Cambridge: Harvard Uni-
    versity Press, 1981.

———. *The New Empire of Diocletian and Constantine.* Cambridge: Har-
    vard University Press, 1982.

Barrett-Lennard, R. J. S. *Christian Healing after the New Testament: Some
    Approaches to Illness in the Second, Third and Fourth Centuries.*
    Lanham, N.Y.: University Press of America, 1994.

Barton, Tamsyn. *Ancient Astrology.* London: Routledge, 1994.

Beagon, Mary. *Roman Nature: The Thought of Pliny the Elder.* Oxford:
    Clarendon, 1992.

Benko, Stephen. "Pagan Criticism of Christianity during the First Two
    Centuries." *Aufstieg und Niedergang der römischen Welt* 2.23.2.1055–
    1118. Berlin: Walter de Gruyter, 1980.

Blumenthal, Henry J., and E. Gillian Clark, eds. *The Divine Iamblichus:
    Philosopher and Man of Gods.* London: Duckworth, 1993.

Blundell, Mary Whitlock. *Helping Friends and Harming Enemies: A Study
    in Sophocles and Greek Ethics.* Cambridge: Cambridge University
    Press, 1989.

Bram, Jean Rhys, trans. *Ancient Astrology: Theory and Practice.* Park Ridge,
    N.J.: Noyes, 1975.

Brenk, Frederick E. "'A Most Strange Doctrine': *Daimon* in Plutarch."
    Classical Journal 69 (1973):1–11.

———. "An Imperial Heritage: The Religious Spirit of Plutarch of
    Chaironeia." *Aufstief und Niedergang der römischen Welt* 2.36.1.248–
    349. Berlin: Walter de Gruyter, 1987.

———. *In Mist Apparelled: Religious Themes in Plutarch's* Moralia *and*
    Lives. Lugduni Batavorum: Brill, 1977.

Brown, Peter. *The World of Late Antiquity 150–750.* London: Thames and
    Hudson, 1971.

Burkert, Walter. *Greek Religion.* Cambridge: Harvard University Press,
    1985.

—————. *The Orientalizing Revolution: Near Eastern Influence on Greek Culture in the Early Archaic Age.* Cambridge: Harvard University Press, 1992.

Burnyeat, M. F. "Aristotle on Learning to be Good." In *Essays on Aristotle's Ethics,* ed. A. O. Rorty, 69–92. (See Rorty.)

Calderone, S. *"Superstitio." Aufstieg und Niedergang der römischen Welt* 1.2.377–396. Berlin: Walter de Gruyter, 1972.

Cameron, Averil. "Eusebius of Caesarea and the Rethinking of History." In *Tria Corda: Scritti in onore di Arnaldo Momigliano,* ed. Emilio Gabba, 71–89. Como: New Press, 1983.

—————. "Eusebius' Vita Constantini and the Construction of Constantine." In *Portraits: Biographical Representation in the Greek and Latin Literature of the Roman Empire,* ed. M. J. Edwards and Simon Swain, 145–174. Oxford: Clarendon Press, 1997.

Cameron, Averil, and Stuart G. Hall. *Eusebius' Life of Constantine, translated with Introduction and Commentary.* Oxford: Clarendon Press, 1999.

Carr, Wesley. *Angels and Principalities: The Background, Meaning and Development of the Pauline Phrase* hai archai kai hai exousiai. Cambridge: Cambridge University Press, 1981.

—————. "The Rulers of This Age—I Corinthians II.6–8." *New Testament Studies* 23 (1976–1977):20–25.

Castelli, Elizabeth A. *Martyrdom and Memory: Early Christian Culture Making.* New York: Columbia University Press, 2004.

Celsus. *On the True Doctrine: A Discourse against the Christians.* Ed. and trans. R. Joseph Hoffmann. New York: Oxford University Press, 1987.

Chadwick, John, and W. N. Mann. *The Medical Works of Hippocrates.* Oxford: Blackwell, 1950.

Clement of Alexandria. *Christ the Educator.* Trans. Simon P. Wood. New York: Fathers of the Church, 1954.

—————. *Clementis Alexandrini Paedagogus.* Ed. M. Marcovich with assistance from J. C. M. van Winden. Leiden: Brill, 2002.

—————. *Stromateis. Books One to Three.* Trans. John Ferguson. Washington, D.C.: Catholic University of America, 1991.

Cohen, David. *Law, Sexuality, and Society: The Enforcement of Morals in Classical Athens.* Cambridge: Cambridge University Press, 1992.

———. *Law, Violence, and Community in Classical Athens.* Cambridge: Cambridge University Press, 1995.

Collins, Derek. "Nature, Cause, and Agency in Greek Magic." *Transactions of the American Philological Association* 133 (2003):17–49.

Conrad, Lawrence I., et al., eds. *The Western Medical Tradition 800 BC to AD 1800.* Cambridge: Cambridge University Press, 1995.

Cook, John G. "Some Hellenistic Responses to the Gospels and Gospel Traditions." *Zeitschrift für die neutestamentliche Wissenschaft und die Kunde der älteren Kirche* 84 (1993):233–254.

Copenhaver, Brian. *Hermetica: The Greek* Corpus Hermeticum *and the Latin* Asclepius *in a New English Translation with Notes and Introduction.* Cambridge: Cambridge University Press, 1992.

Crouzel, Henri. *Origèn et Plotin: Comparaisons doctrinales.* Paris: Pierre Téqui, 1991.

Daniélou, Jean. *Origen.* New York: Sheed and Ward, 1955.

The Dead Sea Scrolls: Hebrew, Aramaic, and Greek Texts with English Translations. Ed. James H. Charlesworth with J. Molgrom et al. Tübingen: J. C. B. Mohr (Paul Siebeck); Louisville: Westminster/John Knox, 1993–.

Dean-Jones, Lesley. *Women's Bodies in Classical Greek Science.* Oxford: Clarendon, 1994.

Debru, Armelle. *Le corps respirant: La pensée physiologique chez Galien.* Leiden: Brill, 1996.

Diels, Hermann, and Walther Kranz, eds. *Die Fragmente der Vorsokratiker,* 7th ed. 3 vols. Berlin: Weidmannsche, 1951–1954.

The Digest of Justinian. Trans. Alan Watson; Latin text edited by Theodor Mommsen with Paul Krueger. Philadelphia: University of Pennsylvania Press, 1985.

Dillon, John M. *The Middle Platonists, 80 B.C. to A.D. 220.* Ithaca, N.Y.: Cornell University Press, 1977.

Dioscorides Pedanius. *De Materia Medica.* 3 vols. Ed. Max Wellmann. Berlin: Weidmann, 1906–1914.

———. *The Greek Herbal of Dioscorides.* Ed. Robert R. Gunther. Oxford: Oxford University Press, 1934.

Dodds, E. R. *Pagan and Christian in an Age of Anxiety.* Cambridge: Cambridge University Press, 1965.

Dover, K. J. *Greek Popular Morality in the Time of Plato and Aristotle.* Indianapolis: Hackett, 1994.

Drake, H. A. *Constantine and the Bishops: The Politics of Intolerance.* Baltimore: Johns Hopkins University Press, 2000.

———. *In Praise of Constantine: A Historical Study and New Translation of Eusebius' Tricennial Orations.* University of California Publications, Classical Studies, vol. 15. Berkeley: University of California Press, 1976.

Drews, Robert. "Diodorus and His Sources." *American Journal of Philology* 83 (1962):383–392.

Droge, Arthur J. "The Apologetic Dimensions of the *Ecclesiastical History.*" In *Eusebius, Christianity, and Judaism,* ed. Harold W. Attridge and Gohei Hata, 492–509. (See Attridge.)

Droge, Arthur J., and James D. Tabor. *A Noble Death: Suicide and Martyrdom among Christians and Jews in Antiquity.* New York: HarperCollins, 1992.

Dvornik, Francis. *Early Christian and Byzantine Political Philosophy: Origins and Background.* 2 vols. Washington: Dumbarton Oaks, 1966.

Edelstein, Emma J., and Ludwig Edelstein. *Asclepius: Collection and Interpretation of the Testamonies.* Baltimore: Johns Hopkins University Press, 1998.

Eger, Hans. "Kaiser und Kirche in der geschichtlichen Theologie Eusebs von Caesarea." *Zeitschrift für die neutestamentliche Wissenschaft und die Kunde der älteren Kirche* 38 (1939):97–115.

Ehrenberg, Victor. "Origins of Democracy." *Historia* 1 (1950):515–548.

Ehrman, Bart D. *The New Testament: A Historical Introduction to the Early Christian Writings,* 2d ed. New York: Oxford University Press, 2000.

Elliott, T. G. *The Christianity of Constantine the Great.* Scranton: University of Scranton Press, 1996.

Engberg-Pedersen, Troels. *Aristotle's Theory of Moral Insight.* Oxford: Oxford University Press, 1983.

Entralgo, Pedro Lain. *The Therapy of the Word in Classical Antiquity.* New Haven: Yale University Press, 1970.

Eusebius of Caesarea. *Die Demonstratio evangelica.* Ed. Ivar A. Heikel.
    Leipzig: J. C. Hinrichs, 1913.

———. *Eusebiou tou Pamphilou Euangelikês proparaskeuês logoi 15.*
    Evangelicae Praeparationis libri XV. 4 vols. in 10. Ed. and trans.
    Edwin Hamilton Gifford. Oxford: e Typograpeo Academico,
    1903.

———. *In Praise of Constantine.* (See Drake.)

———. *Life of Constantine.* Trans. and comm. Averil Cameron and Stuart
    G. Hill. Oxford: Clarendon, 1999.

———. *La préparation évangélique.* 15 vols. in 9. Paris: Éditions du Cerf,
    1974–1991.

———. *Preparation for the Gospel.* Trans. Edwin Hamilton Gifford. Ox-
    ford: Clarendon Press, 1903.

———. *The Proof of the Gospel.* 2 vols. Trans. W. J. Ferrar. London: Soci-
    ety for Promoting Christian Knowledge, 1920.

Evangeliou, Christos. "Plotinus's Anti-Gnostic Polemic and Porphyry's
    Against the Christians." In *Neoplatonism and Gnosticism,* ed. Richard
    T. Wallis and Jay Bregman, 111–128. (See Wallis.)

Farina, Raffaele. *L'Impero e l'Imperatore cristiano in Eusebio di Cesarea: La
    prima teologia politica del Cristianesimo.* Zürich: Pas Verlag, 1966.

Ferguson, Everett. *Demonology of the Early Christian World.* New York:
    Edwin Mellon, 1984.

Fortenbaugh, William W. *Quellen zur Ethik Theophrasts.* Amsterdam: B. R.
    Grüner, 1984.

———. "Theophrastus on Emotion." In *Theophrastus of Eresus: On His
    Life and Work,* ed. William W. Fortenbaugh et al., 209–229. Rutgers
    University Studies in Classical Humanities, vol. 2. New Brunswick:
    Transaction Books, 1985.

Fowden, Garth. *The Egyptian Hermes: A Historical Approach to the Late Pa-
    gan Mind.* Cambridge: Cambridge University Press, 1986.

———. *Empire to Commonwealth: Consequences of Monotheism in Late An-
    tiquity.* Princeton: Princeton University Press, 1993.

Frede, Michael. "Eusebius' Apologetic Writings." In *Apologetics in the Ro-
    man Empire: Pagans, Jews, and Christians,* ed. Mark Edwards et al.,
    223–250. Oxford: Oxford University Press, 1999.

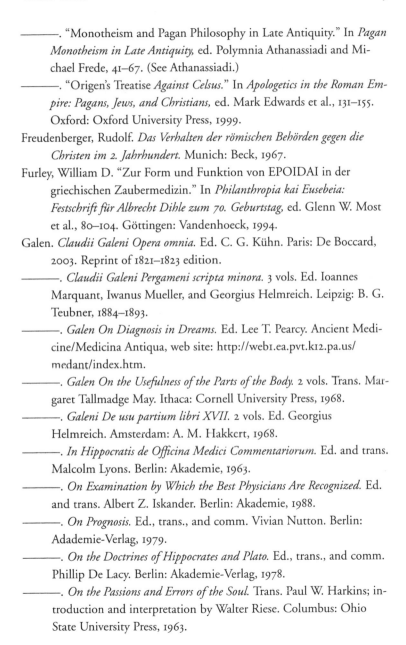

———. "Monotheism and Pagan Philosophy in Late Antiquity." In *Pagan Monotheism in Late Antiquity,* ed. Polymnia Athanassiadi and Michael Frede, 41–67. (See Athanassiadi.)

———. "Origen's Treatise *Against Celsus.*" In *Apologetics in the Roman Empire: Pagans, Jews, and Christians,* ed. Mark Edwards et al., 131–155. Oxford: Oxford University Press, 1999.

Freudenberger, Rudolf. *Das Verhalten der römischen Behörden gegen die Christen im 2. Jahrhundert.* Munich: Beck, 1967.

Furley, William D. "Zur Form und Funktion von EPOIDAI in der griechischen Zaubermedizin." In *Philanthropia kai Eusebeia: Festschrift für Albrecht Dihle zum 70. Geburtstag,* ed. Glenn W. Most et al., 80–104. Göttingen: Vandenhoeck, 1994.

Galen. *Claudii Galeni Opera omnia.* Ed. C. G. Kühn. Paris: De Boccard, 2003. Reprint of 1821–1823 edition.

———. *Claudii Galeni Pergameni scripta minora.* 3 vols. Ed. Ioannes Marquant, Iwanus Mueller, and Georgius Helmreich. Leipzig: B. G. Teubner, 1884–1893.

———. *Galen On Diagnosis in Dreams.* Ed. Lee T. Pearcy. Ancient Medicine/Medicina Antiqua, web site: http://web1.ea.pvt.k12.pa.us/medant/index.htm.

———. *Galen On the Usefulness of the Parts of the Body.* 2 vols. Trans. Margaret Tallmadge May. Ithaca: Cornell University Press, 1968.

———. *Galeni De usu partium libri XVII.* 2 vols. Ed. Georgius Helmreich. Amsterdam: A. M. Hakkert, 1968.

———. *In Hippocratis de Officina Medici Commentariorum.* Ed. and trans. Malcolm Lyons. Berlin: Akademie, 1963.

———. *On Examination by Which the Best Physicians Are Recognized.* Ed. and trans. Albert Z. Iskander. Berlin: Akademie, 1988.

———. *On Prognosis.* Ed., trans., and comm. Vivian Nutton. Berlin: Adademie-Verlag, 1979.

———. *On the Doctrines of Hippocrates and Plato.* Ed., trans., and comm. Phillip De Lacy. Berlin: Akademie-Verlag, 1978.

———. *On the Passions and Errors of the Soul.* Trans. Paul W. Harkins; introduction and interpretation by Walter Riese. Columbus: Ohio State University Press, 1963.

————. *On the Therapeutic Method, Books I and II.* Trans. and comm. R. J. Hankinson. Oxford: Clarendon, 1991.

————. *Selected Works.* Ed. Peter Singer. Oxford: Oxford University Press, 1997.

Gallagher, Eugene V. *Divine Man or Magician?: Celsus and Origen on Jesus.* Chico, Calif.: Scholars Press, 1982.

Gamble, Harry Y. *Books and Readers in the Early Church: A History of Early Christian Texts.* New Haven: Yale University Press, 1995.

Garrison, Fielding H. *An Introduction to the History of Medicine,* 3d ed., revised and enlarged. Philadelphia: W. B. Saunders, 1924.

Geoponika sive Cassiani Bassi scholastici De re rustica eclogae. Leipzig: Teubner, 1895.

Gerson, Lloyd. *God and Greek Philosophy: Studies in the Early History of Natural Theology.* London: Routledge, 1990.

Given, Mark D. "Not Either/or but Both/and in Paul's Areopagus Speech." *Biblical Interpretation* 3 (1995):356–372.

————. *Paul's True Rhetoric: Ambiguity, Cunning, and Deception in Greece and Rome.* Harrisburg, Pa.: Trinity Press International, 2001.

Gladigow, B. "Aberglaube." In *Handbuch religionswissenschaftlicher Grundbegriffe,* s.v., ed. Hubert Cancik et al. Stuttgart: Verlag W. Kohlhammer, 1988.

Glover, T. R. *The Conflict of Religions in the Early Roman Empire.* London: Methuen, 1918.

Gorday, Peter J. "Becoming Truly Human: Origen's Theology of the Cross." In *The Cross in Christian Tradition: From Paul to Bonaventure,* ed. Elizabeth A. Dreyer, 93–125. New York: Paulist, 2000.

Gouldner, Alvin W. *Enter Plato: Classical Greece and the Origins of Social Theory.* New York: Basic Books, 1965.

Gourevitch, Dainelle. "La medicina ippocratica e l'opera *Delle arie, acque, luoghi:* Breve storia della nascità e del potere di un *inganna* scientifico." *Medicina nei Secoli* 7 (1995):425–433.

Graf, Fritz. *Magic in the Ancient World.* Cambridge: Harvard University Press, 1997.

Grodzynski, Denise. *"Superstitio." Revue des Études anciennes* 76 (1974):36–60.

Guthrie, W. K. C. *The Greeks and Their Gods*. Boston: Beacon, 1955.

Hankinson, R. J. "Magic, Religion and Science: Divine and Human in the Hippocratic Corpus." *Apeiron* 31 (1998):1–34.

Hansen, Mogens Herman. *The Athenian Democracy in the Age of Demosthenes: Structure, Principles, and Ideology*. Oxford: Blackwell, 1991.

Hanson, Ann Ellis. "Hippocrates: Diseases of Women I." *Signs* 1 (1975):567–584.

———. "Talking Recipes in the Gynaecological Texts of the *Hippocratic Corpus*." In *Parchments of Gender: Deciphering the Bodies of Antiquity*, ed. Maria Wyke, 71–94. Oxford: Clarendon, 1998.

Harnack, Adolf. *The Mission and Expansion of Christianity in the First Three Centuries*. New York: Harper and Brothers, 1972.

Hester, D. A. "To Help One's Friends and Harm One's Enemies: A Study in the *Oedipus at Colonus*." *Antichthon* 11 (1977):22–41.

Hippocrates. *The Hippocratic Treatises "On Generation," "On the Nature of the Child," "Diseases IV."* Trans. Iain M. Lonie. Berlin: Walter de Gruyter, 1981.

———. *Oeuvres completes d'Hippocrates*. 10 vols. Ed. Emile Littre. Paris: De Boccard, 2003. Reprint of 1839–1861.

Hoffman, R. Joseph. *Porphyry's* Against the Christians: *The Literary Remains*. Amherst, N.Y.: Prometheus Books, 1994.

Hursthouse, Rosalind. "Moral Habituation: A Review of Troels Engberg-Pedersen, *Aristotle's Theory of Moral Insight*." *Oxford Studies in Ancient Philosophy* 6 (1988):201–219.

Hutchinson, D. K. "Ethics." In *The Cambridge Companion to Aristotle*, ed. Jonathan Barnes, 195–232. Cambridge: Cambridge University Press, 1995.

Iamblichus [Jamblique]. *Les Mystères D'Égypte*. Ed. and trans. Édouard des Places. Paris: Belles Lettres, 1966.

———. *On the Mysteries of the Egyptians, Chaldeans, and Assyrians*. Ed. and trans. Thomas Taylor. 3d ed. London: Stuard and Watkins, 1968.

Inscriptiones Graecae. Berlin: G. Reimer, 1873–.

Jaeger, Werner. *The Theology of the Early Greek Philosophers*. Oxford: Clarendon, 1947.

Janssen, L. F. "'Superstitio' and the Persecution of Christians." *Vigiliae Christianae* 33 (1979):131–159.

Jones, W. H. S. *Philosophy and Medicine in Ancient Greece; With an Edition of peri archaiēs iētrikēs.* Baltimore: Johns Hopkins Press, 1946.

Jordan, D. R. "The Inscribed Lead Tablet from Phalasarna." *Zeitschrift für Papyrologie und Epigraphik* 94 (1992):191–194.

Jouanna, Jacques. "The Birth of Western Medical Art." In *Western Medical Thought from Antiquity to the Middle Ages,* ed. Mirko D. Grmek, 22–71. Cambridge: Harvard University Press, 1998.

———. *Hippocrates.* Baltimore: Johns Hopkins University Press, 1999.

Judge, Edwin A. *The Social Pattern of Christian Groups in the First Century.* London: Tyndale, 1960.

Justin Martyr. *Dialogue with Trypho.* Trans. Thomas B. Falls; revised and with a new introduction by Thomas P. Halton; ed. Michael Slusser. Washington, D.C.: Catholic University of America, 2003.

———. *The First Apology.* Fathers of the Church 4. New York: Christian Heritage, 1948.

Kautsky, Karl. *Foundations of Christianity: A Study in Christian Origins.* London: Allen & Unwin, 1925.

Koets, Peter John. *Deisidaimonia: A Contribution to the Knowledge of the Religious Terminology in Greek.* Purmerend, the Netherlands: J. Muusses, 1929.

Kofsky, Aryeh. *Eusebius of Caesarea against Paganism.* Leiden: Brill, 2000.

Kollmann, Bernd. *Jesus und die Christen als Wundertäter: Studien zu Magie, Medizin, und Schamanismus in Antike und Christentum.* Göttingen: Vandenhoeck and Ruprecht, 1996.

Kotansky, Roy. "Greek Exorcistic Amulets." In *Ancient Magic and Ritual Power,* ed. Marvin Meyer and Paul Mirecki, 243–277. Leiden: Brill, 1995.

Kudlein, Fridolf. "Galen's Religious Belief." In *Galen: Problems and Prospects,* ed. Vivian Nutton, 117–127. London: Wellcome Institute for the History of Medicine, 1981.

Lactantius. *The Divine Institutes: Books I–VII.* Trans. Sister Mary Francis McDonald. Washington, D.C.: Catholic University of America, 1964.

Langholf, Volker. *Medical Theories in Hippocrates: Early Texts and the "Epidemics."* Berlin: Walter de Gruyter, 1990.

Lasne, Sophie, and André Pascal Gaultier. *A Dictionary of Superstitions.* Englewood Cliffs, N.J.: Prentice-Hall, 1984.

Levin, Saul. "The Old Greek Oracles in Decline." *Aufstieg und Niedergang der römischen Welt* 2.18.2.1599–1649. Berlin: Walter de Gruyter, 1989.

Lloyd, G. E. R. *Magic, Reason and Experience: Studies in the Origin and Development of Greek Science.* Cambridge: Cambridge University Press, 1979.

Longrigg, James. *Greek Rational Medicine: Philosophy and Medicine from Alcmaeon to the Alexandrians.* London: Routledge, 1993.

Luck, Georg. *Arcana Mundi: Magic and the Occult in the Greek and Roman Worlds.* Baltimore: Johns Hopkins University Press, 1985.

MacMullen, Ramsay. *Christianity and Paganism in the Fourth to Eighth Centuries.* New Haven: Yale University Press, 1997.

———. *Christianizing the Roman Empire (AD 100–400).* New Haven: Yale University Press, 1984.

———. *Constantine.* New York: Dial, 1969.

Malherbe, Abraham J. "The Apologetic Theology of the *Preaching of Peter.*" *Restoration Quarterly* 13 (1970):205–223.

Malina, Bruce J. *The New Testament World: Insights from Cultural Anthropology.* Rev. ed. Louisville: Westminster/John Knox, 1993.

Martin, Dale B. "Contradictions of Masculinity: Ascetic Inseminators and Menstruating Men in Greco-Roman Culture." In *Generation and Degeneration: Tropes of Reproduction in Literature and History from Antiquity to Early Modern Europe,* ed. Valeria Finucci and Kevin Brownlee, 81–108. Durham: Duke University Press, 2001.

———. *The Corinthian Body.* New Haven: Yale University Press, 1995.

———. "Paul without Passion: On Paul's Rejection of Desire in Sex and Marriage." In *Constructing Early Christian Families: Family as Social Reality and Metaphor,* ed. Halvor Moxnes, 201–215. London: Routledge, 1997.

———. "Review essay: Justin J. Meggitt, *Paul, Poverty and Survival.*" *Journal for the Study of the New Testament* 84 (2001):51–64.

————. *Slavery as Salvation: The Metaphor of Slavery in Pauline Christianity.* New Haven: Yale University Press, 1990.

Meeks, Wayne A. *The First Urban Christians: The Social World of the Apostle Paul.* New Haven: Yale University Press, 1983.

Meggitt, Justin J. *Paul, Poverty and Survival.* Edinburgh: T. and T. Clark, 1998.

Meinecke, Bruno. "A Quasi-autobiographical Case History of an Ancient Greek Child." *Bulletin of the History of Medicine* 8 (1940):1022–1031.

Meredith, Anthony. "Porphyry and Julian against the Christians." *Aufstieg und Niedergang der römischen Welt* 2.23.2.1119–1149. Berlin: Walter de Gruyter, 1980.

Merlan, Philip. *From Platonism to Neoplatonism,* 3d ed. rev. The Hague: Martinus Nijhoff, 1975.

Mikalson, Jon D. *Athenian Popular Religion.* Chapel Hill: University of North Carolina Press, 1983.

Miles, Margaret R. *Plotinus on Body and Beauty: Society, Philosophy, and Religion in Third-century Rome.* Oxford: Blackwell, 1999.

Miller, Harold W. "The Concept of the Divine in *De Morbo Sacro.*" *Transactions of the American Philological Association* 84 (1953):1–15.

Moellering, H. Armin. "Deisidaimonia, a Footnote to Acts 17:22." *Concordia Theological Monthly* 34 (1963):466–471.

————. *Plutarch on Superstition: Plutarch's* De Superstitione, *Its Place in the Changing Meaning of Deisidaimonia and in the Context of His Theological Writings.* Boston: Christopher, 1963.

Monoson, S. Sara. "Frank Speech, Democracy, and Philosophy: Plato's Debt to a Democratic Strategy of Civic Discourse." In *Athenian Political Thought and the Reconstruction of American Democracy,* ed. J. Peter Euben et al., 172–197. Ithaca: Cornell University Press, 1994.

Moore, J. M. *Aristotle and Xenophon on Democracy and Oligarchy.* Berkeley: University of California Press, 1986.

Morgan, Michael L. *Platonic Piety: Philosophy and Ritual in Fourth-Century Athens.* New Haven: Yale University Press, 1990.

Nautin, Pierre. *Origène: sa vie et son ouevre.* Paris: Beauchesne, 1977.

Nicander of Colophon. *Nicander: The Poems and Poetical Fragments.* Ed. with introduction, trans., and notes by A. S. F. Gow and A. F. Scholfield. London: Bristol Classical Press, 1997.

————. *Theriaca et Alexipharmaka.* Ed. Otto Schneider. Leipzig: Teubner, 1856.

Nilsson, Martin P. *Greek Popular Religion.* New York: Columbia University Press, 1940.

Nussbaum, Martha. *The Therapy of Desire: Theory and Practice in Hellenistic Ethics.* Princeton: Princeton University Press, 1994.

Nutton, Vivian. "The Chronology of Galen's Early Career." *Classical Quarterly* 23 (1973):158–171.

————. "The Perils of Patriotism: Pliny and Roman Medicine." In *Science in the Early Roman Empire: Pliny the Elder, His Sources and Influence,* ed. Roger French and Frank Greenaway, 30–58. London: Croom Helm, 1986.

Obbink, Dirk. "The Origin of Greek Sacrifice: Theophrastus on Religion and Cultural History." In *Theophrastean Studies: On Natural Science, Physics and Metaphysics, Ethics, Religion, and Rhetoric,* ed. William W. Fortenbaugh and Robert W. Sharples, 272–295. Rutgers University Studies in Classical Humanities, vol. 3. New Brunswick: Transaction Books, 1988.

Ober, Josiah. *The Athenian Revolution: Essays on Ancient Greek Democracy and Political Theory.* Princeton: Princeton University Press, 1996.

Opie, Iona, and Moira Tatem, eds. *A Dictionary of Superstition.* Oxford: Oxford University Press, 1989.

Oribasius, *Collectionum medicarum reliquiae.* 4 vols. Ed. Ioannes Raeder. Amsterdam: Adolf M. Hakkert, 1964.

Origen. *Contra Celsum.* Trans. Henry Chadwick. Cambridge: Cambridge University Press, 1953.

————. *Contre Celse.* Ed. Marcel Borrett. Paris: Editions du Cerf, 1967–1976.

————. *On First Principles.* Ed. G. W. Butterworth. Gloucester, Mass.: Peter Smith, 1993.

Owens, Joseph. *Aristotle: The Collected Papers of Joseph Owen.* Albany: State University of New York Press, 1981.

————. "The Teleology of Nature in Aristotle." *Monist* 52 (1968):159–173.

Patterson, L. "Origin of the Name Panthera." *Journal of Theological Studies* 19 (1917):79–80.

Pears, David. "Courage as a Mean." In *Essays on Aristotle's Ethics*, ed. A. O.
    Rorty, 171–187. (See Rorty.)
Peterson, Erik. *Der Monotheismus als politisches Problem: Ein Beitrag zur
    Geschichte der politische Theologie im Imperium Romanum.* Leipzig:
    Jakob Hegner, 1935.
Pilch, John J. *Healing in the New Testament: Insights from Medical and
    Mediterranean Anthropology.* Minneapolis: Fortress, 2000.
Poole, J. C. F., and A. J. Holladay, "Thucydides and the Plague of Athens."
    Classical Quarterly n.s. 29 (1979):282–300.
Porphyry. *De l'abstinence.* Ed. and trans. Jean Bouffartigue and Michel
    Patillon. Paris: Belles Lettres, 1977–1995.
———. *On Abstinence from Killing Animals.* Trans. Gillian Clark. Ithaca,
    N.Y.: Cornell University Press, 2000.
Price, S. R. F. *Rituals of Power: The Roman Imperial Cult in Asia Minor.*
    Cambridge: Cambridge University Press, 1984.
Prioreschi, Plinio. *A History of Medicine,* vol. 3: *Roman Medicine.* Omaha:
    Horatius Press, 1998.
———. "Supernatural Elements in Hippocratic Medicine." *Journal of the
    History of Medicine and Allied Sciences* 47 (1992):389–404.
Reardon, B. P., ed. *Collected Ancient Greek Novels.* Berkeley: University of
    California Press, 1989.
Rist, John M. *Plotinus: The Road to Reality.* Cambridge: Cambridge Uni-
    versity Press, 1967.
———. "Some Aspects of Aristotelian Teleology." *Transactions of the
    American Philological Association* 96 (1965):337–349.
Rorty, Amélie Oksenberg, ed. *Essays on Aristotle's Ethics.* Berkeley: Univer-
    sity of California Press, 1980.
Ross, W. D. *Aristotle's Physics: A Revised Text with Introduction and Com-
    mentary.* Oxford: Clarendon, 1955.
Sacks, Kenneth S. *Diodorus Siculus and the First Century.* Princeton:
    Princeton University Press, 1990.
Salaman, Clement, Dorine van Oyen, and William D. Wharton, trans.
    The Way of Hermes: The Corpus Hermeticum. London: Duckworth,
    1999.
Salzman, Michele R. "'*Superstitio*' in the *Codex Theodosianus* and the Perse-
    cution of Pagans." *Vigiliae Christianae* 41 (1987):172–188.

Saxonhouse, Arlene W. *Athenian Democracy: Modern Mythmakers and Ancient Theorists.* Notre Dame: University of Notre Dame Press, 1996.

Smith, Andrew. "Iamblichus' Views on the Relationship of Philosophy to Religion in *De Mysteriis.*" In *The Divine Iamblichus,* ed. Henry J. Blumenthal and E. Gillian Clark, 74–86. (See Blumenthal.)

Smith, Jonathan Z. "Towards Interpreting Daimonic Powers in Hellenistic and Roman Antiquity." *Aufstieg und Niedergang der römischen Welt* 2.16.1.425–439. Berlin: Walter de Gruyter, 1978.

Smith, Morton. *Clement of Alexandria and a Secret Gospel of Mark.* Cambridge: Harvard University Press, 1973.

———. "*De superstitione* (*Moralia* 164E–171F)." In *Plutarch's Theological Writings and Early Christian Literature,* ed. H. D. Betz, 1–35. Leiden: Brill, 1975.

Smith, Wesley D. "So-called Possession in Pre-Christian Greece." *Transactions of the American Philological Association* 96 (1965):403–426.

Sorabji, Richard. "Is Theophrastus a Significant Philosopher?" In *Theophrastus: Reappraising the Sources,* ed. Johannes M. van Ophuijsen and Marlein van Raalte, 203–221. Rutgers University Studies in Classical Humanities, vol. 8. New Brunswick: Transaction Publishers, 1998.

Soranus. *Gynecology.* Trans. Owsei Temkin. Baltimore: Johns Hopkins University Press, 1956.

———. *Sorani Gynaeciorum.* Ed. Valentino Rose. Leipzig: Teubner, 1882.

———. *Sorani Gynaeciorum libri IV, De signis Fracturarum, De fasciis, Vita Hippocratis secundum Soranum.* Ed. Johannes Ilberg. *Corpus Medicorum Graecorum* 4. Leipzig: Teubner, 1927.

Temkin, Owsei. "An Essay on the Usefulness of Medical History for Medicine." *Bulletin for the History of Medicine* 19 (1946):9–47.

Theissen, Gerd. *The Social Setting of Pauline Christianity: Essays on Corinth.* Ed. and trans. John H. Schütz. Philadelphia: Fortress, 1982.

Theophrastus of Eresus: Sources for His Life, Writings, Thought, and Influence. Ed. and trans. William W. Fortenbaugh et al. Leiden: Brill, 1992.

Thorley, John. *Athenian Democracy.* London: Routledge, 1996.

Thornton, Timothy C. G. "Eusebius of Caesarea, Constantine II and the Imperfections of Constantine the Great (*Vita Constantini* 4.31 and 4.54)." *Studia Patristica* 29 (1997):158–163.

Trigg, Joseph W. *Origen.* London: Routledge, 1998.

Twomey, Vincent. *Apostolikos Thronos: The Primacy of Rome as Reflected in the Church History of Eusebius and the Historico-apologetic Writings of Saint Athanasius the Great.* Münster: Aschendorff, 1982.

Ulrich, Jörg. "Euseb und die Juden: der origeneische Hintergrund." In *Origeniana Septima,* ed. W. A. Bienert and U. Kühneweg, 135–140. Leuven, Belgium: Leuven University Press, 1999.

———. *Euseb von Caesarea und die Juden: Studien zur Rolle der Juden in der Theologie des Eusebius von Caesarea.* Berlin: Walter de Gruyter, 1999.

Urmson, J. O. "Aristotle's Doctrine of the Mean." *American Philosophical Quarterly* 10 (1973):223–230.

Van den Hoek, Annewies. "Philo and Origen: A Descriptive Catalogue of Their Relationship." *Studia Philonica Annual* 12 (2000):44–121.

Vivian, Miriam Raub. "Eusebius and Constantine's Letter to Shapur: Its Place in the *Vita Constantini.*" *Studia Patristica* 29 (1997):164–169.

Vlastos, Gregory. "Equality and Justice in Early Greek Cosmologies." *Classical Philology* 42 (1947):156–178.

———. *"Isonomia."* *American Journal of Philology* 74 (1953):337–366.

Von Staden, Heinrich. "Anatomy as Rhetoric: Galen on Dissection and Persuasion." *Journal of the History of Medicine and Allied Sciences* 50 (1995):47–66.

———. "'In A Pure and Holy Way': Personal and Professional Conduct in the Hippocratic Oath?" *Journal of the History of Medicine and Allied Sciences* 51 (1996):404–437.

Wallis, Richard T. *Neoplatonism.* New York: Charles Scribner's Sons, 1972.

Wallis, Richard T., and Jay Bregman, eds. *Neoplatonism and Gnosticism.* Albany: State University of New York Press, 1992.

Walzer, Richard. *Galen on Jews and Christians.* London: Geoffrey Cumberlege/Oxford University Press, 1949.

Wenkebach, Ernst, and Franz Pfaff, eds. *Galeni in Hippocratis sextum librum epidemiarum commentaria I–VI.* Leipzig: B. G. Teubner, 1940.

West, M. L. *Greek Lyric Poetry: The Poems and Fragments of the Greek Iambic, Elegiac, and Melic Poets (Excluding Pindar and Bacchylides) Down to 450 BC.* Oxford: Oxford University Press, 1994.

————, ed. *Iambi et elegi Graeci ante Alexandrum Cantati.* 2 vols. Oxford: Oxford University Press, 1989–1992.

Whittaker, John. "Plutarch, Platonism and Christianity." In *Neoplatonism and Early Christian Thought: Essays in Honour of A. H. Armstrong,* ed. H. J. Blumenthal and R. A. Markus, 50–63. London: Variorum, 1981.

Wieland, W. "The Problem of Teleology." In *Articles on Aristotle,* vol. 1: *Science,* ed. Jonathan Barnes, Malcolm Schofield, and Richard Sorabji, 141–160. London: Duckworth, 1975.

Wilken, Robert. *The Christians as the Romans Saw Them.* New Haven: Yale University Press, 1984.

Winkelmann, Friedhelm. *Euseb von Kaisareia: Der Vater der Kirchengeschichte.* Berlin: Verlags-Anstalt Union, 1991.

Winkler, John. *The Constraints of Desire: The Anthropology of Sex and Gender in Ancient Greece.* New York: Routledge, 1990.

Young, Frances M. *The Use of Sacrificial Ideas in Greek Christian Writings from the New Testament to John Chrysostom.* Patristic Monograph Series 5. Cambridge, Mass.: Philadelphia Patristic Foundation, 1979.

Index

Scripture References